THE LAWS OF
DISRUPTION

THE LAWS OF
DISRUPTION

HARNESSING THE NEW FORCES
THAT GOVERN LIFE AND BUSINESS IN

THE DIGITAL AGE

—————

LARRY DOWNES

BASIC

BOOKS

A Member of the Perseus Books Group
New York

Books published by Basic Books are available at special discounts for bulk purchases in the United States by corporations, institutions, and other organizations. For more information, please contact the Special Markets Department at the Perseus Books Group, 2300 Chestnut Street, Suite 200, Philadelphia, PA 19103, or call (800) 810-4145, ext. 5000, or e-mail special.markets@perseusbooks.com.

Designed by Trish Wilkinson
Set in 11-point Minion

Library of Congress Cataloging-in-Publication Data

Downes, Larry, 1959–
    The laws of disruption : harnessing the new forces that govern life and business in the digital age / Larry Downes.
        p.   cm.
    ISBN 978-0-465-01864-2 (alk. paper)
    1. Information technology—Economic aspects. 2. Technological innovation—Economic aspects. I. Title.
HC79.I55D69 2009
338'.064—dc22   2009021607

10 9 8 7 6 5 4 3 2 1

CONTENTS

INTRODUCTION

In the late 1800s, as in the late 1900s, start-ups were running wild.

Railroad speculators, entrepreneurs, and financiers were busy laying redundant track from one end of North America to the other. By 1900, excess capacity had nearly bankrupted the transcontinental railroads. Operators were unable to charge rates that covered ongoing costs, let alone recover their investments. There simply wasn't enough freight to meet the capacity. Shippers knew it and forced the railroads to reduce rates to ruinous levels.

To stay afloat, the railroads invented a unique form of discrimination. Most of the transcontinental tracks began in Chicago and ended on the West Coast but took different routes over the mountains. Shippers to and from Spokane, Washington, for example, could use only the Great Northern Railroad. Knowing this, the railroad developed a rate system that charged shipments from Chicago to Spokane the fare from Chicago to the Pacific and then back to Spokane, even if the freight actually stopped in Spokane. These "back-haul" rates made shipping freight to and from the intermountain regions disastrously expensive. Spokane and other towns fought the system all the way to the U.S. Supreme Court.

The lawyer on the Great Northern case was Brooks Adams. The great-grandson of Revolutionary War leader John Adams, Brooks knew the inevitable result of unfair taxes, whether levied by a distant monarch or a faceless corporation. Reviewing the long history of economic revolutions, Adams argued that legal systems systematically fail to take into account new technologies and their unique properties. Instead, they force-fit new problems into old law. With no clear precedent to determine "fair" rates of rail carriage, the courts had worked their way back to the Middle Ages and the rights of landowners to use the King's Highway, giving far too much deference to the railroads in the process.

Adams demanded a more pragmatic solution: "There is no ancient and abstract principle of right and wrong," he wrote in his brief to the Interstate Commerce Commission (ICC), "which can safely be deduced as a guide to regulate the relations of railways and monopolies among our people, because railways and monopolies are products of forces unknown in former times. The character of competition has changed, and the law must change to meet it, or collapse. Such is my general theory."

Brooks Adams's "general theory" continues to apply one hundred years later. Today, thanks to almost magical improvements in the capabilities and costs of information technology, each of us is developing a parallel existence. Simple information exchanges through e-mail have rapidly evolved into a virtual environment in which relationships are formed, business is conducted, and new information products and services are developed in large-scale group collaborations. We are now living not only our real lives but also a second, digital, life, where distance is irrelevant, time can be started and stopped, and property can be reproduced in an instant with almost no measurable cost.

Ten years after the start of the Internet revolution, however, the inability of rules optimized for an analog world to keep the peace in the digital age has paralyzed much of the legal system. Conflicts over information use, acutely visible in thousands of lawsuits brought by the music industry against its own customers, will soon be joined by nascent fights over privacy, digital civil liberties, technology standards, network control, information crime, and global commerce. As the distance between innovation and the law that regulates it has widened over the past decade, the most alarming result is the speed with which tensions between the two have increased.

These struggles are side effects of the Law of Disruption. First introduced in my earlier book *Unleashing the Killer App*, the Law of Disruption is a simple but unavoidable principle of modern life: *technology changes exponentially, but social, economic, and legal systems change incrementally.* The technology we invent has the potential to change the world at an accelerating pace, but humans can no longer keep up. As the gap between the old world and the new gets wider, conflicts between social, economic, political, and legal systems honed in the age of steam engines and a generation raised on cell phones, iPods, and video games become more acute and more dangerous.

The battle between innovation and the law has reached its defining moment. Nothing can stop the chaos that will follow. Chaos, however, is necessary. The normal evolution of legal systems is slow and incremental. But disruptive technologies, whether railroads or the Internet, ultimately demand dramatic transformation. In science, Thomas Kuhn referred to these breakdowns as "paradigm shifts." In business, Joseph Schumpeter called them "creative destruction." For both men, the process was identical. Bold new experiments, usually the work of young practitioners, directly challenge the core beliefs of the established order, forcing a difficult but critical period of reinvention, followed by another period of normal evolution.

In law, we call it *revolution*—the replacement of one form of government with another.

The Internet revolution is now demanding rules that fit the realities of digital life, particularly the unique properties of information. As an economic good, information can be consumed simultaneously by everyone; in many cases, it becomes more valuable the more it is used. Next-generation media companies including YouTube, Facebook, Wikipedia, Six Apart, Scribd, MySpace, and Twitter exploit those features. They enable a growing community of users to produce, modify, and collaborate on a remarkable range of content. While some of that content is their own, much of it is under the control of large corporations. No matter, say the users. Bits are bits.

As content owners become increasingly desperate to protect their information assets, worlds are colliding. Digital life thrives on cooperation, recombination, and added value. Industrial-era laws, most visibly of copyright and patent, stand conspicuously in the way. It may not take much to overcome them. The Pew Internet and American Life project reports that 72 percent of Americans between ages 18 and 29 say "they do not care whether the music they download onto their computers is copyrighted or not." In China, even the idea that information should be treated as a kind of property was unheard of until the late twentieth century. Laws that can't be enforced are laws in name only. Game over.

This book is the story of these and dozens of similar struggles going on right now. It goes beyond the headlines to reveal the new forces, driven by

technology, that will ultimately determine their outcome. For the most contentious features of digital life, I describe nine emerging principles that are
shaping a new legal code. These nine principles—*the laws of disruption*—
derive from the economic and environmental conditions of digital life. They
are the change agents of the Law of Disruption, closing the gap between legal
institutions of the past and those of the future. My goal is to help you learn
to harness these principles, both for business and for personal gain. To that
end, a "Fast-Forward" section at the end of each chapter offers guidance
for policymakers, business leaders, and consumers hoping to avoid the pit-
falls, smooth the transition, and exploit the opportunities of a fundamental
transformation of law already in progress.

It may seem strange to argue, as I will throughout this book, that markets
generally work better than traditional forms of government in establishing
rules for disruptive technologies. After all, we are now witnessing the most
dramatic market failure since the Great Depression. Business was largely left
alone to manage its own affairs, and business proved unequal to the challenge. Greed, fraud, and irrational behavior took over, silencing the voices
of reason. Banks collapsed, bubbles burst, and venerable institutions went
bankrupt overnight. There was plenty of destruction, to paraphrase Joseph
Schumpeter, although there was little evidence of creativity.

Given this sad history, market forces may seem a poor choice to drive the
creation of a new code of digital life. As we will see, the alternatives are
worse. Judges have little access to the kind of expertise or experience necessary to understand the unique features of innovative technologies. Legislative power is intentionally limited by a variety of checks and balances,
including competing international, federal, and local bodies, as well as the
separation of powers between legislators and the judiciary. Lawmakers are
often beholden more to special interests and lobbyists than to their constituents. Regulators, likewise, are too often the spokespeople for the industries
they oversee, particularly at the moment those industries are threatened by
innovation. As Winston Churchill said, "Capitalism is the worst system, except for all the others."

Regardless of who writes the new laws, one thing is clear. Revolution is
coming. This book will teach you to see the warning signs. It will help you
profit rather than perish from the seismic shifts already in progress. It will

show you ways to smooth your own migration to digital life, and to understand the weakness of the laws that are now in place to regulate it. It will give you the tools to help speed the development of a new code better suited to the accelerating pace of technological change—the new code of the laws of disruption.

DIGITAL LIFE

DIGITAL LIFE

Understanding Second-Order Effects

Throughout modern history, technological breakthroughs regularly surpass the people who invent them. The gap between the potential and the humanly possible, the chief by-product of the Law of Disruption, inevitably leads to dramatic change in the short term. But the real transformation comes later, as human systems—economic, social, legal—struggle to catch up. This chapter introduces the Law of Disruption and its key drivers, Moore's Law and Metcalfe's Law. Together, they have built the foundation for our new existence, our digital life. Now comes the hard part: creating a new body of laws to regulate it, to keep the peace, and to ensure its prosperity.

KILLER APPS IN THE MIDDLE AGES

Disruptive Technologies change the world. But not in the way you might think.

In the darkest days of the Middle Ages, a Germanic king adapted the rigid metal stirrups used in Asia, making them instead from flexible leather. Now soldiers could balance themselves on horseback and still fight, making them far more effective. The stirrup saved Europe, and these new mounted cavalry were celebrated forever after as knights. But that's just the beginning of the story. To maintain the new fighting force, knights needed a source of income. Rather than pay them himself, the king granted the knights the right to collect rents and other tributes from farmers in their domain. Feudalism, landed nobles, and serfdom were born. More knights required more land,

and the king began to take it from the church. Church and state, and the rise of the latter, established a long-lasting pattern of interaction.

The first-order effects of the stirrup were dramatic. Medieval society was saved. The Catholic Church survived and continued to provide social, cultural, and legal continuity with the long-dead Roman Empire. The king emerged as the first leader of a new and powerful empire, the forerunner of modern Europe. On Christmas Day in the year 800, he took the crown from Pope Leo III's hands as the pontiff was about to coronate him, and placed it on his own head. His name was Charlemagne—Charles Magnus, the Great—emperor of the Romans.

The long-term consequences of Charlemagne's simple innovation were, in some sense, even more stunning. The social, economic, and legal systems that developed to support the mounted troops persisted for nearly a thousand years, long after the actual advantage of the stirrup had been neutralized. Charlemagne's empire, in some form, lasted until the age of Napoléon. Even today, you still can't buy property in parts of central London without paying tribute to the Duke of Westminster.

The stirrup is a classic example of what I described ten years ago as a killer application, or "killer app"—a technological innovation whose introduction disrupts long-standing rules of markets or even whole societies. Killer apps establish new industries and transform existing ones. They can even create new empires. Their own inventors may have little idea of the uses for them that people will ultimately discover. And the real impact is often felt long after their introduction. The stirrup, crop rotation, reading glasses, iron rope, the steam engine, railroads, the telegraph, antibiotics, automobiles, the atom bomb, the semiconductor—this is just a short list of inventions whose dramatic introductions were followed by even more dramatic changes to the civilizations that used them.

Saying that the stirrup created medieval Europe is a stretch, but not a big one. As historian Lynn White Jr. put it, "Few inventions have been so simple as the stirrup, but few have had so catalytic an influence on history."

THE THREE LAWS OF DIGITAL LIFE

Charlemagne had the stirrup. We have the computer.

The information age, like the feudal age, began with a simple innovation. On November 6, 1952, Dwight D. Eisenhower was elected president of the

United States in a rout. Although Eisenhower was expected to defeat Adlai Stevenson, no one imagined so lopsided a victory. No one, that is, except a Census Bureau computer named Univac. Univac had been built to tally the census, but its operators programmed it instead to process election results. After only 1 percent of the vote had been counted, Univac correctly predicted an Eisenhower landslide.

Univac weighed 16,000 pounds, performed about 1,000 calculations per second, and cost $750,000. It was the first commercially sold computer in the world, and the first to be used for business applications (General Electric programmed it to calculate its payroll in 1954). It was also the first to be programmed for a task it was not initially designed to perform—a trend that defines modern computing to this day. The Census Bureau's machine was the first; by 1957, forty-six had been sold.

Nearly sixty years after Eisenhower's election, there are now more computing devices in the world than there are people, and their numbers are doubling every few years. The semiconductor, or "chip," was first added to a calculator in 1967, to a toy in 1978, and to a toaster in 1983. A personal computer was first marketed in the early 1980s. Despite unfathomable advances in the computer's power and abilities, the price of computing has dropped steadily for thirty years. Today's PC costs 16 percent of what it did in 1981, but is nearly five hundred times more powerful. More than a billion have been sold.

As chips have become cheaper and more prevalent, their impact has moved from the world of computers and high technology to every aspect of modern life. Computers are the central driver of productivity gains across industries. Software has become a key source of new consumer products and services. The average automobile now has more than one hundred microprocessors and its own operating system. Even product packaging is becoming intelligent. Soon, more than a trillion items will be able to send and receive data about their price, whereabouts, and expiration dates.

The ubiquity of computers in business, however, has been eclipsed by their takeover of our personal lives. As e-mail and Web browsing have given way to virtual reality games, intelligent cell phones, and social networking, we are each developing a second, parallel, existence. Human beings thrive on interaction, and computers have given us remarkable new tools to connect, collaborate, and communicate with one another. In 2008, consumer Internet usage surpassed business use for the first time, opening a gap that is expected to widen over the next decade. We have our real lives, and now we also have digital lives.

In our digital lives, we can simultaneously chat with friends in different time zones or explore alternative identities in role-playing games. We can let our computers scour the Internet looking for things that interest us— auctions for obscure collectibles, music by artists liked by people who like the same books as you do, or just random content (blogs, photo images, YouTube videos) fed into our personal home pages. And we are no longer tethered by wired connections. All of our information is now available wherever we go on a variety of devices. Nearly 20 percent of American homes had dropped landline service by 2009, relying entirely on cell phones. "Computing," as Nicholas Negroponte wrote in his 1995 classic, *Being Digital*, "is not about computers anymore. It is about living."

Digital life is the unintended side effect of cheap computing power and the ubiquitous network standards known as the Internet. Initially invented in the 1970s, the Internet had the modest goal of connecting the mainframe computers of U.S. government agencies and defense contractors. As more computers joined the network, however, the Internet mutated into something far different and much more interesting. Today, it connects billions of devices and billions of people. It moves information at ever-increasing speeds along a nearly infinite set of pathways, shortening distances and eliminating borders.

Three related principles—Moore's Law, Metcalfe's Law, and the Law of Disruption—explain the power and promise of digital life. Taken together, they provide its natural laws—its physics—overseeing its unique forms of time, space, and gravity.

Moore's Law: Faster, Cheaper, Smaller

In 1965, Gordon Moore, the founder of Intel, made an astonishing prediction. In a brief article titled "Cramming More Components onto Integrated Circuits," he claimed that the number of transistors on his chips would double every year or two without increasing their cost to users. His promise is now known as Moore's Law: every twelve to eighteen months, the processing power of computers doubles while price holds constant.

Moore's Law is the result of technological breakthroughs that reduce the size of transistors, coupled with manufacturing improvements that greatly reduce the frequency of defects. With each new generation, producers yield slightly larger chips made with slightly smaller transistors. Neither Moore nor his competitors have yet to break Moore's Law, and there is every reason to believe they will continue to deliver on it for the rest of our working lives.

The application of Moore's Law boils down to one remarkable fact: computers continue to get faster, cheaper, and smaller. As a result, they become more powerful by a factor of two with every succeeding generation. Computer memory, data storage, and data communications have their own rough approximations of Moore's Law. Improvements in fiber-optic cables (which transmit data at the speed of light) and the development of optical switches translate to data communication costs that are rapidly approaching zero for most uses. One fiber-optic cable can carry millions of simultaneous telephone calls.

Total data storage has also expanded exponentially. In 1980, IBM sold refrigerator-sized disks for its mainframe computers that stored about 1.2 gigabytes of data at a cost of $200,000. Today, Wal-Mart sells 4-gigabyte drives—enough to store about 3,000 books—that are the size of a paper clip and cost only $5.00. GE announced in early 2009 a breakthrough that will increase the storage capacity of CDs by 100,000 percent. IBM is working on technology that will store data in individual atoms and build circuits out of a single molecule.

Because chips are the raw material in the construction of digital life, the implications of the faster-cheaper-smaller principle are profound. Consider a few examples:

1. *Deflation.* Basic commodities like oil, electricity, or cotton tend to become more expensive over time, with cost increases working their way through the rest of the system. Computer prices, on the other hand, have stayed the same, or gone down. Miniaturization leads to computers in more and more products, increasing economies of scale and pushing costs down even faster.

2. *Abundant resources.* Oil, natural gas, coal, and many of the sources of electricity are nonrenewable—as they are used, they are also used up, raising prices and limiting further increases in productivity. But the major ingredient of semiconductors is silicon, the second-most abundant element on earth.

3. *Zero marginal cost.* For most manufactured goods, such as automobiles, price is based on the sum of the cost of developing the goods (research and development as well as marketing), the marginal cost of producing each item (including materials, distribution, and customer service), and a profit margin. Software—the programming that tells computers what to do—can be marketed, manufactured, and distributed electronically, giving it a marginal cost that is close to zero.

Perhaps the most compelling example of Moore's Law in action is not in business at all, but in the world of toys. From the moment in early 1999 when Sony announced its second-generation home video game console, the PlayStation 2, it was clear this would be no mere plaything. PS2 games provide three-dimensional animations that are convincing enough to give many adults motion sickness. Because the games are networked, PS2 users around the world can play them against each other, building powerful communities of users who, in many cases, are coauthors of new game modules or other new uses for the software. Sony sold more than 1 million PS2s in Japan on the first day they were available. To date, Sony has sold more than 150 million PS2s.

Built fifty years after the Univac, the custom processor in the PS2 can execute more than six billion instructions per second. Roughly speaking, that makes the PS2 the equivalent of 22 million Univacs. That many Univacs would fill an area larger than the city of Seattle, and in 1952 would have cost more than $16 trillion, considerably more than the current gross domestic product of the United States. The PS2, on the other hand, is the size of a small laptop computer. It sells for $99.

Seven years later, in 2006, Sony launched the PlayStation 3. The PS3 features even more lifelike graphics, full networking capability, and the ability to download and play high-definition movies. Thanks to Moore's Law, PS3 is thirty times more powerful than PS2. That translates to about 660 million Univacs, enough to fill the entire state of Washington. And their cost, in 1952 dollars, would exceed the total money supply of the world.

Metcalfe's Law: Value Expands Exponentially

While those numbers are settling in, consider the second defining principle of digital life. Metcalfe's Law, formulated by networking pioneer Robert

Metcalfe, explains a phenomenon anyone with a telephone already understands. The more people you can reach, the more reasons you find to reach them. One telephone is useless. A few phones have limited value. A billion phones create a vast network. As the number of connected devices in any network increases, the number of possible connections between them grows exponentially. Each new connection, therefore, adds far more value than the one that preceded it. To paraphrase Metcalfe's findings, the usefulness of a network is the square of the number of users connected to it.

The key to Metcalfe's Law is the knee in its curve, the point at which there are enough users so that each new node adds not a few but a few million new connections. Here's how it works. If you have a network of two telephones, the total number of possible connections is two (I call you, you call me). Add a third phone and we add not two but four additional links, still not very exciting. The millionth new phone, however, adds not two or even two hundred but *two million* new potential calls, making the network even more attractive for the next million users, and the millions after that. Add three-way and conference-calling features, and the number of possible connections explodes.

Networks—railroads, computers, or individuals speaking a particular language—exert a kind of magnetic pull. The more users, the stronger the pull. Reaching the inflection point gives the network increasing momentum, or what is sometimes called "the tipping point." Eventually, absent any economic or technical constraints, networks grow to the point where every possible connection is made. At that point they become so much a part of our lives that they are almost invisible. To reach the tipping point, however, networks must attract as many users as quickly as possible, drawing in the next, bigger, wave. The best way to do that is to keep the cost of entry low, perhaps by subsidizing or giving away equipment the user needs to connect and then charging little for access and use.

For information technology, Moore's Law makes it relatively easy to keep the costs of connection low. Digital networks are built on hardware that gets cheaper all the time, allowing new applications to take full advantage of Metcalfe's Law. That's one important reason digital networks have developed so much faster than earlier networks like, say, the railroad or the telephone, where giving away free service wasn't an option. These early technologies also didn't benefit from the additive value of standardization. Railroads in the United States did not settle on a uniform gauge until the 1880s, making interconnections between lines in the North and South complicated, slow, and expensive. Telephones added dials only in 1931, though the need for human operators had constrained growth for some time. Without self-dialing, today's phone system would require more operators than there are human beings to work it.

The protocols for exchanging information over the Internet are both standardized and more robust. New applications simply grow their user bases on top of the existing network infrastructure. The more users there are, the more appealing the application becomes, a phenomenon that economists refer to as "network effects." As demonstrated by applications such as YouTube, Facebook, and Twitter, network effects in digital life are easier to establish than in the physical world. YouTube and Facebook, for example, reached the top-ten most visited Web sites in 2008, only three years after being launched. With the cost of the network paid for by its customers, Internet phone company Skype signed up 400 million users in its first five years. Its software actually improves as each new user downloads it.

The Law of Disruption: The Distribution of Change Is Uneven

As Moore's Law continues its relentless journey into the realm of smaller, cheaper, and faster, new applications arrive more quickly. As they do, Metcalfe's Law is there to spread them around. Together, Moore's Law and Metcalfe's Law have created a new environment—the world of digital life. It goes beyond the creation of a first- and now second-generation of Web-based products, services, and devices. Digital life is a virtual location where relationships are formed, business is conducted, and new products and services made entirely of information are designed, launched, and consumed.

As with other great innovations, however, human beings and social institutions need time to adjust to this new reality. The stirrup quickly transformed military strategy, but its success led to conflicts between church and state, between kings and their subjects, and between new landowners and subsistence-level farmers. The huge social changes wrought by the stirrup took centuries to play out. The same is true of later inventions. The steam engine ushered in the industrial age, but also generated a century of wars over the ownership of raw materials and access to new markets. The invention of nuclear weapons dramatically ended World War II, but left the world in perpetual anxiety about the potential for total annihilation.

In the gap between the speed with which people respond to change and the much greater potential of the technologies we invent, the greatest conflicts in human history occur. This unavoidable struggle between old and new is explained by the third law of digital life: the Law of Disruption. According to the Law of Disruption, *technology changes exponentially, but social, economic, and legal systems change incrementally.* As the new world runs increasingly ahead of the old, social systems invariably break down, only to be dramatically reinvented to better suit the new environment to which human beings have already relocated. Periodic upheavals are unavoidable; unexpected and unintended phenomena are natural by-products.

In some sense, the Law of Disruption codifies what we have already learned from a thousand years of killer apps. Their initial impact can be dramatic— even revolutionary. But the real change may come years later. In the long run, as human beings reorder their lives to adjust to the new realities, the second-order effects of innovation are both more dramatic and more systemic.

Ten years into the Internet revolution, we're only just starting to see the impact of the Law of Disruption. Newspapers, which originally shrugged off digital technology as a novelty, are fighting for their lives. Manufacturers now routinely source their materials and even their processes from a global market of suppliers. Even leading high-tech companies—including those whose products started the chain reaction—sometimes find themselves outpaced by entrepreneurs with little more than a good idea.

Still, the most difficult change has only begun. As digital life evolves a culture and an economy that fit its new reality, it is increasingly clear that the legal system of the old world doesn't work anymore. Our current laws were forged during the Industrial Revolution, the last great technological leap. They are built on assumptions about ownership, citizenship, and limits of time and distance that don't apply in digital life.

Just as the Industrial Revolution replaced the feudal law of medieval Europe with a new law of merchants and markets, the information age is forging its own legal principles, ones better suited to regulate the new activities, relationships, and transactions it supports. In the past ten years, conflicts over digital citizenship, global electronic commerce, and rights to new information products and services have strained an already fragile legal system. Digital life brings with it profound opportunities, but the systems in place to oversee it have reached the breaking point. Our social, economic, and legal institutions now face a wrenching transformation.

AT THE ACCIDENT-PRONE INTERSECTION OF INNOVATION AND LAW

Business and economics have already been remade by digital technology. Innovation is now reinventing law. The Law of Disruption is running head-on into the statutes, regulations, judicial opinions, and treaties that today regulate businesses and consumers in their digital lives. So far, law has shaped (and sometimes distorted) the key features of digital life. Now the process is going the other way.

Dramatic change is unavoidable. The processes and institutions that create laws are slow and methodical, replete with redundant checks and balances. The authority of regional and national governments is generally limited, with some rights reserved for local institutions. In most jurisdictions, legislation requires passage in both an upper and a lower body. Party politics and the influence of lobbyists and other nongovernmental organizations often stalemate each other, keeping real reform at bay. These controls reduce the risk of tyranny, but they also create a system that is ill-fitted to respond to the rapidly evolving needs of citizens living a digital life.

Courts and judges are even less well suited than legislators to bring the law up to date. The job of the judiciary is to interpret the law, not to improve it. Judges in most courts are generalists, trained only in a process of conflict resolution applicable to a wide range of problems. Few understand modern technology. When forced to weigh in on problems at the border of physical and digital life, courts have limited access to outside expertise. Even in the best of circumstances, judges can solve only the particular conflicts of the parties standing before them. They cannot reach out to answer or even raise the larger questions.

Faced with the daunting task of reconciling existing law with the Law of Disruption, judges are understandably frustrated. In the famous 1984 *Betamax* case, movie studios sued Sony, the maker of the first home videocassette recorder, claiming that its very existence violated their right to control the use of entertainment content. The Supreme Court disagreed.

"One may search the Copyright Act in vain for any sign that the elected representatives of the millions of people who watch television every day have made it unlawful to copy a program for later viewing at home," the Court wrote, "or have enacted a flat prohibition against the sale of machines that make such copying possible." Rejecting the movie studios' demand that the Court ban the VCR, the Justices directed the studios to look elsewhere for relief. "It may well be that Congress will take a fresh look at this new technology, just as it so often has examined other innovations in the past. But it is not our job to apply laws that have not yet been written."

Faced with disruptive technology, as *Betamax* demonstrates, economic forces of the old world always resist the transformation to a new legal paradigm, pitting innovation against the dusty laws of the past. Digital technology is hardly the first innovation to force policymakers to choose between the two. In the United States, the creation of national railroads and the concentration of capital they made possible inspired the Progressive movement, which fought to reclaim government, at least in part, from a few powerful corporations. President Theodore Roosevelt embraced the Progressive agenda and broke up the monopolies, not because he was a liberal but because he believed it was a necessary safety valve to avoid revolution. His fear was well founded. In Russia, a very different kind of uprising replaced the aristocracy of the czars with that of the Soviet Politburo. One transformation was largely nonviolent. The other was not.

We stand today at a similar crossroads. At the accident-prone intersection of innovation and law, clashes between business and consumers, business and government, and governments and their citizens are growing in frequency and in volume. Fights have broken out over information ownership, network neutrality, privacy, spam, wiretapping, pornography, and gambling. These and hundreds of other struggles pit laws written during the industrial age against the Law of Disruption. As in every earlier conflict of its kind, the outcome is certain. A new body of law, one better suited to our digital lives, will ultimately emerge. Only the timing and the path we'll take to get there are in doubt.

Business leaders can no longer separate innovation from the laws that circumscribe it. The design of new products and services, increasingly launched on a worldwide basis, must follow the rules of hundreds of potential regulators, including local tax authorities, price-setting boards, advertising overseers, and consumer safety agencies. Web sites may require compliance with laws protecting those with disabilities, or with antidiscrimination laws protecting gender, minority status, sexual orientation, or age. Contractual limits on a distributor's "territory" become impossible to enforce when consumers have the ability to shop worldwide for the best prices and terms. This is particularly true for information products, which are simply downloaded to the user's computer from anywhere on the network they happen to reside.

As digital pioneers build new homesteads online, they too need to understand the increasingly complex web of rules and regulations that determine what they can and cannot do there. As information becomes the measure of value in a postindustrial economy, consumers increasingly find themselves caught in the crossfire in fights between businesses and between governments. Consumer electronics manufacturers, for example, continue to develop exciting new products that allow users to enjoy a variety of media in new formats and with added conveniences, including next-generation digital video recorders (DVRs) such as TiVo and Moxi. Content owners, echoing the battle over the Betamax, still argue that some or all of the uses of these devices violate their rights and ought to be banned.

Content owners are also fighting consumers over how new services can or cannot be used. Apple's Steve Jobs took the side of his customers (and, naturally, the best interests of Apple) in pushing music publishers to offer digital songs through iTunes without copy-protection technology that limited the devices on which they could be played. He appears to be winning that battle. But another Apple product, the iPhone, follows exactly the kind of "closed" model Jobs elsewhere condemns. Despite outrage from customers and threatened intervention by European regulators, the iPhone works only on cellular networks approved by Apple.

Sometimes the conflicts are between rapidly converging industries trying to control who has access to customers and who will profit from them. The Hulu service, launched by some of the largest broadcast networks, lets users watch television programs on their computers and bypass the gatekeeping function of cable companies. Hulu made cable providers nervous enough, but when the makers of a software product called Boxee built an interface to stream Hulu content from the computer directly to the user's television, the cable companies blew their tops. They demanded that the networks participating in Hulu shut Boxee out, technically and legally. Hulu complied. Dazed, NBC Universal chief Jeff Zucker explained, "We want to find an economic model that makes sense."

Increasingly, consumers reject these artificial limits. What's more, the collaborative technologies of social networking applications make it easier for users to speak with a single voice, putting pressure on both companies and governments to take consumer demands seriously. Just ask Facebook. In early 2009, company lawyers made what they considered minor modifications to the site's privacy policy. Such documents are generally written in dense legal terminology, made up mostly of boilerplate language no one actually reads. At least, that was what the lawyers thought. In reality, the residents of digital life have become sensitized to the potential abuses embedded in these documents and, whether they understand them or not, pay close attention to any changes.

Here, a few of Facebook's more paranoid users noted the revisions and argued, not entirely correctly, that they signaled a dramatic shift in policy. Facebook, they believed, was giving itself ownership of all user content, even that of users who decide to leave the site. Rumors of dark motives by Facebook's owners quickly spread, fanned by the very tools for sharing information that Facebook provides. The company was flooded by a torrent of angry complaints from users. A Facebook group called "People Against the New Terms of Service" quickly signed up 120,000 members. Unflattering headlines appeared in mainstream media ("Facebook Hoisted on Its Own E-Petard," "Facebook Backtracks on Use Terms"). Within days, Facebook CEO Mark Zuckerberg was forced to reverse course, and returned the document to its original form.

Zuckerberg's "about-facebook" signaled something more than just bad lawyering or poor customer communications, though both were involved. The company's entire value is based on good relations with its users. That asset cannot be maintained when the terms of service (TOS) are dictated rather than negotiated. "More than 175 million people use Facebook," Zuckerberg noted humbly on his blog, making it the sixth most populated "nation" in the world. Going forward, he promised, the documents that define the Facebook community will be written in collaboration with users and in language that everyone can understand. "Our terms aren't just a document that protect our rights; it's the governing document for how the service is used by everyone across the world. Given its importance, we need to make sure the terms reflect the principles and values of the people using the service."

Terms of service, privacy policies, license agreements, and other legal documents are the governing instruments of digital life. They are its Magna Carta, its Constitution, and its Universal Declaration of Human Rights. They are also the starting points for a new body of law—a government of the people, by the people, and for the people of the Internet. Long the exclusive province of specialized lawyers, they are now the responsibility of the lawmakers, senior executives, and users who want to help form a more perfect union. Facebook's users executed a bloodless coup, perpetrated in a matter of days by rebels with little understanding of the law they were nevertheless determined to overthrow. Welcome to business and life in the digital age.

FAST-FORWARD: THE LAWS OF DISRUPTION

Frederick Jackson Turner, historian of the American West, famously argued that law on the frontier adapted to the unique properties of its environment. As fur traders gave way to ranchers and ranchers to railroad tycoons, the law evolved to suit their changing needs. Unwritten rules became charters, territorial laws, and state constitutions. Gunfights, posses, vigilantes, and the summary justice of the hanging tree passed on to sheriffs, circuit-riding judges, and frontier lawyers. But no matter how civilized the West became, frontier law never reverted to the original form of the former colonies or the European precedents the colonists brought with them. Instead, the law of the frontier became the law of the United States.

The American frontier was fueled by free land. The digital frontier is fueled by free information. Just as Turner elegized that the "wilderness masters the colonist," so too will the Law of Disruption increasingly define interactions in digital life. The Law of Disruption is its "code of the West," driving the creation of new rules better suited to its unique conditions.

This book explores nine critical areas where technology, driven by the Law of Disruption, is dramatically rewriting the rules of business and life. In each, industrial-era laws are being overthrown. In their place, new principles have emerged to create a code of law applicable to the digital age. These new principles are the *laws of disruption*—emerging rules for digital life shaped not by courts or legislatures but by Moore's Law, Metcalfe's Law, and the

Law of Disruption itself. They are the keys to resolving today's most bitter conflicts at the border of physical and digital life.

The laws of disruption are divided into three groups, reflecting the major components of digital life:

1. *Private life*—The struggle of digital citizens to control private data and ensure fundamental rights for their digital selves
2. *Public life*—The efforts of businesses to secure a robust technical environment and a competitive market free of unfair competition, protectionist policies, and dangerous new forms of crime
3. *Information life*—The development of economically sound rules for the control and use of information products and services, balancing incentives for creators with the need for reuse and collaboration of a new kind of consumer

THE LAWS OF DISRUPTION

PRIVATE LIFE

1. **Convergence**	When Worlds Collide
2. **Personal Information**	From Privacy to Propriety
3. **Human Rights**	Social Contracts in Digital Life

PUBLIC LIFE

4. **Infrastructure**	Rules of the Road on the Information Highway
5. **Business**	All Regulation is Local
6. **Crime**	Public Wrongs, Private Remedies

INFORMATION LIFE

7. **Copyright**	Reset the Balance
8. **Patent**	Virtual Machines Need Virtual Lubricants
9. **Software**	Open Always Wins ... Eventually

Understanding the laws of disruption is essential to plotting a course through the minefields of digital life, a frontier society prone to rapid booms and even faster busts, to winners and losers changing places in an instant, to consumer revolts and life-or-death lawsuits. Those who learn to harness them will shape the legal contours of digital life. They will lead the development of new markets and gain invaluable competitive advantage when launching digital products and services. Even more, they will determine whether digital life becomes a true democracy or a tyranny of the masses—a utopia guided by fundamental human rights or a virtual mob armed with pitchforks and torches, ready to burn every new innovation as a Frankenstein's monster.

Our digital lives hang in the balance.

THE WEIRD
ECONOMICS OF INFORMATION

Non-rivalrous Goods and the Problem of Transaction Costs

Digital technology has transformed the market from one based on industrial production to an information economy fueled by ideas. To understand the opportunities and the risks of living a digital life, we need to understand the key ways in which information behaves differently—indeed, often the opposite—from traditional assets like oil, timber, and other commodities. Information, for example, doesn't get used up, costs little to distribute, and often improves in value the more it is used. This chapter looks at the economic properties of information and the stresses they create for a property rights system designed around the scarcity of manufactured goods.

HEROES

It was a fight over nothing.

In 2008, 12,000 members of the Writers Guild of America staged a withering strike against the major Hollywood studios. It lasted three months, interrupted dozens of TV series, and delayed several big-budget movies. Reportedly, the two sides collectively lost more than $2 billion. The sole issue in the dispute was when and how revenues from Internet and other digital distribution of entertainment would be allocated. But so far, no such revenues exist.

Online distribution of movies and especially TV is a recent phenomenon, powered by ever-faster data transmission speeds, the continued spread of broadband technologies into the home, and improved protocols for file compression. It seems certain that profitable models for delivering Hollywood content to computers, personal digital assistants (PDAs), cell phones, and other non-TV devices will emerge. But in these early days, as with music before it, it isn't clear what those models will be. Will they be supported by advertising? Will content be pay-per-view or purchased? Meanwhile, as with earlier less bandwidth-intensive content, much of the innovating is being done by users of YouTube, BitTorrent, and all the variations, who in the interest of speed and experimentation don't bother with the niceties of obeying the law (Viacom has a $1 billion lawsuit in progress against YouTube and Google).

Why did the two sides risk so much fighting over revenue that doesn't yet exist from channels that haven't been invented? The writers say they took a stand in large part because they did not do so in the early days of videocassette sales and rentals. When the profitable models finally arrived, the writers believed they got a much worse deal. Because media sales and rentals now represent the largest share of entertainment income, missing the boat has been painful for the writers.

The studios argued that until it is clear how and when money is to be made from digital distribution, preassigning residual royalties to writers would limit the studios' ability to experiment with different distribution and partnership models. (They made the same argument with regard to videotape.) Ultimately, new residual rates were agreed to for categories including downloaded rentals and sales, ad-supported streaming media, short clips, and promotional uses. Whether these prove to be favorable rates, or even the right categories, remains to be seen. Either way, media will continue to migrate to the Internet at the expense of other forms of distribution.

THE FIVE PRINCIPLES OF INFORMATION ECONOMICS

It's hard to say if anyone made the right decisions in the writers' strike, in part because the tools for valuing intellectual creations, even for present uses, are terrible. You will look in vain at the balance sheets even of companies whose sole assets are information (much of the entertainment industry, as well as professional services such as doctors, lawyers, and consultants) to find any useful measure of the current or future value of the company's real assets. Even though management gurus sing the praises of developing a company's "intellectual capital," financial reporting systems ignore it.

Accountants refer to all the valuable information in your business—your information assets—as "intangibles." As the name suggests, these are assets that never take a physical form the way factories and inventory do. Unlike physical assets, information assets are generally not counted in toting up the total worth of an enterprise. For the most part, a company's human resources, brands, and good relationships with customers and suppliers—let alone its copyrights, patents, trade secrets, and trademarks—are left off the books. The value of the company's information, at least as far as accounting is concerned, is pretty much nothing.

Why? Accountants have argued for years that information and other intangibles are so different economically from material goods that traditional methods of valuation just don't apply. As an asset, they point out, information behaves precisely the opposite of its tangible counterparts. Capital assets lose value as they are used, equipment becomes obsolete, and raw materials are depleted. Brands and reputations become more valuable the more they are exercised, in theory generating revenue forever. You cannot determine the price of a logo or a customer relationship with the same tools you use to depreciate a tractor.

That might be true, but it doesn't explain why accountants have done so little to develop valuation techniques that do apply to information assets. The result, in any case, is that few managers understand what they are or how they work. Even CEOs of large companies regularly get it wrong when they talk casually about "trademarking an idea" or "copyrighting a word." (You cannot do either.)

As information becomes more central to the economy, the failure to account for its value has become dangerous. Executives, especially in public companies, are compensated on the health of their companies' balance sheet. To the extent that information value doesn't appear there, it's understandable that many companies don't put much, if any, effort into developing or even managing those assets.

That's unfortunate, because the strategic cultivation of information assets can pay off in dramatic ways. Consider Harrah's Entertainment, which operates casinos in most places in the world where gambling is legal. When former business school professor Gary Loveman joined the company as chief operating officer in 1998, he decided to look for underutilized assets off the balance sheet. He found them, of all places, in the data warehouse. Like most casino chains, Harrah's had implemented a rewards program that gave customers special benefits for using their membership cards while playing slot machines. Harrah's was collecting vast amounts of information on its "factory floor," but had done very little to put that data to good use.

According to Loveman, a detailed review of the collected information deflated some long-standing assumptions about how Harrah's made money. Most of the company's profits came from just 25 percent of its customers. Those customers were not, however, the "cuff-linked, limousine-riding high rollers we and our competitors had fawned over for many years." Instead, Harrah's discovered that the high-profit customers were regular visitors, many of them recent retirees. They made frequent trips to the casino and spent steadily, if modestly, at its gaming tables, restaurants, and hotels. Harrah's quickly reconfigured most customer-oriented operations, including check-in, complimentary meals, and special promotions, orienting them toward the actual, as opposed to the presumed, best customers.

The result was a changed enterprise, one that consistently outperforms its competition. Even though the balance sheet never reported the value of the diamonds Loveman found when he looked in his data mine, his information assets were by no means worthless. In 2006, Harrah's was sold to a private equity partnership at a price that valued the information at more than $1 billion, representing a 30 percent premium over the price they might otherwise have received. Today, Gary Loveman is still CEO of the company, a position he has held since 2003.

The writers' strike and the Harrah's story teach one important lesson about the economics of information: just because its value is indeterminate doesn't mean it's worthless. Not by a long shot. The writers and producers clearly didn't think so, nor did the buyers of Harrah's. Just to take another easy example, search giant Google has $20 billion in assets (mostly cash) on its balance sheet. But the company, even on the lowest day of the stock market in ten years, was worth nearly $100 billion—more than five times the book value. Somebody has figured out, at least in part, how to value the information assets.

Digital life is made up of a wide range of information types, including private data, speech, news and entertainment, business practices, and information products and services such as films, music, inventions, and software. The laws of disruption, as we'll see in the coming chapters, organize themselves around the behavior of these information types. So before diving into the specifics, we need to understand a few key facts about information economics.

Let's start with what it is economists do know. Most goods in our industrial economy, everything from stirrups to computers, fall into a category known as rivalrous goods. Rivalrous goods are those that can be possessed by only one person at a time and whose use is limited to that person or with whomever she might share it. If I own a barrel of oil, for example, then you don't own it unless I sell it to you, in which case I no longer have it. Once it's used, it's gone forever—no one has it anymore.

There is, however, another kind of economic good—the non-rivalrous good. Non-rivalrous goods can be used by everyone at the same time; limiting access to them is difficult if not impossible. The classic example is national defense. The army protects everyone, including those who don't pay their taxes. Defensive missiles can't be programmed to leave your house unguarded.

Information is also a non-rivalrous good. Once a composer completes a piece of music, everyone can perform it simultaneously. There is cost associated with its creation, and perhaps with marketing the finished product to interested performers. But the composer incurs no additional cost no matter how many times the work is played. When we're all done, the composition is still there. In fact, it becomes more valuable the more freely it's shared—it becomes more popular, maybe even a "hit."

Until recently, however, many types of information could not be easily distributed without first being copied to physical media such as books, newspapers, or, in the case of the song, tapes and records. In that transformation, it lost its non-rivalrous properties, looking more like the barrel of oil than like national defense. It's easy to limit access to the barrel of oil—there's only one, after all. The song, which can be duplicated, is harder to control, but it's still possible to exclude those who didn't pay for a copy or pay for the right, as in radio, to broadcast it.

For information products, the ability to exclude is a function of law—the law of copyright, which makes it a crime to duplicate information without permission. Copyright gives the composer the exclusive right to make or authorize copies. At the same time, it outlaws the production of copies by anyone else, including someone who purchased a legal copy. By limiting both the production and the use of the song, copyright transforms non-rivalrous information into a rivalrous physical good.

As digital technology makes it easier to distribute the song electronically, the alchemy of copyright is disappearing. Given the Internet, as everyone knows, it is now much harder to limit who gets to hear the song and when. Although legally the composer can exclude those who do not buy authorized copies of his work, his ability to police that right is increasingly expensive, often costing more than it's worth. You can't really stop people from humming your tune, for example, even if they do it out loud. And now you can't really stop them from sharing copies of a digital recording, either.

There are, however, important reasons for using law to treat information as a rivalrous good. Laws that grant copyrights to composers are aimed at maximizing the value of the up-front investment that information producers must make. If copyright didn't exist, you could simply buy a recording of the song, reproduce it, and sell your own copies. Because your total investment would be only the cost of a single copy, your version would likely be cheaper. The composer would find it difficult to recover his creative investment, making him less likely to undertake his important work in the first place. Ultimately, everyone would be worse off.

Still, copyright neutralizes some of the valuable features of non-rivalrous goods. Fortunately, this special power is limited. Even with copyright, some forms of sharing are perfectly legal. Libraries can loan out the same copy of a recording to as many people as want to hear or play it, one at a time. Fans who purchased their own copy are likewise more than welcome to loan it to their colleagues, or even to resell their copy to a used record store or through online services such as Amazon Marketplace or eBay. Copyright also has a time limit. In the United States, for example, copyright lasts from 70 to 150 years. After this period, the work becomes the property of the public to use however it wants. It becomes forever after a purely non-rivalrous good.

Moreover, copyright applies to the composer's particular expression of the work, not the underlying ideas. The ideas in a song (love conquers all, love stinks) are non-rivalrous from the moment the song is written. Consider a 1996 case involving sports statistics. In the days before the Web and wireless data devices, Motorola sold a device called Sportstrax. Employees of the service watched sporting events on TV and entered key information such as who had the ball or who had scored into a computer system. A few minutes later, Sportstrax customers would be paged with short updates. The company was soon sued by the National Basketball Association, which claimed the pager violated their copyright in the broadcast of games.

The court disagreed. Sporting events are not "authored," the judges noted, and are therefore not protected by copyright in the first place. Game data, including interim scores, are non-rivalrous. Today, pagers have given way to cell phones that can take photographs and access the Internet. Popular television programs such as *American Idol* have armies of fans who watch the show and write blogs about each performance even as they're watching them. So long as the actual performances aren't being copied, however, the commentary is perfectly legal.

The challenge for copyright and other laws controlling access to information, however, has always been to strike the right balance between incentives for creators and the value that the public derives from unlimited use. It's a balance that is constantly being unsettled by the Law of Disruption. On the one hand, information technology has greatly lowered the cost of creating and distributing information, including books, movies, and recorded music. The same technology has also made it far easier to make and distribute unauthorized copies, in many cases perfect replicas of the original.

This is only the start of the weird behavior of information as an economic good. The five principles described below summarize the rest.

1. Renewability

Information cannot be used up. Once it has been created, it can be used over and over again. In the end it is still there, in exactly the same condition as it began. Most new information, moreover, is created from other information, making it a renewable energy source. In electronic form, neither its production nor its use generates waste products that damage the environment. In that sense, information is the ultimate "green" energy.

The online encyclopedia Wikipedia, for example, is not written by hired experts. It is written by volunteers, who post articles on subjects they either know or think they know something about. Within certain limits, anyone else can edit, correct, or change entries. Over time, the articles evolve into a useful and reliable form. No money changes hands in either the creation of Wikipedia or its use.

2. Universality

Everyone can use the same information at the same time. Blog entries, news articles, and YouTube videos can be enjoyed simultaneously by an unlimited number of people.

Each consumer, moreover, may have a completely different reason for consuming the same information, and perhaps her own unique response to it. She may even be inspired to respond with information of her own creation. Facebook is made up entirely of user-generated content. Users in the same groups are constantly commenting on the status updates, photographs, and other information posted by their friends, and inviting each other to join interest groups or play information games.

3. Magnetism

Rivalrous goods operate under the law of supply and demand. The greater the supply, the lower the price you can charge for it, and vice versa. The value of information, on the other hand, is a function of Metcalfe's Law. It increases exponentially as new users absorb it. The more places my brand or logo appears, the higher the value customers attach to all my goods. Use makes the brand more, not less, valuable.

The increase in value accelerates as the information spreads, creating a kind of magnetic pull that generates network effects. Since no one owns the protocols that make up the Internet, these standards have spread easily, resulting in the explosive growth that began in the 1990s. The standards are now more valuable than they were when only a few people used them.

4. Lack of Friction

The more easily information flows, the more quickly its value increases. In electronic form, information can move in any direction at the speed of light.

It experiences no decay along the way, arriving at its destinations in the same form as when it departed. For many kinds of information, including languages, religious doctrines, and advertising, the ease of transfer helps to improve society—or at least the profits of those who disseminate it. The cheaper it is to "spread the word," the more likely and quickly it will be spread.

There's a paradox here, however. The frictionless spread of information can undermine the incentives for its production. Content producers, including authors, musicians, news organizations, and movie studios, invest heavily in the production of new information. To recover their investment, producers must charge for its use. Economically, however, even the simplest payment schemes (subscriptions, for example) slow the natural tendency of information to move freely. Since information flows along the path of least resistance, markets look for ways to avoid fees. In that sense, new technologies often subvert old business paradigms, even when the inventors of those technologies didn't intend for them to do so.

5. Vulnerability

Information does share one property with tangible goods; it is not indestructible. Value can be destroyed through misuse. If you license your company's name (and reputation) to an inferior product or a product that does not have or make a clear connection to your brand, you risk confusing consumers about what your brand stands for. Value can also be destroyed by a third party, perhaps a competitor offering a knockoff product that looks like yours but is of lesser quality. Or an identity thief can appropriate your name and credit history to borrow money from banks or credit card companies. When the thief disappears, not only is the money gone, so is your reputation.

Information can also be a victim of its own success. It is now so easy to produce, distribute, and consume information that users are experiencing overload. Today, Web sites, e-mails, blogs, text messages, and even "tweets"— brief messages that reflect the thoughts of a user on the popular Twitter service—all compete for users' limited time. As the sources of information and the volume produced expand rapidly, consumers find it more difficult to limit their exposure to information of real value.

It's easy to see these principles in action in digital life. Think about Google. One might wonder how a company can be worth anything, let alone $100 billion, when it charges absolutely nothing for its products and services. You can search Google's databases and use its e-mail service day and night without spending a penny; you can store photos on its Picassa photo service, create documents with its online word processing software, download Google maps, and share videos on its YouTube service for free. Indeed, the company is determined to have as many people as possible take complete advantage of it.

Even though the databases and other services are what consumers want and therefore represent the true source of the company's value, Google doesn't hoard those assets as if they were barrels of oil to be used only when necessary. It treats them instead as non-rivalrous goods that increase in value the more people use them. The company isn't being generous. Google makes all its money by renting out advertising space to companies whose products and services complement the things consumers do when they are using Google. If information wants to be free, then let it be as free as possible, and make all the profits from the collateral effects of Metcalfe's Law.

For social networking sites, just giving away content isn't good enough. They have to find ways to get users to help them develop their Web sites in the first place. Companies like Facebook, MySpace, and their professional equivalent, LinkedIn, are constantly adding free tools and "gadgets" to make their products more compelling. Once the sites reach their tipping points, the search for ways to make money begins in earnest, including premium services and targeted advertisements. But thanks to the weird economics of information, there remain powerful reasons not to charge the users—ever.

THE PROBLEM OF TRANSACTION COSTS

The frictionless transfer of information and the problem of information overload suggest that the economy of digital life is a kind of machine. Like the best engines, it can operate with remarkable efficiency—provided its parts are kept lubricated and free of foreign matter. Already, technologies operating under the Law of Disruption have ruthlessly eliminated waste in our increasingly efficient digital lives. Still, the information economy is not perfect. It suffers, like its physical counterpart, from a kind of inefficiency, what Nobel Prize–winning economist Ronald Coase first called "transaction costs."

Coase first came to the United States from England in 1931. Only twenty years old, Coase had a revolutionary agenda. Already struggling to reconcile the socialism of his youth with the free-market sensibility of his professors, Coase saw big companies as proof that centralizing activities could work on a grand scale. If he could learn how big companies did it, Coase imagined, then perhaps the lessons could be applied to big governments as well. Oddly enough, no one had ever asked why companies existed, and certainly no one had ever thought to ask the people who were running them.

What Coase learned made him swear off socialism forever, and led to the publication of an article that changed economic thinking forever, contributing to Coase's Nobel Prize in Economics sixty years later. There was a price, it turned out, not only to whatever was being bought or sold but also to buying or selling it. Buyers and sellers had to find each other and then negotiate deals and consummate them. None of this activity was especially easy, much less free. In his article, Coase argued that companies were getting bigger because markets were just too expensive.

Coase called the price of doing a deal its "transaction cost." The existence of transaction costs, he believed, explained why companies were internalizing more and more activities, especially repeated functions like buying raw materials and marketing. The firm was cheaper than the market. To understand why, let's take a simple example. Say you work for an average-size company and you've run out of paper clips. Almost assuredly, you will get your paper clips not by leaving your office to drive to the office supply store but by going down the hall to the supply cabinet, where your company's purchasing department maintains an inventory of paper clips. Your company will, in fact, keep such basic supplies on hand as a matter of course, without giving much thought to the cost of carrying this inventory, even if buying and distributing office supplies have nothing to do with what your business does. Your company is likely to keep paper clips on hand even if there was no discount for buying in bulk.

Why? Even if you could get paper clips on your own for the same price, you still have to go out and get them. This means finding the stores that carry them and learning how much they charge. Then you have to choose between the closest store and the one with the best price. At the checkout stand, you need to make sure you are really charged what the store advertises. If the clips are somehow defective, you have to take them back and demand replacements or some other remedy.

And that's just for a simple transaction. Imagine instead that you were buying raw materials needed to manufacture a jet airplane. There is the additional effort of negotiating a price, writing a contract, inspecting the goods, and, potentially, invoking the legal system to enforce the terms and conditions. Better, you say, to own the supplier or at least to buy in bulk and avoid all that trouble. That "trouble" is transaction costs.

Working from Coase's basic idea, economists have now identified six main types of transaction costs:

1. *Search costs*—Buyers and sellers finding each other in increasingly broad and distributed markets.
2. *Information costs*—For buyers, learning about the products and services of sellers and the basis for their cost, profit margins, and quality; for sellers, learning about the legitimacy, financial condition, and need of the buyer, which may lead to a higher or lower price.
3. *Bargaining costs*—Buyers and sellers setting the terms of a sale, or contract for services, which might include meetings, phone calls, letters, faxes, e-mails, exchanges of technical data, brochures, meals and entertainment, and the legal costs of contract negotiations.
4. *Decision costs*—For buyers, comparing the terms of the seller to other sellers, and processes such as purchasing approval designed to ensure that purchases meet the policies of the organization; for sellers, evaluating whether to sell to the buyer instead of another buyer or not at all.
5. *Policing costs*—Buyers and sellers taking steps to ensure that the good or service and the terms under which the sale was made, which may have been ambiguous or even unstated, are translated into expected behavior from the parties. This might include inspecting the goods and any negotiations having to do with late or inadequate delivery or payment.
6. *Enforcement costs*—Buyers and sellers agreeing on remedies for incomplete performance. These include everything from mutual agreements for a discount or other penalties to expensive litigation.

As this list suggests, transaction costs range from the trivial (turning over the box to see the price) to amounts greatly in excess of the transaction itself (imagine if you were seriously injured by a defective paper clip flying off the shelf and sticking you in the eye). Economists Douglass North and John Wallis have estimated that up to 45 percent of total economic activity consists of transaction costs. Eliminating them entirely would translate to a staggering $4.5 trillion in annual savings in the United States alone, eliminating much of the work done today by accountants, lawyers, advertisers, and many government agencies.

Firms are created, Coase concluded, because the additional cost of organizing and maintaining them is cheaper than the transaction costs involved when individuals conduct business with each other using the market. But what functions should a firm perform internally? The answer is only those activities that cannot be performed more cheaply in the market or by another firm. In fact, as Coase says, a firm will tend to expand precisely to the point where "the costs of organizing an extra transaction within the firm becomes equal to the costs of carrying out the same transaction by means of an exchange on the open market." For some activities, say plumbing, the open market works relatively well, and the need for plumbers to form large firms to avoid transaction costs has never arisen. For the large-scale operations of Boeing and General Motors, which required coordination, heavy capital investment, and complex distribution systems, the firm is the only economically viable solution.

Coase believed economists should turn their attention to the practical problem of uncovering transaction costs wherever they occur and eliminating those that are unnecessary. Doing so, he hoped, would help reduce the need for government intervention. A great deal of regulation and liability laws, Coase argued, were unconscious efforts to overcome transaction costs for certain types of activities, such as accidents and pollution. But the regulations themselves generate so many transaction costs that in many cases doing nothing at all would have produced a better result. To find out how much law and regulation are optimal requires a better understanding, once again, of the costs.

Coase had hoped his elegant proof would get economists working on the real problem at hand. Ironically, all he did was make economics more esoteric. Instead of lowering themselves to the kind of empirical research that was common in other social sciences, economists simply dispose of Coase in an opening footnote. They "assume a frictionless economy" and then proceed to develop elaborate mathematical models of behavior in a purely theoretical universe. Rather than join his quest, most economists retreated to more abstract models of economic behavior.

Increasingly frustrated with his economist colleagues, Coase instead took up residence at the University of Chicago's law school. Economists, he came to see, avoided information, and misused the few sources, such as government data, that they had. Economics had become a shell game. "If you torture the data enough," he wrote, dismissing much of modern economic analysis, "nature will always confess." If that was all economists could do, Coase decided he was no economist. Awarded the Nobel Prize in 1991, Coase began his acceptance speech on a note of despair. "In my long life I have known some great economists," he told the committee, "but I have never counted myself among their number nor walked in their company."

Look at the performance of the economy over the past twenty years and it's easy to sympathize with Coase's frustration. The "rational" stock market still booms and busts. Cyclical industries continue to overexpand and then overcontract. Efforts at creating an open global economy without trade barriers are met with rioting mobs. National banking regulators read every tea leaf they can find and still go to bed at night wondering if they cut rates too soon or too late, too much or too little, or even if it makes an iota of difference. While most economists fiddle with their formulas, the economy is burning. Without a better understanding of the nature of transaction costs, we'll never be able to predict—let alone improve—what seem to be the most basic elements of economic behavior.

That, in any case, is the real world. In digital life, the problem is not only less severe but also solvable. The free flow of information made possible by Moore's and Metcalfe's laws is decreasing the friction of transaction costs in a variety of interactions. From global price comparisons to searches of much of the world's store of knowledge to auctions for anything and everything, the cost of deal making is plummeting. The Law of Disruption, in fact, is driving down all six of the transaction costs. That is what makes it so disruptive in the first place. Consider a few examples:

1. *Search costs*—Technology connects people across geography, time, and national borders. Automatic notifications for obscure collectibles on eBay, finding old friends through the "People You May Know" fea-

ture on Facebook, or letting your TiVo pick programs for you that it thinks you might like to watch—each of these reduces search costs, sometimes dramatically. Restaurant and other business reviews available directly on cell phones make it easier to find just the right place no matter where you are. One iPhone application uses GPS technology to help you find your car in a crowded parking lot.

2. *Information costs*—Technology creates standard data structures that can be searched and consolidated over a growing network of computers. The asymmetry of sellers concealing data has eroded, radically changing the way people buy cars, real estate, and investment securities. Free or subscription services including CarFax, Zillow, and Yahoo Finance give buyers an abundance of valuable information that before may have been inaccessible at any price. Online dating services such as Chemistry.com increasingly use sophisticated profiling technology to suggest matches most likely to be compatible.

3. *Bargaining costs*—The exchange of information can now take place digitally, and is captured in databases for easy reuse in subsequent transactions. Instant publication of classified ads on Craigslist means many local transactions are completed within minutes. Business-to-business transactions increasingly rely on libraries of standard terms. The nonprofit association ACORD, for example, uses the XML data standard to create standard forms used by insurance, reinsurance, agents, and brokers offering life, property, and other lines of products.

4. *Decision costs*—Visibility to expanded online markets gives both buyers and sellers a truer picture of minute-to-minute market conditions. Several insurance Web sites, including Progressive.com, provide instant quotes and comparisons to the prices of their competitors. Cell phone users can compare prices from online merchants while shopping at retail stores, putting added pressure on merchants to match or beat those prices or offer other incentives, including delivery or after-sales support. Online gamers can check the reputation of potential participants to decide whether to allow them to join their teams.

5. *Policing costs*—Transactions conducted with system-to-system data transfers create a more complete record of the actual performance of the participants, which can then be captured and queried. For goods

purchased online, most merchants now provide direct access to detailed shipping and tracking information from expediters such as UPS or FedEx or even standard delivery from the postal service. Some, including Dell Computers, provide information further up the manufacturing process, allowing customers to see where their products are before they're even assembled. Most software products now collect bug and other failure information in real time, automatically installing updates and repairs. Players of the online World of Warcraft game can "speak" directly to in-game employees or robots when they have a problem.

6. *Enforcement costs*—Electronic records can simplify the process of resolving disputes over what was agreed upon or what did or did not occur. Online payment services such as PayPal offer elaborate dispute-resolution functions that include mediation and arbitration when buyers and sellers cannot resolve their differences, along with insurance and guaranteed satisfaction. All are supported by the collection of end-to-end transaction data documenting the actual performance of buyer and seller. Bloggers can quickly whip up electronic mobs to put pressure on companies, politicians, or celebrities whose behavior they feel does not comply with agreed-upon standards.

FAST-FORWARD: CONFLICTS AT THE BORDER

The Law of Disruption adds an important dimension to Coase's observation about business organizations. As transaction costs in the open market approach zero, so does the size of the firm—if transaction costs are nonexistent, then there's no reason to have big companies, period. For products constructed entirely or largely out of information, we now stand on the verge of what Don Tapscott and Anthony Williams call "peer production," where just the right group of people come together to apply just the right set of skills to solve complex problems, whether of business or otherwise.

Efficiency translates to savings of time, money, and waste. Productivity, customer satisfaction, and the availability of customized products and services have improved dramatically. Keeping in touch across time zones and long distances gets easier, as does organizing diverse groups of people for social, political, or business reasons. The average consumer can now edit an online encyclopedia, post news and photos as a citizen journalist, or operate a home-based business that can produce and distribute just about anything.

Now for the bad news. Our current legal system, forged in the factories of the Industrial Revolution, was designed to maximize the value of rivalrous goods. It can't be easily modified to deal with the unique economic properties of information. Worse, the crushing overhead of regulations and lawsuits, which may no longer be cost-effective even in the physical world, adds even less value when applied to the lower–transaction cost environment of digital life.

Increasingly, the old rules do little more than hold back innovation for the benefit of those who can't or don't know how to adapt to the economics of digital life. In many cases, inefficient laws are propped up by failing businesses that are not eager to see their advantages erased. Sometimes those fighting transformation are powerful business interests, including large media companies, real estate agents, and even some of the technology companies whose products fuel the revolution.

Resistance may also come from the users themselves. In digital life, private information can be invaluable in deciding who to interact with, either for business or for interpersonal transactions. As the Law of Disruption brings more private information online, powerful emotions have come to the surface. Citizens in much of the world believe their rights to privacy are being violated, not only by businesses but by their classmates and neighbors. Perhaps most worrisome of all, governments are taking advantage of lower transaction costs to improve the technology of surveillance, raising fears of the dystopic world described by George Orwell in his novel *1984*.

Lower transaction costs have also proved useful to criminals and terrorists, who operate freely and anonymously in digital life. Sometimes their crimes exploit the vulnerability of information, as in identity theft and other forms of Internet fraud. More ominously, virtual gangs are able to attack the infrastructure of the Internet itself, releasing viruses and other harmful software that incapacitate servers, destroy data, or, in the case of spam, simply waste people's most precious resource: time.

Perhaps the most difficult problems of information economics, however, involve the plasticity of information in electronic form. Technology has made it possible to realize the remarkable potential of information to be shared and even enhanced by as many people as are interested in it. Inevitably, every new innovation that supports this creative urge runs headlong into laws protecting information as a kind of property—that treat non-rivalrous goods as rivalrous goods. Although such laws are still necessary, they have proven unduly rigid in their current form, sparking some of the most vitriolic fights on the digital frontier.

The Three Laws of Digital Life and the weird economics of information have created a perfect storm. Our industrial-age legal system will not survive it. After the flood, the nine laws of disruption, introduced in the following chapters, will guide the construction of new codes better suited to digital life. Implementing these principles will require a great deal of coordination and collaboration. Most of all, it will require considerable courage on the part of those who live in both the physical and the digital worlds. So we begin, appropriately enough, at the border that currently separates them.

PRIVATE LIFE

LAW ONE: CONVERGENCE

When Worlds Collide

As wireless access and cheap mobile computing become ubiquitous, the world of the physical and the world of the digital are merging. On the border, some of the most difficult problems of law appear. Where do our digital activities take place? What law applies? Are judges, legislators, and law enforcement officers competent to enforce behavioral standards on our avatars? As this chapter demonstrates, the best and most effective code for the intersection of industrial and information economies is a market-based solution—software code written by the Law of Disruption.

HELP!

It seemed like a good idea at the time.

In 1981, a still young Apple Computers was sued by the other Apple Corporation—the one founded by the Beatles to control their catalog of hits. The dispute involved the relatively arcane world of international trademark law, confusing even for lawyers who specialize in it. Though the logos of the two companies (the rainbow drawing of an apple in the one case, the detailed photograph of half an apple in the latter) are obviously different, the Beatles argued that consumers could be confused into thinking the companies were related, and tried to force Apple Computers to change its name.

Lawyers for the two companies came up with a way they thought would let both Apples exist. In a complicated, poorly drafted agreement, the companies set aside the trademark dispute and agreed that Apple Computers would stay out of the music business and Apple Corporation would stay out of the computer business. But a few turns of Moore's Law later found Apple's Macs being used to compose and mix music, and the two companies clashed again. In the midst of a 1991 trial that lasted more than one hundred days, a new agreement was reached. This time, they agreed to split the baby in half. Apple Computers' exclusive fields of use would now include "computer software of any kind on any medium," while Apple Corporation's exclusive fields of use included "music and/or musical performances; regardless of the means by which those works are recorded, or communicated, whether tangible or intangible." The truce, apparently, was to last forever.

Forever turned out to be one eternity too long. In 1999, a college sophomore named Shawn Fanning figured out he could combine the Internet, encoding standards for music files, and high-speed access to the Web from his dorm room, creating the notorious Napster service. Though the service was shut down after a few glorious years, Napster invented a new way of distributing music. Ten years after the two Apples resolved their differences, the computer company launched the iPod digital music player and iTunes store on the Web, transforming Apple from a second-tier computer company into the leader in digital music. Peer-to-peer sharing of bootleg music files went legal and mainstream. iTunes has changed the way most people buy, store, and listen to music.

The Beatles were not pleased. Apple Corporation sued again, arguing that the launch of iTunes broke the 1991 agreement. Did it? There's no doubt, as the Beatles argued, that iTunes sells music "recorded or communicated" in an "intangible" form. Nor can it be disputed, as Apple Computers countered, that the iTunes music store sells songs in the form of "computer software." Neither side seems to have considered what would happen if those "exclusive" fields combined into one new business. Carving up markets evolving at the speed of the Law of Disruption proved impossible.

So iTunes does and does not violate the agreement, an impossible legal mess unintentionally created by the companies' lawyers. In his opinion resolving the case, Justice Edward Mann wrestled for a few dozen pages with the agreements before deciding in favor of Apple Computers. He could just as easily have ruled the other way, as the judge acknowledged. "If the intention of the lawyers who drafted the 1991 agreement was to create obscurity and difficulty for lawyers to debate in future years, they have succeeded handsomely," he wrote with British understatement.

Eight months later the companies settled, agreeing this time that Apple Computers would own all Apple-related marks and license back to the Beatles the ones they use. The companies also announced that at long last the Beatles would begin offering their music in digital form via the iTunes store. That may have been the point of starting up the litigation again in the first place. Had the Beatles won the lawsuit, or even an interim ruling, it would have improved their bargaining position. Given estimates that the Beatles' recordings might be worth as much as $600 million to iTunes, why not incur modest legal fees trying to improve that number? "We love The Beatles, and it has been painful being at odds with them over these trademarks," a relieved Apple CEO Steve Jobs announced. Lawsuits may slow the pace of business transformation, but consumers ultimately get what they want.

THE LIMITS OF ANALOGY

Apple v. Apple began as a fight over trademarks. All along, however, the real governing body of law was the Law of Disruption, and in particular the subsection on convergence. Worlds are colliding as new markets and new applications emerge from the primordial soup of the Internet. Cell phones, text messages, and digital images bridge the gap between family and friends in the real and digital worlds. High-definition televisions and DVRs bring the fidelity and versatility of theater entertainment into our homes. Amazon and Netflix are moving quickly from managing atoms to moving bits—through the Kindle electronic book reader for Amazon and digital downloads of movies and other media for both.

The convergence of the physical and the digital, of the industrial and information economies, generates some of the messiest disputes between the law of property and the Law of Disruption. The results are complicated and often indeterminate. Until recently, the two worlds more or less kept to themselves, which was just as well. Efforts by legislators in the physical world to regulate activities in digital life are poorly received by the often rebellious natives.

In 1996, for example, President Clinton signed the Communications Decency Act, which banned pornography on the Internet. The CDA, as even its authors knew, was clearly unconstitutional on First Amendment grounds. The U.S. Supreme Court dispensed with it before it ever went into effect.

Still, Web site operators were outraged at the audacity of a single nation claiming moral ownership of digital life, and immediately declared a day of mourning. They shut down their Web sites, literally turning the Web black for a day. John Perry Barlow, a lyricist for the Grateful Dead and the co-founder of the Electronic Frontier Foundation (EFF), dispatched his now famous "Declaration of the Independence of Cyberspace." Expressing disgust with politicians who were trying not so much to regulate a new medium about which they knew nothing but rather to appear to be legislating, Barlow declared the Internet off-limits to the governments of the physical world. He promised not a violent revolution but a war of attrition. "You have no moral right to rule us," Barlow wrote, "nor do you possess any methods of enforcement we have true reason to fear." The document was reprinted so many times that a *Wired* magazine story about it the following month didn't bother to include the text.

Barlow's predictions proved prescient. In the years since the CDA was enacted, governments at all levels and across geographies have tried to regulate, tax, constrain, ban, encourage, or disparage thousands of new applications that have been released into the roiling waters of the Internet. In nearly every instance, those efforts have failed.

Perhaps the only thing all this legislating has done is to solidify resistance among the increasingly wealthy and powerful residents of what Barlow called the "civilization of the Mind." There are now dozens of nonprofits lobbying on behalf of Internet users, and hundreds of blogs devoted to discussions of Internet governance, law, and general outrage at any effort by physical governments to intervene.

As technological convergence brings the two worlds ever closer, the old and the new laws that govern them are increasingly at odds. What to do? This chapter explores the rapidly evolving rules that mediate between the fading law of the industrial age and the emerging law of digital life. Ultimately, the Law of Disruption takes charge, but its invisible hand often performs cunning tricks that create both threats and opportunities for digital pioneers and the merchants who serve them.

On the border, as the Apple case suggests, short-term thinking by lawyers can have unfortunate side effects. The disputes that follow are complicated by the fact that distinguishing intentions from reality often falls to men and women in robes. Although I have great respect for the judiciary as a whole, judges will be the first to acknowledge that they are poorly cast as arbiters of conflicts spawned by the Law of Disruption. As federal appellate judge Richard Posner explains, "The judiciary, unlike the executive and legislative branches, has no machinery for systematic study of a problem." If "the subject is new, the court will not have the time or resources to bone up on it."

Rather than rely on expertise they do not have, judges are trained to resolve cases through an analytical lens known as "legal reasoning." The process of legal reasoning is one of sorting and selecting analogies. A judge is presented with a problem of law. Each of the parties offers her own set of earlier judicial opinions that she believes resolves the matter in her favor. When lawyers argue before a judge, they argue from precedent. This problem is analogous to one already decided by other judges perhaps in parallel or superior courts, and the same rule announced in those earlier cases must be applied here. Success in court is determined by which of the opposing sets of cases the judge finds most resembles the problem at hand.

But what happens when the subject of a dispute doesn't particularly resemble any previous set of facts? Consider two recent cases that asked what might seem to be a simple question: what is eBay? In both cases, retailers of name-brand merchandise (Tiffany's in the United States, Louis Vuitton in France) tried to hold eBay liable for damage to their brands caused by the sale of counterfeit or gray-market merchandise sold through eBay's marketplace.

Though the company has been in existence for ten years, describing what service they provide—or even who their real customers are—baffled courts in the United States and France. In the end, the cases boiled down to an analogy. Is eBay like a department store, where the merchandise of many different manufacturers is sold for a markup? Or is it more like a community bulletin board in a grocery store, where customers post want ads and "for sale" listings on index cards? Under long-established law, department stores are responsible for ensuring the authenticity of the merchandise they handle, while the grocer maintaining a bulletin board is not.

EBay's business includes elements of both. Like a department store, it exercises considerable control over the market, policing complaints from customers, offering payment and shipping support, charging fees based in part on the final sale price of a listing, and even, for its most active merchants, offering employee-like services including health insurance. Like a bulletin board host, on the other hand, eBay never handles or even sees firsthand the merchandise that its buyers and sellers exchange.

The U.S. court decided in favor of eBay and dismissed Tiffany's claims. The French court decided against eBay and ordered the company to pay $63 million in damages. Yet U.S. and French law regarding counterfeit goods is largely the same. Was the U.S. court swayed by evidence that eBay offered Tiffany's extensive tools to monitor auction listings on the site and report likely counterfeits for investigation and cancellation? Was the French court influenced by the fact that eBay is an American company and Louis Vuitton the owner of many famous French brands? Did it matter that some of the listings in the French case involved not counterfeits but items being sold outside the brands' tightly controlled distribution channels?

The short answer is that we don't know. Judicial opinions read like a Sherlock Holmes mystery. The judge begins with the bewildering and contradictory evidence, and then calmly and confidently leads the reader through the legal rules that end, inevitably, with a simple conclusion. The best arguments of the losing side are deflated; the cases that support them are explained away. Helpful details, including the judge's legal philosophy, are left out. In the eBay cases, both decisions read as completely reasonable applications of the same law.

What does eBay do now that a court in one country has approved its practice for handling counterfeits while another has rejected it, with perhaps many other countries to weigh in? As a virtual provider of marketplace services, eBay's auctions take place everywhere and nowhere. Whose law applies when the seller is in one country and the buyer in another, especially when judges in those locations have created very different rules to apply to new kinds of transactions? The result is a mess.

Both decisions are on appeal, meaning that higher courts are reviewing the opinions for legal errors. (Popular media and blogs regularly report lower-court decisions as if they are final and determinative. As we'll see, however, appellate courts can issue dramatic reversals, a possibility that increases in cases that pose novel questions of legal interpretation.) EBay, depending on the final outcome, may have to change its business practices based on the country in which a seller or a buyer lives, or close its marketplace to whole classes of merchandise. Given the volume and rapid evolution of digital commerce, judge-made edicts may simply be impossible to follow, discouraging future innovation. If enough courts come up with enough contradictory rulings, the company may be unable to continue operating at all.

WHEN NETWORKS CONVERGE

Judges are not the only ones struggling to rationalize innovative technologies with deep-rooted rules. Regulators, and the industries they oversee, are also struggling to adjust old ways of managing competition to meet the new realities of digital life. Driven by Moore and Metcalfe's Laws, the Internet has begun to absorb older network technologies, including telephone, radio, and, more recently, television. Cable, telephone, and Internet providers are increasingly offering one-stop shopping. Converging technologies offer new options for consumers but challenge the business assumptions of established companies.

Each of the affected industries has had a long history of complex government regulation. But the rules of the game and the players are now in flux, leaving regulators unable to say how these new services fit into decades-old legal frameworks. Do Internet phone calls, which many companies offer for free, have to be taxed to pay for emergency services? Do Internet radio stations, which can be set up and run by hobbyists, have to pay the same royalties as traditional radio? Do television programs "broadcast" over the Internet have to comply with decency standards? If so, whose?

Innovative new services are caught in the middle. The aptly named Pandora, for example, allows users to create custom Internet radio "stations" based on artists or songs they like. Almost from their inception, however, Pandora and other Internet stations have been fighting for their lives. After years of negotiations, music publishers convinced the U.S. Copyright Royalty Board in early 2007 to adopt new royalty rates that would have effectively ended most services. A settlement later appeared to be in the works that would save Pandora, a deal finally agreed to in mid-2009.

Regulators flip-flop on what rules apply to whom, egged on by the companies they traditionally deal with, which are themselves unsure how to respond to the seismic shifts in their industries. Internet phone provider Skype continues to argue that its architecture can't support routing 911 calls to local emergency providers, despite requirements that it do so. The U.S. Supreme Court continues to struggle with decency rules in an era when the vast majority of viewers do not receive programming over the air—the only place those rules apply.

Improvements in consumer electronics are a regular source of conflict. In 2006, cable TV provider Cablevision was sued by TV networks, including the Cartoon Network and other content providers, over a proposed change to what is still an emerging new technology—the digital video recorder. DVRs are computer-like devices that allow viewers to record programs from their television. Unlike the older VCRs they are rapidly replacing, DVRs use cheap disk drives to store far more programming. They also include sophisticated software that allows users to record and replay programs in a variety of ways or even to let the DVR choose programming for them based on prior viewing history. Increasingly, the DVR allows viewers to watch the programs they want when they want to, without regard for the time, day, or channel choices made by broadcasters. Within the next five years, analysts predict more than 40 percent of all U.S. homes will have one.

To consumers, the value of DVRs has been obvious. Their radical and unpredictable reshaping of the television industry, however, has already brought those who make or offer the technology into court. The earliest challenges have been to the very idea of the DVR. In 1984, the U.S. Supreme Court famously held that content owners could not ban VCRs, even though technically every time viewers taped a program they were making a "copy" of it without permission. Up until now, courts have uniformly held that DVRs are similar enough to VCRs that the same rule applies, though they have looked poorly on features that allow DVRs to automatically skip over commercials as they record.

The Cablevision case, however, challenges management decisions more than it does the technology. Cable providers such as Cablevision that include DVR rentals as part of the price of cable service face a logistical nightmare. DVRs are popular and evolving rapidly. It isn't practical to service or replace millions of units installed in customer homes every time an upgrade or a new generation becomes available. So Cablevision proposed to simplify their computing architecture by replacing in-home DVRs with network DVRs stored and managed centrally in branch offices. The features would be the same. Subscribers would continue to program the DVR from their television screen to record the programs they want to watch later. The recordings, however, would now be stored at Cablevision's facilities. All that would change is the physical location of the hard drives.

The television networks argued that network DVRs broke the law. Recording, storage, and replay by the consumer on a Cablevision-supplied box at their home is legal, but relocating the devices to a branch office is not. Why? With the proposed service, each time the viewer subsequently pressed the "play" button on their remote control, the cable company would have to resend the program from the networked DVRs to the viewer's TV. That, the networks argued, was an unauthorized "public performance"—in effect, a rebroadcast of the program without permission of the owner. Moving the box a few miles transformed a legal activity into a copyright violation.

That argument sounds ridiculous, but under current law the networks were probably right. In a muddled opinion, the appellate court dove deep into the technical details of networked DVRs. Since the copy transmitted from the networked DVR when a viewer ultimately hit "play" was a copy made specifically by and for that user, the court held, the subsequent resending of the program was not a transmission "to the public" and therefore did not violate copyright law. The court combined a dubious understanding of the technology with a strained reading of the law to find in favor of Cablevision. Cablevision was allowed to proceed with deploying the network DVRs—the right solution if not the optimal process for reaching it.

An obvious question not asked by either party was why content owners who supply programming to Cablevision and other cable companies were suing in the first place. Copyright had nothing to do with it. As viewers increasingly write their own schedules, the Cartoon Network and its fellow plaintiffs worry that advertisers won't pay premium rates for time and day of the week. The networks may also worry that DVRs will give cable operators better viewing information and therefore better leverage in paying for programming in the future. Anything that can slow the deployment of DVRs, on this view, is good for the networks. So any chance they get, they sue.

It's a familiar story at the border of physical and digital life. When new technologies offering improved value to consumers are released into the ecosystem of an existing industry, they always disrupt existing business relationships, some of which may not have changed in decades. New value ultimately translates to new profits. In the short term, however, there are always participants whose piece of the pie may shrink. Lawsuits, if nothing else, throw a wrench in the gears of innovation as litigation grinds its way through the courts, skewing the operation of the Law of Disruption. If plaintiffs can convince or just confuse the judge, that's even better. The legal opinion becomes a valuable bargaining chip in negotiating—at the winner's preferred pace—for a reallocation of the profits that the new service ultimately generates.

These days, using the courts to block the Law of Disruption is a popular management tool. But it doesn't substitute for an actual strategy. Litigation is expensive and time-consuming. The outcome is impossible to predict. The Beatles appeared to have won a lasting victory in 1991, until technology undid it. In the Cablevision case, dozens of parties, including nonprofit advocacy groups, wrote briefs that fervently argued one side or the other. The networks won the early rulings. Then, in a flash, they lost everything. In fights at the border of converging industries, the only guaranteed winners are the lawyers.

There's another danger to using the legal system to work out the details of how new technologies will be deployed: customers don't like it. The process of carving up new value among innovators, existing service providers, and governments is confusing, secretive, and frustrating, and consumers are increasingly suspicious. To them, the protracted litigation and regulatory proceedings represent unneeded delay. And private settlements often translate to higher prices for new products and services. In the 1980s, digital audiotape manufacturers and content owners worked out a deal that traded clumsy copy protection and royalty payments for a promise not to use the courts to block introduction of DAT. Consumers rejected the technology, however, in part because of concessions that only they had to pay for. The technology is now effectively dead. On the border of physical and digital life, customers prefer to travel much closer to the theoretical speed of the Law of Disruption.

DIGITAL VICE

The most innovative uses of convergence technologies usually begin in the world of digital vice: gambling, drinking, violent video games, and pornography. Vice Web sites were among the first to introduce video, live streaming of Web cams, real-time multiplayer games, and many other improvements to the initially text-based World Wide Web. Internet pornography is one of the leading categories of electronic commerce, generating more than $57 billion a year. It is a long-standing maxim in the Internet business that these industries are worth watching closely, if only because the latest innovations in digital technology arrive there first.

Not surprisingly, it is also in these industries where collisions between old law and the Law of Disruption most often occur. Regulators and courts around the world have been dragged into border conflicts about everything from the online sale of cigarettes, efforts to regulate the violent content of video games (tried and failed on First Amendment grounds in at least nine states), and attempts to curb Internet pornography. When the World Trade Organization ruled in 2004 that the U.S. ban on Internet gambling violated international trade law, some congressmen indicated they preferred a trade war to compliance. "It cannot be allowed to stand," said one, "that another nation can impose its values on the U.S. and make it a trade issue."

Often the mere threat of regulation is enough to change the behavior of nervous executives, especially of public companies. New York attorney general Andrew Cuomo, for example, has been pressuring Internet providers to shut off access to newsgroups he believes harbor child pornographers. In a letter to cable giant Comcast, he criticized the company's reluctance to sign his "Code of Conduct." The refusal put Comcast "at the back of the pack in the race to fight this scourge," he wrote, adding ominously that the company's refusal "would likely be surprising to Comcast's millions of customers across the country." When the letter became public, the company signed on.

In nearly every case, legal conflicts rarely turn out to be about the morality of the activity in question. Instead, most are simply turf battles between global and national or federal and state legislatures over who gets to regulate the vice, and therefore who gets to tax or at least benefit from the largesse of its lobbyists. In the United States, states regulate matters of morality and family life, but the federal government has the exclusive power to manage commerce between states or between the United States and other countries. The intersection of these two powers has long been a source of conflict. The Law of Disruption, here as elsewhere, is making the problem worse. In some sense, all Internet commerce is interstate, if not global, especially at the border of physical and digital life.

Efforts by local regulators to control global activities always fail one way or another. Consider the cautionary tale of Pennsylvania's Child Sexual Exploitation Unit. Formed in 2008, the CSEU consisted of three law enforcement agents assigned to surf the Web looking for images they believed constituted child pornography. When they found something they thought qualified, notices were sent to Internet service providers including AOL, Verizon, and WorldCom, demanding that the ISPs block access to the offending sites for their Pennsylvania customers. (German and UK regulators, among others, maintain similar "blacklists" of offending sites.)

Pennsylvania was out of its depth, technologically as well as legally. Lawmakers seemed unaware that ISPs don't host most of the offending content. They merely provide their customers access to the Web sites in question. Moreover, given the Web's architecture, the only way to block sites from Pennsylvania users was to cut off access to all of the ISPs' customers, not just in Pennsylvania but around the world. Which is precisely what the companies did.

There were other problems. Many of the pages deemed unacceptable by Pennsylvania were created by individual users of Web-hosting services, in which one Web address holds the pages for thousands of sites. Compliance with the locking orders required the ISPs to cut off all the hosted sites, not just the ones with the challenged content. In one case, the state ordered ISPs to cut off a Spanish Web host with more than 500,000 sites, including an official geological survey of Spain and the International Philatelic Club. Worse, the CSEU never checked to see if the offending images were removed or relocated, leaving the addresses blocked forever. Because the site owners themselves weren't contacted, a new owner might someday acquire a previously banned address and never know it.

Some five hundred notices were sent before the law was ultimately declared unconstitutional, by which time as many as 1.19 million Web sites having nothing to do with child pornography had been blocked. By comparison, only 376 sites with content that may or may not have included child pornography (the determinations were based entirely on the opinions of the three CSEU staff members) were blocked, a ratio that the judge found illegally interfered not only with interstate and international commerce but with free speech rights as well. "There is little evidence that the act has reduced the production of child pornography or the child sexual abuse associ-ated with its creation," the judge wrote. "On the other hand, there is an abundance of evidence that implementation of the Act has resulted in mas-sive suppression of speech protected by the First Amendment."

A close look at another recent fight shows an even darker side to the turf wars of convergence. In 2005, a small California winery challenged state laws, including those from Michigan and New York, which banned the direct import of alcohol by consumers. States claim these laws deter underage drinking, but in doing so they also stop adult residents from joining winery clubs that make periodic shipments directly from the vineyards. As the pop-ularity of wine and the ease of use of the Internet simultaneously expanded, West Coast wineries have grown frustrated by the restrictions.

The case pitted the federal commerce power, which prohibits states from discriminating against out-of-state businesses, against the Twenty-first Amend-ment. Passed in 1933, the amendment ended America's experiment in national Prohibition but left the states the exclusive right to regulate or even ban alcohol sales within their borders. (Some counties still ban all alcohol sales, both retail and in taverns.) One clue that moral considerations are not the only issues in-volved, however, was that neither state banned the purchase of out-of-state wine. They simply required that it be sold through local distributors licensed and taxed by the state. In-state wineries, which both Michigan and New York have, were exempt even from the ban on Internet sales.

The states, in other words, weren't trying to reduce alcohol consumption in general or even prevent it among minors. They were using the Twenty-first Amendment to protect local industries, including in-state wineries and liquor wholesalers. Indeed, wine is not the only commodity to face local bans. In the face of new competition from digital providers, states are raising increasingly convoluted barriers to each other's products. Web sales have been outlawed at the state level for everything from contact lenses to dog medication to caskets. As with the wine case, every regulation claimed some legitimate interest in keeping out-of-state suppliers out. But courts have consistently struck them down for what they really are—protectionist regulations.

As improvements in technology make more intricate webs of national and even global commerce possible, local efforts to protect native industries look more and more suspicious. The goal of Michigan and New York was not to protect minors. It was to protect the wholesalers. The real authors of the bill were the merchants, who preferred not to compete with electronic commerce, no matter how slight a risk it posed. Ultimately, the U.S. Supreme Court struck down all the restrictions. Banning Internet sales, the Court noted, was part of an "ongoing, low-level trade war" among the states. The Court brushed aside the states' claim of protecting children as what it was— mere posturing.

What's disappointing in all of these cases is that they demonstrate how often the best interests of its citizens are clearly not the priority of local governments. Instead, regulators appear beholden or worse to the industries they oversee. Instead of fighting for consumers, the states fight against them. Most cases challenging protectionist laws are brought instead by public-interest law firms. In the wine sales case it was the Washington, D.C.–based Institute for Justice, which has fought a variety of local restrictions on Internet commerce. The institute's general goals seem simple enough: "First, governments shouldn't be permitted to favor certain industries or businesses over others. And second, they shouldn't be able to erect irrational barriers to entry." Threatened by rapid change at the hands of the Law of Disruption, however, local governments continue to try both.

ANTISOCIAL NETWORKING

At the fringes of digital life, where technology increasingly mimics and even exceeds the opportunities for human interaction, digital pioneers are experimenting with a range of new ways of living and communicating. Whether in online versions of popular role-playing games such as World of Warcraft, Lord of the Rings Online, and RuneScape; social networking sites that include Facebook, MySpace, and LinkedIn; or total virtual environments such as Second Life, users can combine real information about themselves and their interests with made-up facts and pure fantasy. All of this information is used to enhance their relationships with real people or form purely fictional—even intimate—connections with the avatars of others.

Given human nature, it didn't take long for these new environments to inherit some of the social diseases that plague the real world. Digital life now suffers from outbreaks of defamation, stalking, sexual predation, theft, and fraud. Not surprisingly, calls for various forms of policing—private, public, and self-regulation—quickly followed the appearance of this antisocial networking. In the near future, at least, traditional law enforcement is unlikely to play a significant role in solving these problems. They lack the technology, budgets, and most of all the frame of mind to understand the nature of the problem, let alone craft a solution.

Regulators, however, can't resist the temptation to interfere when lurid facts emerge. The results are usually clumsy and unhelpful. In 2008, for example, South Korean movie star Choi Jin-sil was accused by bloggers of driving another actor to kill himself when he was unable to repay a $2 million loan she had made to him. His fans attacked her mercilessly online, and Choi told authorities that she "dreaded" the Internet. In 2008, Choi herself committed suicide.

The Korean government seized on Choi's death as an excuse to crack down on a variety of Internet behavior that it apparently didn't approve of. Nine hundred agents from a Cyber Terror Response Center began scouring the Web for slander and what it considered Web "bullying." The country's Communications Commission ordered some of South Korea's larger portals to register users by name and social security number before allowing them to post comments about anything. In response, opposition leaders pointed out that existing defamation laws were perfectly adequate to address the real-life consequences of unlawful Internet conduct. They accused the government of trying to impose martial law on the Internet to distract Koreans from scandals of their own.

In the United States, regulators are increasingly concerned with risks posed by social networking sites. As services such as MySpace and Facebook mushroom in popularity, prosecutors fear that minors are being exposed to inappropriate content and dangerous adult participants. MySpace balked at requests from a number of states to turn over the names of registered sex offenders who had profiles on the site, while New York attorney general Andrew Cuomo singled out Facebook for failing to protect teenagers from sexual predators. Under threat of litigation and new laws, however, both companies agreed to a variety of technical changes to protect young users. MySpace, for one, pledged to combat harmful materials on their site, better educate parents and schools, cooperate with law enforcement officials around the country, and develop new technology for age and identity verification.

Pressure on the social networking sites may or may not reduce the risk of harm to minors. The poor track record of legislators responding to perceived new harms in digital life, however, suggests that making law in the wake of sensational news stories only makes things worse. In 2006, for example, Congress amended federal communications law to define a new crime: "cyberstalking." Federal and state law already deals with stalking in the physical world, but Congress apparently believed those statutes were inadequate to deal with incidents where stalkers had used the Internet as part of a campaign of harassment against their victims.

The legislative process, with multiple committees and horse trading between parties, the House and Senate, and Congress and the White House, is not designed to micromanage emerging technologies or the unfortunate side effects that may come with early use. We have already seen the danger of using "legal reasoning" to analogize old cases to new activities. The cyberstalking statute reveals a similar problem with legislation. The result here is incomprehensible legislation that in practice does nothing. Despite Congress's good intentions, the cyberstalking law is poorly thought out, poorly drafted, and almost surely unconstitutional.

As is often the case with bad laws, most of the problems come right at the beginning—in the section marked innocently as "definitions." Slightly simplified, the law defines cyberstalking as:

- any use of the Internet
- using either a communications "device" or "software"
- to communicate with another person
- without disclosing your identity and
- having the "intent to annoy"

A simple drafting error makes the law obsolete before we even get to the substance. The definition of "Internet," borrowed from an older law, inadvertently leaves out wireless communications and Internet services offered by nontraditional telecommunication providers, including cable companies. This is a common problem with laws that attempt to specifically regulate emerging technologies. Emerging technologies change at the speed of Moore's Law, leaving statutes that try to define them by their technical features quickly out of date.

Courts, however, will often look past or otherwise correct obvious errors, in which case we move on to the bigger problems. The definition sounds nothing like what most people would think of as cyberstalking. The problem is that the new crime grafted onto an earlier statute that dealt with obscene phone calls. The poor fit is obvious. In the case of an obscene call, a caller harasses his victim by speaking or other verbally obscene communications. The calls take place between the offender and the victim, with the offender failing to identify himself. These terms have been expanded to cover Internet communications. Despite calling the new crime "cyberstalking," however, all the law prohibits is the equivalent of a harassing phone call using the Internet instead of a phone.

But how does an obscene phone call translate to Internet behavior? Online communication is usually text based, and may be communicated to many recipients. Most digital communication, moreover, is not fully identified. I might use "ldownes" as a user name when posting to a blog or discussion board or when sending e-mail. In both cases, absent other data, I haven't disclosed my identity, and not because I am trying to keep it a secret.

As for the final element, the law is unclear on whom the offender must intend to annoy. Where phone calls have one target, Internet communications often have no particular recipient in mind. Anyone who has ever read even the most serious-minded blogs knows that many of the postings, both by those managing the original content and by those responding to it, have at least in part the intent to annoy some readers. So long as these messages are posted, the sender has committed the crime of cyberstalking. That is true even if the message is never read, or never read by a particular victim, or read by someone other than the person the offender intended to annoy. Under the law's literal definition, in fact, just posting a criticism *of the statute itself*, so long as you intend for your criticism to annoy someone—perhaps its authors—constitutes a crime, punishable by up to two years in federal prison.

Even worse, as one of my students pointed out, "cyberstalking" would include his throwing his Blackberry at me from the back of the room. The Blackberry, after all, is an "Internet device or software," and throwing it is a use intended to "communicate." If his intent was to annoy me, the crime is complete even if my back is turned and I never knew he did it. The communication would have been received by his fellow students, who are unlikely to have found it annoying in the slightest.

Whether Congress was right that a new law was needed, one thing is clear. The statute seems pretty far from what I suspect most people would think constitutes stalking in digital life. It's no surprise, then, that since its passage very few prosecutions for cyberstalking have taken place. In the cases that have, the real stalking was of the traditional variety—in person and over the phone. E-mail messages simply supplemented the bad behavior.

In many cases, technology-specific statutes fail because the technology changes. Here the problem was more basic. Its authors either didn't know what behavior they were trying to criminalize or became hopelessly lost in analogizing it to the much simpler problem of obscene phone calls. The result was the unintended criminalization of a broad range of behaviors I suspect weren't even considered in the drafting and negotiation of the bill.

FAST-FORWARD: LIFE ON THE EDGE, LAW ON THE BORDER

The cyberstalking law is unfortunately not an isolated case. Fueled by outrageous but likely anecdotal online behavior and a lack of understanding for how technological innovations actually work, bad legislating at the border of physical and digital life is all too typical. In many cases misbegotten laws so obviously violate constitutional provisions—here, perhaps, the First Amendment—that they are voided by courts before the ink is even dry. Cynical lawmakers may even pass them fully expecting them to be overturned, giving legislators cover to tell constituents they tried to put Internet miscreants behind bars but were blocked by "activist" judges. Others prove so nebulous that they are unenforceable, or come without the budget appropriations that would allow the agencies and offices charged with enforcement from trying. In many cases, they sit on the books, ready to spring to life at some point in the future when changes to the technology have outpaced the text, making them, often, the source of unexpected or even opposite results from the intention of their drafters.

Judges can't be expected to resolve these border conflicts, either. Reasoning by analogy doesn't work when the Law of Disruption is constantly creating new forms of interaction in our increasingly real digital lives. Digital music, electronic marketplaces, DVRs, and social networking applications are not "like" anything else. They are something new, as are many of the products and services developed using new digital technologies. The law is ill-suited to adapt to such rapid changes. When disputes involving new innovations are taken to traditional courts, confusing and ultimately destructive applications of old concepts to new situations inevitably follow.

The unhelpful techniques of courts and judges make litigation a dangerous way to conduct negotiations over new products and services, but competitors and others may force you into court. What to do? Companies may not be able to avoid lawsuits, but most executives can do a much better job of anticipating them. The more radical the innovation, in fact, the more likely it is that competitors will use the courts to slow or stop your progress. That's a natural consequence of the Law of Disruption. The tendency for technological innovation to change the rules of an industry is invariably faster than the industry wants to change. Law is one of the principal weapons of resistance.

A radical shift is also needed in the role of company lawyer. The legal staff needs to be integrated into the business and in particular into the innovation process. IBM, which fought government antitrust battles long before Microsoft was even born, was constantly at the mercy not so much of the Department of Justice but of its own lawyers. Former CEO John Opel is reported to have said that the legal department was the only one in IBM that didn't have a budget, and it exceeded it every year. It might be funnier if it wasn't true.

The company lawyer up until now has operated pretty much as a lone ranger or as a necessary evil, depending on one's point of view. Not anymore. If the general counsel isn't part of a company's strategic decision making, the business is asking for trouble. If the general counsel doesn't know what strategic decision making is—that is, if she doesn't understand business in general, let alone the particular business of her client—trouble has probably already arrived.

Businesses on the digital frontier need lawyers who are experts not just in law but in business. This is especially true for in-house counsel. That is largely heresy today. Most corporate lawyers keep themselves far from the details of the businesses they serve. They see themselves instead as risk managers. If they're asked their opinion about matters of corporate strategy, future products and services, or new technologies, they view their job only as pointing out the downsides, the dangers, and the reasons not to innovate.

When the Internet became a strategic technology in the late 1990s, CIOs learned to be full participants of the executive team. We need to begin training lawyers to do the same.

What about consumers? Clearly, the residents of digital life cannot rely on their elected representatives in the physical world to promote their interests. Unfortunately, unelected regulators and other administrators are often just as beholden to entrenched business interests with whom they've interacted perhaps for decades. During the Industrial Revolution, widespread dissatisfaction with railroad pricing and other practices led to the creation of the Interstate Commerce Commission. But rather than redress customer grievances, the ICC quickly became the agent of the industry it was meant to oversee. Regulatory agencies created as part of the post-Depression New Deal, similarly, have long since become captured by their respective industries. The Food and Drug Administration, Federal Communications Commission, Securities and Exchange Commission, and others see themselves more as cheerleaders than watchdogs. Agencies can be a powerful force for resisting change by businesses trying to avoid transformations to their industry midwifed by the Law of Disruption.

New laws or new regulations are rarely the solution in any case. The lawmaking process is intentionally slow, making it a poor fit for solving problems that may be only temporary side effects of rapidly cycling innovation. Even as new applications breed new social problems, legislators should be wary of crafting laws that are too specific or enacted before it's clear the problem won't mutate into something else or otherwise resolve itself.

In some sense, it doesn't matter what lawmakers do. New laws can single out a few random victims, but regulators can't really control behavior taking place in a world where they don't live. Making law from a distance—whether by Congress in the digital age or Parliament during the American colonial period—only foments unrest. Faced with bad laws and clueless lawyers, consumers have grown adept at avoiding regulations they don't like. The Law of Disruption gives them all the ammunition they need to do so.

As real life and digital life continue to converge, courts and regulators do the most benefit by doing nothing. The rapidly changing and ad hoc nature of new interactions can better be overseen by market forces. In digital life, the uneven leverage between consumers and business is coming increasingly into

balance, minimizing the kinds of collective-action problems that traditionally require government intervention. For better or worse, consumers are
now part of the process of creating new products and opening new markets.
Increasingly, consumers will resolve their grievances with businesses and with
each other through ad hoc forms of government, forming digital posses to
put pressure on companies whose behaviors and practices they dislike.

The market is not perfect, but it at least has the ability to rapidly prototype solutions to new problems, rejecting quickly those that don't work out.
Businesses that learn to harness the collaborative capabilities of citizens living their digital lives will profit. Those who fight it will suffer or die.

LAW TWO: PERSONAL INFORMATION

From Privacy to Propriety

Though no one can quite agree on its dimensions or source, most people believe they have a right to privacy. A grassroots consumer movement in the United States and Europe aims to protect that right against the particular pressure it comes under in digital life. This chapter proposes a working definition for "privacy" in the context of its economic value both to society and to individuals, and offers a rant-free solution to the problem. The citizens of digital life should acknowledge their right to privacy, but create a market where individuals and businesses can buy and sell all or part of that right. This approach has already been tested by grocery stores and other "loyalty" cards, though many consumers may not realize that that's what they were doing when they signed up.

A MULTIMILLION-DOLLAR PHONE BOOK

General Motors was about to be sideswiped by the Law of Disruption.

In 2002, the company's human resources department wanted to issue an electronic update to the company telephone book. The simple task proved nearly impossible. First, GM contacted every European employee in their native language to ask for written permission to include their number. For employees who objected, GM offered the services of a third-party negotiator to mediate for them (no one took them up on the offer). Then the company convinced more than two hundred affiliated companies to sign written agreements not to abuse the information if they happened to see it.

The permissions and agreements, along with applications, forms, and affidavits, were next submitted for review to regulatory agencies in more than a dozen countries. Even then, GM was able to publish the phone book only because the U.S. Department of Commerce negotiated a truce in the war GM had inadvertently driven into—a war between the European Union and everyone else.

The fight over the GM phone book was a fight about privacy. In 1995, Europe adopted a sweeping directive to protect what it calls "personally identifiable information" about its citizens. Under the directive, no PII may be stored, distributed, or otherwise used without the express permission of the person to whom it refers. No data may be exported outside the EU to countries who do not follow the directive. The subject of any PII stored in any database, including records not stored electronically, has the right to review her information and may apply to local courts for relief for any breach of the directive.

Even though the telephone numbers GM wanted to list were for office phones bought and paid for by GM, connecting them to the names of employees clearly made them personally identifiable. Consequently, the project required compliance with privacy laws in every European country in which GM had employees. Because the directory would be "exported" electronically, the company also had to certify it would follow EU rules even in countries that don't require them, including the United States. As GM's chief privacy officer, Bob Rothman, explains, "Any information associated with an individual is private: a phone number, address, hat size, or even the name of a pet. We couldn't put the names of our European employees in the directory. How can you be a functional international company and not know who's working for you?"

You may have never heard of the European Union's 1995 Directive on Privacy, but chances are good that if you do business in Europe you will . . . soon. In the European legal system, directives describe end results that the EU wants to achieve. National legislatures, under EU law, "have to adapt their laws to meet these goals, but are free to decide how to do so." This means that every member country has its own slightly different set of rules for implementation and separate agencies for enforcement. In Germany, employers are required to track an employee's religious affiliation, which is illegal in France. French employers must track sick days, which is illegal in Germany.

Since 1995, global corporations have spent billions hiring chief privacy officers and other privacy-compliance staff, negotiating with business partners, and engaging the EU's privacy machinery. Since U.S. law does not comply with the directive, the Department of Commerce has negotiated a "safe harbor" program that allows information exchanges between U.S. and European companies, provided the U.S. companies are certified as complying with European law in seven key areas. (Hundreds of companies are now certified.) Failure to follow the law can lead to harsh penalties, including fines or prison for business owners, data controllers, or anyone else who handles the information. The range of activities that now require the involvement of company lawyers has expanded dramatically.

The privacy directive was passed before the Internet became the world's data communications network. Since 1995 the sheer volume of information—personally identifiable and otherwise—that has become digitized and can be cheaply transported around the world has grown by orders of magnitude. Thanks to Moore's Law, that cost continues to fall, and, thanks to Metcalfe's Law, the value of sharing information increases geometrically. The Law of Disruption has clearly overtaken the European law of privacy, and for the moment the mismatch is costing a fortune.

PRIVATE FROM WHOM?

We've jumped headfirst into the maelstrom known as the "privacy debate." In the past few years there have been at least a dozen books published on privacy in the digital age. Most are polemics that waste little time before accusing those who disagree with them of Hitlerian aspirations. Database owners, according to one law professor, "make people vulnerable by stripping them of control over their personal information." Internet marketers operate "a web of thoughtless decisions made by low-level bureaucrats . . . and a way of relating to individuals and their information that often becomes indifferent to their welfare." On the other side, a conservative think-tank fellow derides privacy advocates (or "privocrats" as she calls them) as "vigilantes" and "sneering know-nothings" engaged in "charlatan crusades."

Privacy, clearly, evokes an emotional, even visceral, response in most people, making it difficult if not impossible to talk about rationally. That, unfortunately, is a problem shared by many features of the information economy. Technology is being applied in ways that revolutionize not just business life but our personal lives as well. Buying books and paying bills on-line makes many people nervous enough, but the Law of Disruption doesn't wait for us to catch up. Political life, family life, even religious life have, in recent years, moved online at breakneck pace. As soon as you sign up with one online service, another one—better, faster, more customized—comes along.

The closer technology gets to matters that are central to our basic sense of self—of who we are—the more likely it is that our first response to it will be an emotional one. In an exercise I use with business students, getting agreement on what information is and is not private dissolves into chaos. Is your street address private? Your e-mail address? Internet Protocol (IP) address? Everyone just gets upset. So even if we lack the basic tools—even the basic vocabulary—to resolve the privacy problem, the imperative to do so gets stronger with each new generation of hardware and applications.

The first step to solving this mess is to understand that there are not one but *several* privacy problems. Each involves the desire of individuals to keep information from others. The costs and benefits of privacy, however, vary based on who it is we want protection from—family and friends, employers, news media, governments, or criminals. Each category of PII user is subject to different levels of restrictions, some legal and some simply social conventions. From least to most protective, these are:

- *Family and close friends*—Generally speaking, we consider only our most intimate thoughts and activities private from family and friends. To invite you to dinner, I need to know your schedule, telephone number, dietary restrictions, and who else we know in common with whom you may not get along. Under American law, minors and the infirm elderly have almost no privacy from guardians and caregivers.
- *Employers and business colleagues*—Employers in the United States are legally free to listen in on your phone calls, copy your computer files, and rifle through your desk. They can disclose any information they find. Business colleagues may also need detailed information about us (and we about them) to complete transactions of mutual benefit. To loan you money, I need to know your credit history and

your bank details. Once the transaction is complete, much of this information is no longer relevant and may be deleted or forgotten.

- *News media*—In most democratic societies, the press is given a wide berth in investigating and reporting the private details of the lives of famous and even ordinary citizens when their activities are considered representative or otherwise newsworthy. The fear of government censorship is generally stronger than concerns about abuse of the free-speech privilege, especially in the United States. In the Internet age, however, an expanding definition of news media (e.g., bloggers and other "citizen journalists") makes almost everyone a reporter and almost everyone a subject.

- *Government*—Governments are viewed suspiciously when it comes to PII about their citizens. The public sector's collection and use of private data are closely regulated. In general, only information necessary to enforce the law can be demanded or even independently obtained. In the United States, the 1974 Privacy Act prohibits agencies that collect PII from disclosing it, even to other agencies. During times of national crisis (war, outbreak of disease), however, government access to private information about everyone tends to expand. For inmates or convicted felons, on the other hand, very little information is considered private.

- *Criminals*—Criminals, by definition, are those who use PII for destructive purposes, including fraud, defamation, and, more recently, technologically enhanced crimes such as identity theft. Though discussions of privacy often deal with the problem in the abstract, nearly all privacy-related laws are focused on keeping PII from criminals.

Before we review how digital life has strained the concept of privacy, we need to dispel one pervasive myth. For Americans, there is no constitutional right to privacy from anyone other than the government. Absent a few specific laws, you have no legal protections of any kind against the collection and use of your PII by advertisers, the paparazzi, or your in-laws. That may come as a surprise to you. It always does to my students, many of whom can't let go of this misconception even when they learn the truth. The *idea* that Americans have a universal right to privacy, invokable against anyone, is one of the most persistent myths in American law. But consider a few contrary facts:

- Employers can lay claim to any information they find regarding their employees. Colleagues, whether business or personal, can dig into any public records about your past, so long as they don't break into your home or misrepresent themselves in the process. Beyond a few specific rules about credit scores and medical history, there are few laws limiting how businesses can collect and report PII about customers, prospects, or consumers in general.

- In 2006, Hewlett-Packard was derided for spying on members of its own board of directors to determine who was leaking embarrassing information about the company to the press. The company even hired private investigators who pretended to be the directors in order to obtain copies of their cell phone records. After months of investigation, prosecutors concluded that no criminal law had been broken. Pretending to be someone to get their cell phone records was outlawed only after the HP scandal outraged the public. Indeed, intercepting and recording cell phone transmissions in their entirety were perfectly legal until 1986.

- The media, particularly in the United States, still enjoy broad immunity in their collection and use of PII. The Nixon administration was unable to preempt publication of the pilfered Pentagon Papers, despite plausible concerns about national security. Even those whose information is being reported have little recourse. Under long-established precedent, newspapers cannot be sued for libel even if the information they publish is wrong so long as they make reasonable efforts to validate it before publication. A 1989 Supreme Court case even held that the names of rape victims may be reported from public records such as police files.

PRIVACY VERSUS TECHNOLOGY

American privacy law, such as it is, largely protects citizens from their own government. The EU, on the other hand, has created a vast government bureaucracy to protect its citizens from each other. The conflict between privacy law and the Law of Disruption, however, has put both approaches under significant strain. In the near future, the differences may prove irrelevant.

Even before the Internet age, technology regularly eroded the anonymity of both public and private life. Samuel D. Warren, a prominent nineteenth-century Boston lawyer, was outraged when a photo of his daughter's 1890 wedding appeared in the *Washington Post*. Warren and his law partner, future Supreme Court justice Louis Brandeis, published a powerful indictment of the press in the *Harvard Law Review*. They called for laws to protect "the acts and sayings of a man in his social and domestic relations" from the "ruthless publicity" of the papers. They defined this new right to privacy, famously, as the "right to be left alone."

For the most part, however, Warren and Brandeis's call for laws to protect the right to be left alone has gone unanswered. Meanwhile, digital technology has vastly expanded the amount of information about us that is easily accessed. The right to be left alone, if such a right ever existed, is now almost impossible to enforce. The invention of cameras, telephones, automobiles, fingerprinting, blood analysis, and, more recently, global positioning systems, cell phones, sensors, and other surveillance equipment has made it easier and arguably safer to interact with one another. At the same time, these innovations reduce the range of our anonymous activities.

Technology, inevitably, leads to the collection of more and more data, ultimately in digital form, that memorialize more and more of what we do, when we do it, and with whom. Is that bad? On one side of the scale is the value to the individual of maintaining private, sometimes embarrassing, preferences. On the other side, public records about our business transactions, photographs of our property and public appearances, and medical records that reveal communicable diseases are of value to everyone else.

Today, information is constantly on the move. The architecture of the Internet, which routes small packets of information through whatever set of connections is least busy at any given moment, means that information regularly crosses national borders (if only transiently) even when the sender and receiver are only a few miles apart. As the costs of data storage, processing, and communications plummet, companies and even individuals are increasingly storing their data where it is most often processed, a concept known generally as "cloud" computing. In the cloud, data are stored and processed by service providers who operate the applications that use it, whether it is e-mail managed by Gmail or information about your customers stored by Salesforce.com, Oracle, SAP, and other application providers.

Cloud computing is just the tip of the iceberg. The real privacy crisis isn't about the storage and use of current data sources, but rather the dramatic expansion of new data in the coming decade. Ten years ago I was introduced to an energetic brand manager at Procter & Gamble named Kevin Ashton. Ashton engaged my consulting colleagues to evaluate a technology that, although it had already been around for many years, was about to get cheap enough to reveal its true potential. That technology is called radio frequency identification, or RFID. It is a combination of hardware, software, and data standards that allow specialized, increasingly inexpensive computer chips to send and receive small amounts of information over radio frequencies. Since 1995, governments and manufacturers of large items like trucks, airplanes, and railcars have used RFID to "tag" items that send and receive continuous information about their location, ensuring they are where they are supposed to be. RFID uses almost no power—in many cases, just static electricity in the air around it.

Ashton realized that as the price of RFID tags or "Electronic Product Codes" fell from hundreds of dollars to fractions of a dollar, RFID could replace the static bar codes printed on package labels. Thanks in large part to work Ashton did to establish a standard format and data-exchange protocols for EPCs, we are now on the verge of a new world for data creation, exchange, and use throughout the manufacturing, distribution, and retail supply chain. Companies are already experimenting with EPCs to track items from warehouses to retail location, and to reduce theft for high-cost items such as perfume. Tagging prescription drugs to ensure accuracy and eliminate counterfeits is just on the horizon. Once RFID tags become cheap enough, perhaps in another five to ten years, it will be cost-effective to include one on every item in commerce. The EPCs will be printed on the packaging using magnetic inks—literally "printed" circuits.

The design of EPCs differs from that of static bar codes in one crucial respect. Bar codes scan to a general description ("roll of Bounty paper towels"), but each EPC is given a unique ninety-six-bit identifier that distinguishes it from every other item of its kind, indeed from every other thing in the world. The EPC's identifier is its Internet address, and it can send and re-

eive data about itself using the same networks humans use for more sophis-
icated interactions. Even though EPCs will send and receive only minimal
data (price, location, and lot and item numbers), the rollout of EPCs will
add roughly a trillion new devices to the Internet.

This "Internet of things" has both exciting and terrifying potential. For
manufacturers, distributors, and retailers, RFID promises a new era of efficiency. EPC promises complete life-cycle information from the point of manufacture to the point of sale for every item produced, shipped, and sold, what
have called elsewhere the "information supply chain." As the ISC takes
shape, basic business activities move from the world of estimates and focus
groups to true scientific disciplines. Activities that have relied on guesswork,
intuition, and small and outdated sample data will be transformed, including
manufacturing planning, pricing and promotion, inventory control, market-
ng, and forecasting.

For consumers, RFID will mean improvements in price, availability, and
he utility of commercial goods. Waste, theft, and obsolete inventory will be
reduced, keeping prices low. Promotions and advertising will be tailored to
maximize relevance and availability. According to consumer market consultants, consumer benefits will include "simplified, automatic cooking instructions; improved product recall capabilities; in-home monitoring of freshness
dating; consumer-level automated replenishment; and ongoing item registra-
tion and security."

There's more. EPCs can communicate anytime they are within range of a
reader device. So there's no reason, at least technically, to end the collection of
information at the point of sale. EPCs in your home could, in theory, communicate with each other and back up the supply chain as far as the manufacturer, who in turn can let you know when products are about to run out,
break down, or expire. When enough data from enough users are collected
and consolidated, manufacturers can use data about consumption and use
(the toothpaste always gets used with the dental floss, the milk and the cereal
go together, multiple brands of the same product live side by side in your
cupboards) to change product lineups and offer special promotions. After-
sale services such as repair and return, upgrades, maintenance, or replacement of consumable parts will experience the same kind of revolution as the
supply chain.

The after-sales potential of EPC data has proven to be controversial even in the theoretical stage. You probably flinched a little at the idea of your appliances and cabinets polling their contents and sending information through your home network back to retailers, distributors, and manufacturers. Our possessions may have an information life of their own, one that may extend beyond our ability to understand or even supervise. The use of that information may reveal facts about us that even we aren't aware of. (My TiVo seems to think I have an interest in home remodeling programs. If so it's a latent interest.)

It doesn't take much more to conjure images of a dystopian future. We share an innate fear that our technology will somehow get together to enslave us. Popular movies like *The Matrix* and *The Terminator*, where humans serve machines rather than the other way around, are popular for a reason. Under the Law of Disruption, fear of new technology can be almost as powerful as the technology itself.

Meet Katherine Albrecht, a Harvard graduate student who in 1999 was working on her Ph.D. thesis in education. According to Albrecht, she read about tests that Wal-Mart and some of its suppliers were running with prototype EPCs, and she saw the nascent technology as something deeply dangerous. Albrecht left Harvard to launch an aggressive, worldwide anti-RFID campaign, which she named Consumers Against Supermarket Privacy Invasion and Numbering, or CASPIAN, after a hero in C. S. Lewis's *Chronicles of Narnia*.

Though CASPIAN was never much larger than Albrecht herself, it proved a formidable obstacle to RFID tests around the world. She appeared on radio and TV and in newspapers around the world, demanding an immediate end to RFID. She called for boycotts of participating stores and merchants, including Procter & Gamble, Levi's, and Ahold. In her book *Spychips: How Major Corporations and Government Plan to Track Your Every Purchase and Watch Your Every Move*, Albrecht argued that RFID technology will destroy the foundations of modern civilization. "The threat they pose," she said in one interview, "is on a par with nuclear weapons."

The merchants never knew what hit them. The tests were designed simply to see if signals could be sent and received in warehouses and on store shelves without interference from other signals, including electricity and cell phones. Frankly, the proponents of the technology had only the most basic idea of how the data flow would function. RFID tags are still years away from being cheap enough to replace bar codes. No one expected consumers would care at all about the tests. Certainly, no one anticipated a grassroots protest movement, fueled by Albrecht's inexhaustible energy and fiery rhetoric. It was as if one day in 1895 Guglielmo Marconi's first experiments using radio waves to transmit information for Lloyd's of London was met by villagers bearing torches and pitchforks, convinced that Marconi was trying to summon Satan himself.

That's not a metaphor. In 2003, Albrecht acknowledged that the source of her passion against RFID was religious. "When I was eight years old," she said, "my grandmother sat me down after a visit to a grocery store and told me that, 'There will be a time when people will not be able to buy or sell food without a number,' referring to the Mark of the Beast, Revelations 13. I made a promise to myself at eight years old that if there were ever a number to buy or sell food, I would stop what I was doing and fight it." Albrecht's objection to EPCs, in other words, is that they literally signal the coming of the Apocalypse, a connection she made explicit in her book *The Spychip Threat: Why Christians Should Resist RFID and Electronic Surveillance*.

Albrecht lives in a particularly dangerous gap between technological potential and human adaptation. Human beings cannot absorb change as quickly as technology brings it about. Although most people learn to suspend their anxiety, others turn to religion, protest, or violence to help them cope. The Luddites attacked the weaving machines of Lancashire in 1811, believing them to be possessed. Ted Kaczynski, the Unabomber, sent explosives to those he believed were hastening the arrival of a bleak inhuman world ruled by machines. Katherine Albrecht appears on TV and at government hearings, calling for the banning of EPCs or, as she calls them, spychips. Forty years ago, journalist Alvin Toffler gave this phenomenon a name. He called it "Future Shock." It is the most dangerous side effect of the Law of Disruption.

Albrecht isn't alone, at least not in her general and growing unease over technology and its effect on privacy. Preemptive anti-RFID laws have been introduced in seven states, including California and Washington. Beyond RFID, privacy advocates, including the American Civil Liberties Union (ACLU), EFF, and other nonprofit groups, see the loss of anonymity everywhere. Internet "cookies" track how users navigate a Web site. Governments have granted themselves increased surveillance powers as part of the "war on terror." Stolen personal information is used to defraud consumers and financial services firms. Few see the dangers of new technologies in quite the apocalyptic terms Albrecht does, but none of us feels entirely comfortable with the speed with which technology is rewriting the private-public equation.

WHO CARES?

Pseudomillenarians like Albrecht inhabit one end of the spectrum in the privacy debate. The other, metaphorical miles away, is perhaps represented best by technology leaders, including Sun Microsystems chairman Scott McNealy, who announced, "You have zero privacy anyway. Get over it." Oracle CEO Larry Ellison put it even more bluntly: "The privacy you're concerned about is largely an illusion. All you have to give up is your illusions, not any of your privacy."

It's hard to translate feelings into rational conversation. That's a lesson in and of itself—every new technology that improves our ability to collect, store, and use information, whether business, personal, or political, is likely to invoke strong feelings. Failing to anticipate that response, as the early experimenters with RFID learned, isn't likely to stop the technology. It can, however, substantially and unnecessarily delay its deployment. Worse, it may lead to unfortunate legislation that shapes the way the technology is used in unanticipated and nonproductive ways.

The tsunami of new information can't be avoided. The value of that data will compel its use. Regulators can put constraints on RFID and other technologies, but the market will find ways around them . . . eventually. So let me ask a stupid question: who cares about privacy anyway? In the abstract, the answer is everyone. In practice, consumer behavior tells a very different story.

Even as CASPIAN and other antitechnology advocates rail against RFID as the end of the world, most consumers already carry a device that tracks their every movement with far more power and precision than an RFID tag ever will. A few years ago, I had the good fortune to be skiing in the Alps on the border of France, Switzerland, and Italy. Throughout the day, I noticed that my friend's cell phone was constantly signaling new messages for him. At lunch, I asked him what was going on that was so important. It turned but that each time we crossed a national border, invisible on the ski slopes, his cell phone duly checked itself in to Swisscom, France Telecom, and Telecom Italia. The text messages were letting him know who was now providing coverage. Better than any human border patrol, the phone companies, all of them at least in part government owned, knew and logged his every step.

The ubiquity of cell phones has opened a wide gap between privacy in the abstract and privacy in practice. Carriers constantly check the location of every phone, whether or not in use, and monitor its movements. Indeed, cell phone companies offer geographically specific services to their customers that are based on using PII (your current location), including maps and directions, local restaurant and retail guides, and even services that show on the map when friends are nearby. Such data, not surprisingly, has proven invaluable for law enforcement, too, both to determine the whereabouts of a suspect and, increasingly, for real-time tracking of criminals and stolen property.

Parents of lost or wayward children or elderly adults are also making good use of location data, setting up perimeters that, when crossed, alert the proper authorities. The kids, meanwhile, use services such as Sprint Nextel's Loopt, Google's Latitude, and Helio's Buddy Beacon to find each other (but block their parents). The iPhone already boasts dozens of applications that rely on GPS data of the user's whereabouts to provide contextual information. These include Yelp (which uses GPS to find restaurants and cafés near your phone) and Njection Mobile (which alerts drivers to upcoming speed traps).

On the Web, the most popular innovations of the past few years are social networking applications designed to help people share what is clearly private information—your tastes and preferences, your response to last night's television programs, or even, in the case of Twitter, a 140-character miniblog about what you are thinking about right this minute. One study by AOL found that 84 percent of respondents said they wouldn't disclose their income online, but then 89 percent went ahead and did it anyway. Another study found that 41 percent of two hundred random Facebook users revealed their e-mail and street addresses and even their phone numbers to a complete stranger who invited them to be "friends."

Researchers are perplexed by these results, declaring a "privacy paradox." People value their privacy, but then go out of their way to give it up. There's nothing paradoxical about it. We do value privacy. It's just that we're willing to trade it for services we value even more. Consumers intuitively look at the information being requested and decide whether the value they receive for disclosing it is worth the cost of their privacy.

We don't do a perfect job, but probably close to it. If I don't give an e-commerce Web site my name, address, and credit card information, I can't buy goods. If I don't give the bank my Social Security number, I can't open an account. If I don't show my ID at the airport, I can't fly. At the same time I'm suspicious when an informational Web site asks for my home address and phone number, or when an e-commerce site wants to know my credit card number before I've completed a transaction. If it's not obvious why a piece of information is being requested, I'm not likely to give it up—in fact I become suspicious of the entire interaction.

In digital life, it turns out there is usually considerable value to giving up PII. Every time you walk into a video store in the physical world, the relationship with the merchant more or less starts over. But because Netflix knows your complete rental history, it can recommend films you are likely to want to see. RFID-based electronic "fastpasses" save us time at the toll plaza and may ultimately be used to reduce road congestion, even though we understand that the Department of Highways can now track our vehicles. Interactions with other people, whether social or business, require us to trade information. Cell phone users and social networkers broadcast PII because that's the basis on which human relationships operate, even with people we don't know.

The confusion over what we think we want and what we actually want has dangerous consequences when governments try to mediate one or the other. Google and other search engine companies learned that lesson the hard way in early 2007. For months, the press was filled with stories about governments in the EU and the United States condemning the companies for retaining data about user searches for up to two years. The search companies argued they needed the data to improve their services, but privacy advocates feared more insidious motives. EU privacy agencies called Google the winner in a "race to the bottom" for consumer privacy protection. So Google abruptly changed course and agreed to keep search data for only eighteen months, and later, under continued criticism in the United States, for only nine months.

Across the hall, however, law enforcement agencies of the same governments were calling for more, not less, data retention. Following terrorist bombings in Madrid in 2004 and London in 2005, the EU passed another directive, this time *requiring* member countries to implement laws requiring the retention of Internet and cell phone usage data. The Netherlands has proposed a retention period of eighteen months, while the Czech Republic, France, Spain, and the UK set it at one year. A full set of requirements has been delayed, but Google promised the agencies it would keep search data for twenty-four months, a decision that was applauded in both Europe and the United States. In the furor over privacy, no one seems to have noticed the irony of one set of regulators demanding complete anonymity while another, in the interests of effective law enforcement, insisted on the preservation of the very same data.

All the while, the companies continue to point out that they don't keep personal information in the first place. Google, contrary to dozens of newspaper stories that assume otherwise, doesn't know or keep records of "your" searches, because it neither knows nor cares who "you" are. All the search engines know is that the same computer initiated a particular combination of searches—information they use to improve the quality of the suggestions they make even as you're typing. Google only sees the Internet Protocol address of the computer that made the request. It is true that IP addresses can be linked to an individual if the Internet service provider retains a record of which customer had that address (usually reset when a user powers off their equipment), but that would normally require a court order to access.

So no matter what Google is doing with the search data, Google has no idea who is associated with an IP address—it's only by combining Google's data with data to which the company doesn't have access that identification is possible. Even then, the IP address is "personal" only if the person using the computer is the one to whom the account is registered. That is not the case, for example, when many people are sharing a wireless Internet connection or if the user is at work, sharing an IP address with hundreds of people.

Anxiety over the Law of Disruption leads consumers to lobby their governments to take action against innovations they don't fully understand. The result is laws and regulators that don't solve any real problem but unintentionally add costs and delays to the deployment of new technologies. Here, exasperated Web-service companies are being whipsawed by schizophrenic demands from consumers and a patchwork of state, federal, and international privacy laws. Many are now calling for a single uniform standard that would at least give companies something to aim for. But individual governments can't even decide if they're for or against retention. Actually, they can The answer is both.

The Rise of the Privacy Market

Solving the privacy problem begins by pinpointing the source of all this froth. Information has value. Private information is valuable when it's kept secret, but in many cases it's even more valuable when it's shared. What we're experiencing isn't moral collapse or signs of the Apocalypse. It's market failure.

Part of the problem is a lack of transparency about who wants our information and what they'll do with it. Today, most business uses of PII are innocent and appropriate. But the more PII that companies have, or so privacy advocates argue, the more tempted they will be to package and resell that information to marketers who, in turn, will bury us in personalized advertising. The fear is that our data will be used against us. Will it? That depends on whether you see targeted advertising as a vice or a virtue.

As I write this I am watching election returns from the 2008 U.S. presidential campaign on the CNN Web site. Because my ISP is the cable company, the IP address assigned to my computer easily translates to my zip code—but nothing more, and nothing that would constitute PII. Still, CNN is using that minimal information to reconfigure a portion of the screen to show particular local election results ("My Races"). There's nothing invasive about their knowing where I live, since they have no way of knowing who I am among thousands of people who live in my zip code with me. That they determined the information without having to ask simply saved me the trouble of entering it.

Cable Internet provider Charter Communications has gone further. The company informed its customers in 2008 that it would begin tracking the Web sites they visited and use the information to target specific advertisements in banner ads as they surf the Web. The information collected would be only about how the computer is being used. Though Charter could connect that to the name of the account holder, there's no reason to do so for the purpose of sending a targeted banner ad. Indeed, assuming that the Web sites visited by the users of a particular account are PII, the privacy invasion here and elsewhere is being done not by humans but by software. Still, some members of Congress immediately raised concerns with the company, hinting that the practice amounted to illegal wiretapping. Activists are currently lobbying Congress, the Federal Communications Commission, and the Federal Trade Commission (FTC) to act preemptively against Charter.

Advertisers would like to spend as little as possible to get people to buy their products and services. Without any information, let alone PII, most broadcast advertising is little more than a shot in the dark. "Half the money I spend on advertising is wasted," retail pioneer John Wanamaker famously said. "I just don't know which half." At the same time, digital communication is cheap, so there's little incentive for an individual advertiser to limit herself to likely customers. That's why spam is so dangerous. No individual spammer has a reason not to send his messages to everyone. If spam isn't controlled, however, the sheer volume of irrelevant messages being sent can make e-mail unusable for everyone.

Targeted advertising may be an annoyance, or it may prove to be a godsend. Perhaps if advertisers know more about us, they can impose less advertising on us, and maybe more of what is advertised may actually be of interest. Direct marketing professionals, at least in public, claim they don't want or need any PII. If they had only basic demographic information for each address (age, sex, zip code), their pitches would be far more effective than they are today, meaning you'd get less of them, and those you did receive would be more likely to be relevant. That case, however, has not been made to consumers. In an early 2009 survey conducted by privacy monitor TRUSTe, only 28 percent of respondents said they were comfortable with advertising based on their online behavior.

Realistically, the arrival of targeted advertising on our screens, cell phones, and PDAs is unavoidable. The twenty-first-century economy is based on consumption—even privacy advocates have to eat and travel and buy vacuum cleaners. Spending is driven by marketing, or so manufacturers believe.

Thank goodness they do. Much of the valuable information content available on the Internet, and so many of the useful services we use every day, is free. Why? Not because of some utopian dream of inventors or even because of the remarkably low transaction costs of the digital economy. The content is free because the costs of the services—blogs, stock quotes, even home movies posted on YouTube—are underwritten by advertisers. If we don't read and respond to ads, we'll have to pay for these services some other way. How much did you pay Google this year? Nothing, same as last year and next year. Newspapers, radio, and television, at least in the United States, have been sponsored by ads almost from the time they were invented. All the Law of Disruption has done here is to make the ads more relevant, giving them the appearance, at the same time, of personalization and invasiveness. In both cases, it's an illusion.

The first step to solving the privacy problem is to understand that privacy is less about indiscriminately protecting information that may be personal and more about understanding who wants to use it and how we can value it. Through a variety of legal, moral, and social conventions, we've already established an elaborate set of protocols that enable millions of exchanges every day largely without incident or transaction costs.

The second step is to take a sober look at our PII and realize that, with the special exceptions of governments and criminals, nobody cares much about it anyway. Business colleagues, merchants, and our friends and families already have too much information to work with. The Law of Disruption is accelerating the gap between what we capture and what we can use. By and large, when someone asks for information from us, there's usually a good reason to believe they're asking for only the minimal amount they need.

In practice, people care far less about privacy than they do in theory. Consumers recoil reflexively at every announcement of a new technology or service that might capture PII. Even when its intended use is entirely inert, they demand their governments do something to stop it. At the same time, as citizens they are outraged when a crime occurs for which police have failed to capture adequate video or other surveillance data. So governments demand PII be retained and turned over to law enforcement and antiterror agencies.

The problem isn't that privacy is eroding in the information age. The problem is that those who decry its loss greatly exaggerate its existence in the first place. Privacy is at least partially, as Larry Ellison says, an illusion, and the danger of losing it is mostly academic. Increasingly, the privacy debate is one we have entirely with ourselves, ending in stalemate. When your information is being captured and logged, the natural human response is suspicion or worse. Why do they want this information? What are they going to do with it? What's the risk that it will be exposed in some way that will embarrass me? But if you're running any kind of business, you can't understand why anyone objects to your collecting basic information you need to provide better service, customize your future offerings, or offer discounts and special pricing.

My dog has a digital ID chip embedded just under the skin, a precaution most parents would find abhorrent—until their child is lost. RFID technology including the VeriChip from Applied Digital Solutions is already being used to create bracelets that tag Alzheimer's patients, paradoxically giving them more freedom of movement. Police can inform GM of stolen vehicles that, using the OnStar service, can be remotely disabled. For every nightmare scenario, there are two practical, socially beneficial uses of technologies that, although they reduce the privacy of some group of users, offer offsetting benefits to everyone that more than compensate for the loss.

Real or perceived abuse of PII, on the other hand, can disproportionately destroy value. The Social Security Administration should have been commended for an early Internet application that allowed users to review all of their salary and Social Security deposits online, a service launched in 1998. To protect against the data's being seen by someone other than the participant, the agency required the user to validate her identity with her full name, Social Security number, date and place of birth, and mother's maiden name. That's more validation than any bank requires for actual access not just to account information but to the assets themselves. Still, the idea of online Social Security data made people nervous. Under pressure from Congress, the agency removed the service, which has never been replaced. Instead, the SSA sends all the information in printed form by mail. Which is safer? (The most significant source of ID theft, as we'll see, is stolen mail.)

The final step in resolving the privacy problem is to separate the emotional value of PII from its economic value. There is a simple solution to the privacy problem, and it begins by recognizing that information is a commodity. PII, like any other economic good, is exchanged only when someone who wants it values it more than the person who has control over it. Then, if the necessary market structures are in place to enable a low transaction-cost exchange, a trade occurs. The vast amounts of data that are traded on a daily basis and the speed with which such transactions are increasing in every facet of life suggest that a market for information trading not only exists but is increasingly robust. As technology improves, it is spreading from business to social and even intimate activities.

To resolve the privacy problem, businesses and governments need to recognize that it is not violations of their "right to be left alone" that people object to, but unfair exchanges of value. The problem is not one of privacy, in other words, but of propriety. The solution to that problem is to establish markets for buying and selling information, including PII, that put consumers on even ground with everyone else, allowing them to market their information based on their own priorities and preferences.

Some signs of an emerging market for private data are already visible and demonstrate how little actually need be done to get it up and running. When a consumer signs up for a loyalty card, either on a Web site or in the grocery store, a contract is formed (as an experiment, read one of the agreements you already signed). The consumer sells the merchant her rights to future transaction data. In exchange, the merchant offers discounts or other concessions. Take a look at the receipt from your last food purchase—if your "club card" savings were 5 percent, then 5 percent was the amount the store was willing to pay for the right to know what you bought, including the fact that it was you who bought it.

Knowing which items are purchased from a particular store at a particular time by a particular customer is valuable to the merchant, not because he can now hold your preferences hostage but because that knowledge can be used to stock the store more efficiently in the future. He can also use the information to offer you incentives to change or connect related preferences (you buy baby wipes, so here's a coupon for a new brand of disposable diapers). Without the consumer's cooperation, the merchant can't get the full value of transaction data; likewise, consumers benefit most when merchants can aggregate data from a lot of customers to find interesting patterns. The private data market is a series of millions of joint ventures, formed virtually and, for the most part, without the need to negotiate terms.

Think, too, of the frequent-flyer or other affinity marketing programs you willingly signed up for. The airlines, grocery stores, and video rental clubs value the ability to track your transactions and use that data to focus their offerings to you. You value the discounts or free merchandise you get in return. The airline isn't interested in knowing that you're making a lot of trips to Southern California so they can blackmail you (assuming there's someone you don't want to know about the trips). They're interested in finding patterns in the behavior of all their frequent flyers that suggest changes to their routes or prices.

The privacy debate turns out not to be about privacy at all. It's about economics. Who owns the data? How much is it worth? What uses are licensed and for how long? Under what conditions can the seller revoke his rights, or demand a higher price? We don't need a pledge by merchants or laws written to preserve the integrity of a consumer's existential sense of self. Rather, we need a functioning market for buying and selling information created whenever two people, two companies, or any combination engage in some activity and therefore generate some new data.

FAST-FORWARD: THE MARKET FOR PRIVATE INFORMATION

Business leaders, regulators, and consumers can either engage a rational dialogue and solve the privacy problem quickly or continue to posture and accuse. Whether or not they do, the availability of new data sources—a side effect of the continued operation of the Law of Disruption—will force a solution to the privacy problem. It may not come quickly, and the process of getting there may not be efficient. There will be embarrassing missteps and catastrophic breaches of social mores along the way. Still, the problem will be solved. All the fearmongering does—all it ever does—is to skew the deployment of innovation, often to the detriment of those making the most noise.

In the worst-case scenario, the solution will be generational. Raised by technology, young people today have an innate appreciation for the economics of information exchange. They understand that no matter how valuable data might be when kept secret, hidden, and hoarded, its value multiplies when shared, added to, and built upon. Not surprisingly, this next generation of consumers, business leaders, and regulators has a radically different view of privacy. Adults fret about the possibility of a rogue refrigerator revealing our eating habits to someone who might actually care. Kids, on the other hand, tell each other everything—in instant messages and texting; on their MySpace, Live Journal, and Facebook pages; in their Flickr photographs and Twitter postings. They all aspire to be celebrities, and fame comes from having more people know more trivia about you than they do about someone else. They're in constant communication with each other, and share everything. They're the Too Much Information generation, but only by the standards of their parents and grandparents.

So even if we don't solve the privacy problem, the next generation of information users will. While we agonize over abstract problems, they will be busy enjoying their digital lives. We may leave behind a crazy quilt of unenforceable rules and regulations, but as we'll see in the following chapters, they will always find ways around them.

Most people have a deeply psychological attachment to the idea of privacy. As an emotional attachment, it is largely impervious to rational argument. Like a belief in God or that the Chicago Cubs will someday win the World Series, there's no point in arguing about it. In order to make sense of privacy in the digital age, however, we must at least accept the fact that privacy is not what we think it is. Just as important, we need to recognize that the emotional reasons we assume otherwise strongly influence our behavior as consumers. If you have trouble imagining selling private information, consider the Web sites, retail relationships, and family and social interactions, including social networking applications, where today you freely give it away.

In the future, you'll sell information about your transactions in exchange for discounts, rebates, or even a cut of the profits that come from their use. A new breed of metamerchants will emerge to package and resell data back to producers and retailers. The information brokers will include companies already fluent in the economics of information, including Google, Yahoo, Microsoft, and eBay. But don't count out GE, Wells Fargo, and Wal-Mart. Already, start-ups including BlueKai and eXelate Media are buying and selling information collected from Web site cookies using what the companies call "behavioral exchanges."

Businesses today simply react (poorly) when a privacy breach or new technology upsets their customers. That passive strategy must end. Business leaders must take the initiative in the privacy debate. Establishing the privacy market will require significant public education, helping consumers see the value of sharing information. Appropriate incentives must be offered. Trade associations, which by and large do not have privacy on their radar, need to be activated. For now, don't ask for information you don't need or won't use. Recognize the generational differences as well as regional ones, and work toward a postprivacy society.

Businesses must also understand that the response to private data collection and use is visceral. Treat it accordingly. The public relations nightmare of RFID will be repeated as long as businesses fail to recognize the importance of making the case for the value of the information that will be collected by new technologies and applications. The technology may not be mainstream yet, but legislation is already being passed to regulate it—or worse. Don't wait until the Law of Disruption has opened an unclosable gap.

There's an appropriate role here for governments. Since the dawn of capitalism, policymakers have proven adept at creating the necessary infrastructure for new markets. The existence of police and courts, for example, largely deters participants from cheating, keeping enforcement costs low. Rather than micromanage the emerging market for information exchange whenever something goes wrong, legislators and regulators should focus on establishing standard contracts, clear definitions of what is and is not PII, and simple and cheap mechanisms for resolving breakdowns and punishing destructive—that is, criminal—behavior.

The United States and Europe begin this process at opposite starting points. In the United States, PII is owned by whoever creates it; in Europe, it is owned by whomever it refers to. The difference offers the opportunity to test empirically a long-standing theory of economics. Ronald Coase famously argued that in markets with minimal transaction costs, the initial allocation of property rights is irrelevant. The parties, Coase said, will bargain until the user who most values the property becomes the owner by agreeing to pay the highest price. If the initial owner values the property the highest, no exchange needs to occur.

As noted earlier, the biggest failing of the information market is the lack of good metrics (or any metrics) for valuing information and other intangibles. If legislators really want to help solve the privacy crisis, they would do well to require accountants and investment industries to establish the kinds of valuation rules already required for tangible property. Then establish initial rules as Europe did and then let the market bargain for the most efficient uses.

If Coase is right, we may soon find that there's no practical difference between the different approaches to privacy in the United States and Europe. American consumers will bargain to retain PII they truly value. Europeans will sell those data that, in the end, they don't really care to keep secret. Either way, the information will find its way to the most valuable use—the use that most benefits everyone.

Law Three: Human Rights

Social Contracts in Digital Life

Individual rights in digital life have eroded badly during the "war on terror." Much of the electronic surveillance that now takes place does so secretly, without warrants or other requirements of democratic societies. The only protection most of us are left with is the sheer volume of information and the lack of funding for governments to sift through all of it. The Law of Disruption, in other words, is standing in for the Bill of Rights. As a code of frontier law, that's not surprising—the same thing happened in the American West. We can at least do a little better, as this chapter proposes, by establishing a few principles of digital civil liberties, and then writing the software to enforce them.

Unconventional Wisdom

It's funny what you can find when you read beyond the headlines.

In a rare showing of international cooperation, the Council of Europe (an organization of forty-seven countries that predates the EU) recently implemented a new treaty to help deter the spread of Internet crime. The "Convention on Cybercrime" includes many sensible provisions aimed at unifying global computer-crime laws. It also closes loopholes that made it possible for criminals to escape prosecution by locating their activities offshore. The treaty went into force in 2004 and is open to any nation to sign; so far forty-six countries have adopted it. In 2006, the U.S. Senate ratified the treaty, making it immediately binding. The Department of Justice hailed the convention as a responsible, efficient response to escalating global crime made easier by the growth of digital life.

An odd coalition of communication providers and civil liberties groups, however, raised strong objections. The businesses were concerned about new requirements for online services, including the retention and preservation of user data and the creation of technical back doors that allow police to monitor real-time traffic. Though many of these requirements are already part of U.S. law, the treaty authorizes agents in any signatory country to force foreign service providers to comply. Adding insult to injury, the cost of responding to investigatory requests, regardless of their source, is borne entirely by the provider. As communication companies read that provision, law enforcement agencies around the world can now outsource much of their investigative costs to the private sector, with no controls of any kind.

Civil liberties groups worried about another kind of cost—the erosion of basic rights. Under the convention, law enforcement agencies can not only demand compliance but also order the service provider not to reveal that a user's data was taken. Hypothetically, an order to search your data may already have been issued. You would never know. Service providers can fight orders that require them to preserve and turn over data, but in many cases they won't bother. The information, after all, is not the companies' but that of their users.

The convention also requires cooperation no matter what kind of foreign investigation is being performed or by whom. Signatory countries must cooperate with each other even when the activity in question wouldn't be criminal—and may indeed be protected—in the other country. If France is investigating the sale of Nazi memorabilia on eBay, the United States must cooperate, even though such transactions are not illegal in the United States. If Latvia objects to blog entries critical of its government, Latvia can demand that the Justice Department subpoena records from any service provider in the United States. As the ACLU put it, "The broad scope of the Cybercrime Treaty and the vast number of potential signatories threatens the core liberties of Americans and will obligate the United States to use extraordinary powers to do the dirty work of other nations."

In announcing passage of the treaty, Attorney General Alberto Gonzales acknowledged these tensions but failed to dispel them. He issued a statement praising the convention's potential to aid law enforcement, but promised not to comply with the treaty in ways that violated the rights of Americans. (Such statements have no legal significance.) So far, there have been no reported cases of the convention being invoked in the first place. That may be because the subject of the investigation simply didn't object—or was gagged from disclosing that they tried.

Netizen Kane

The Convention on Cybercrime is part of a growing body of laws aimed at regulating online behavior. While the last two chapters reviewed government efforts to regulate digital businesses on behalf of their constituents, here we turn the problem around. *How do governments, for better or worse, regulate online citizens?* Do the physics of digital life create a world in which our online selves are freer or more carefully controlled? Do our rights in digital life depend on where our physical selves are located—what country we are in—when we log on?

The rights of citizens to be free of government interference are known as civil liberties; more broadly, our core freedoms in interacting with each other are known as human rights. These protections include lofty concepts such as the freedom of speech, the right to a speedy trial and to confront witnesses against us, and freedom from unreasonable search and seizure—all basic principles of democratic society. In the physical world such rights may be inherent in the legal system, or encoded in historical documents such as the Magna Carta, Bill of Rights, and Charter of Fundamental Rights of the European Union.

There is, of course, no universal set of rights that all governments recognize and respect. Under civil law, criminal defendants are presumed guilty until proven innocent; in the United States, the presumption is the opposite. China has no free press. America doesn't recognize, as Canada and Sweden do, a right to affordable health care. These differences, some large and some small, are what distinguish the national character of one country from another.

Digital life, however, exists in no particular country. When the rights of digital citizens (or "netizens" as they are sometimes called) conflict with governments trying to impose their regulatory will, the question is not only what rights apply but whose? Put another way, will netizens enjoy the best of all possible freedoms or the least common denominator? In 2008, Thailand blocked local access to YouTube for four months until Google agreed not to allow anyone to post videos that criticized its king or otherwise offended Thai sensibilities. The Thai restriction now applies to all Google content worldwide. Earlier, Indonesia and Pakistan blocked the video site until it removed films deemed offensive to Muslims. Pakistan, by accident, implemented its ban in a way that made the site inaccessible worldwide for several hours, a frightening demonstration of just how easily technology can be bent to the whims of overzealous regulators. China has blocked YouTube and threatened search providers Google and Baidu, promising to "purify the Internet's cultural environment and protect the healthy development of minors." A race to the bottom is in progress.

Leading figures in government, academe, and the business of technology, however, have higher hopes. Already, civil liberties organizations from the physical world have set up shop in digital life. Native organizations, including the pioneering Electronic Frontier Foundation, have operated since the dawn of the Internet age. The Internet has its freedom fighters, sit-ins, protests, boycotts, and civil disobedience. Together with more libertarian politicians in the physical world, a ragtag alliance has proven itself able to organize quickly and often effectively when interlopers appear. This chapter reviews their contentious efforts to create a bill of rights for online behavior.

WHERE SPEECH IS REALLY FREE

Perhaps the most remarkable feature of Internet economics is that digital information moves with almost no transaction costs. This has proven a boon not only to buyers and sellers of digital goods but for any interaction that requires the exchange of information. Commercially, companies can now easily share vast amounts of data instantaneously. Industrial buyers can review detailed specifications online and automatically transfer purchase orders, pricing, contracts, and other documents traditionally involved in business-to-business exchanges. Consumers can research the purchase not only of digital products but of all manner of goods and services, including cars, large appliances, and even real estate. When pre- or postsales service is required, retailers have dramatically lowered their costs by offering e-mail, online chat, or do-it-yourself service options, in many cases enlisting other customers to help answer questions as part of user community forums. Wikipedia, the online encyclopedia, has almost three million articles, written, edited, and verified by an army of anonymous volunteers.

On the Web, speech is "free" in every sense of the word. So it's not surprising that one of the fastest-evolving uses of Internet technology has been in the political arena. The 2008 U.S. presidential campaign took place largely in the world of digital life, where candidates spoke directly to voters through the Web, volunteers coordinated through social networking sites, and bloggers captured every moment and discussed them endlessly with their readers. During the primaries, CNN sponsored one debate for each of the political parties in which all of the questions came in the form of YouTube videos posted by ordinary citizens.

This is the kind of free speech the founding fathers could have only dreamed about. Before the age of cheap computing and communications, speech was effectively limited to those who could afford radio, television, and print media. Now every citizen has not only the freedom to speak but also the means to do so as equal members of the body politic.

The Law of Disruption has revolutionized communication, in part because there are few traditional laws to interfere with it. Long before the digital age, the inventors of modern democratic government understood both the liberating potential of communications technology and the latent danger of government censorship. To ensure that speech remains as free as technology permits, most democracies build in strong protections against government interference. In the United States, the First Amendment flatly declares that Congress "shall make no law . . . abridging the freedom of speech." In Europe, the Charter of Fundamental Rights guarantees freedom of thought, expression, and information.

These are some of the strongest protections that netizens have against regulatory intrusions of any kind. Still, we should pause for a moment to dispel a few widely held myths about what free speech really means. First, like the right to privacy, it is a right *only against* the government. In the United States, private employers may place any restriction they like on what you say on the job. With a few exceptions, they may even fire you for things you say at home or in public. Children have no free speech right to assert against their parents, no matter how loudly they try. You have no right to complain about the poor quality of my merchandise while standing inside my store. Primary schools and universities can and do punish students for speech they don't like. In 2007, a student at Hamline University in Minnesota was suspended and ordered to get a mental health evaluation after sending e-mails to university officials arguing that students should be permitted to carry concealed weapons on campus for self-defense. In an earlier case, a University of Michigan student was suspended for posting short stories on his blogs that featured violent imagery, including torture and mutilation.

Even the prohibition against government censorship is not as black-and-white as the First Amendment suggests. Supreme Court justice Oliver Wendell Holmes Jr. famously wrote that free speech "would not protect a man falsely shouting fire in a theater and causing a panic." Despite freedom of speech, you can be jailed for perjury, which is the crime of lying under oath. Courts have also allowed laws that restrict the time, place, and manner of speech. No one has the right to stand in the middle of a freeway blocking traffic in order to give a lecture on the shameful conduct of legislators and lobbyists. The FCC has the right to ban obscene language over the public airways. (Until he moved to unregulated satellite radio, "shock jock" Howard Stern was fined ten times.) The European Union's Racism and Xenophobia Directive, likewise, outlaws remarks "carried out in a manner likely to incite violence or hatred," including statements made online. Though the list of exceptions is still relatively small, "no law" doesn't really mean what it says.

Still, political speech is at the core of the First Amendment, and in the United States, courts have looked skeptically at any efforts to restrict it. In 2009, a federal appeals court rejected a California law banning the sale or rental of violent video games to minors as an improper restriction on speech. The 1996 Communications Decency Act, an early effort by Congress to ban pornography on the Internet, was blocked almost as soon as President Clinton signed it. All nine justices of the Supreme Court later agreed the act was unconstitutional, citing the vagueness of terms such as "decency." Vague and overbroad restrictions, the Court noted, have the potential to suppress political speech.

Anonymous political speech is also protected. Before and after the American Revolution, unsigned pamphlets and editorials, including *The Federalist*

Papers, played a major role in shaping the emerging nation. This lesson seems to have been forgotten in a recent case in New York City, where local prosecutors ordered the operators of city politics Web site Room 8 to disclose the true identities of some of its bloggers. The owners of the site were warned that even disclosing the demand to the targets of the investigation could constitute a crime. Room 8 contacted a public interest lawyer, who challenged the order on First Amendment grounds. The prosecutor immediately withdrew it, refusing to say why it had been issued in the first place. The damage, however, was done. One of the posters, identified only as "Dissident Republican," deleted all of her postings from the site and stopped answering e-mails from Room 8's operators.

Political speech on the Internet for the most part has enjoyed the same protection it does in physical space. In Malaysia, the courts recently intervened to order the release of a well-known blogger, Raja Petra Kamarudin, a member of the royal family who had been detained for two months on charges that his criticism of the government threatened national security and insulted the Prophet Muhammad. Raja Petra had been arrested under a 1960 act that was intended to curb communism but had been consistently used to squelch political speech ever since. In the United States, courts have trimmed back some of the Patriot Act's more draconian features, including provisions that gag communication companies from disclosing they have been ordered to turn over customer information.

In some cases, however, lawmakers have gone further to restrict online political speech than they might in physical space. German officials regularly prosecute Web site operators for providing links to radical newspapers and providing access to violent video games, pornography, and other "youth-endangering" content that prosecutors generally ignore in the physical world. The military government of Burma shut down the country's access to the Internet altogether after photos of the brutal crackdown on demonstrations by Buddhist monks in 2007 led to increased international pressure on the regime.

Online speech, in any event, goes far beyond the world of politics. Human beings have a remarkable ability to absorb communication technology for personal use, keeping close pace with the Law of Disruption's ability to generate new applications. It's little surprise that the Internet has revolutionized every imaginable form of social interaction. Without the need for expensive printing equipment, supplies, and distribution, anyone with a computer can publish their own newspaper, and millions already do—more than a hundred million blogs have been cataloged so far. Teenagers stay in constant touch with their families and each other using cell phones and text messages. Social networking applications open the possibility of a wider range of friends and acquaintances from around the world and new ways of interacting with them.

In the wider world of Internet speech, legislators and courts have proven unable to resist the urge to interfere. Since the Supreme Court overturned the Communications Decency Act, Congress has made two further attempts to regulate sexual content on the Web. The first, the Child Online Protection Act, was blocked almost immediately after its passage in 1998. (It was finally put to death eleven years later.) Legal challenges also dogged COPA's successor, the Children's Internet Protection Act, which limited its scope to schools and libraries receiving Internet subsidies from the federal government. The Supreme Court narrowly upheld CIPA in 2003, noting that adult library patrons could demand removal of the required Web site filters. In all these cases, the Court has made clear that any law that treats Internet speech more harshly than the published kind will not pass muster.

Lingering in many of the voided laws is at least a whiff of hypocrisy. The Internet is an easy political target. Legislators frequently use digital life and its perceived anarchy as a stalking horse for moral, political, or even religious judgments. Since its inhabitants are scattered around the world, offending its residents is unlikely to cause political backlash. The Internet has no natural constituency to vote the bums out. Passing laws that are obviously unconstitutional or unenforceable may seem pointless, but it gives legislators the ability to rail against immorality and take an unfair stab at "activist" judges at the same time. Constituents can't blame their lawmakers for not trying.

The absence of an organized political base among Internet users is rapidly disappearing, accelerated by anti-Internet legislating and other posturing. In addition to public interest groups such as the ACLU and the EFF, clinical programs at leading law schools including Harvard and Stanford have stepped in to take on local and national cases. Blogs specifically focused on issues of Internet law are some of the most active on the Web. Internet users are increasingly aware of the harm that overbroad regulation can cause, and are translating that awareness into aggressive lobbying and litigation.

Still, civil liberties suffer even when bad laws are quickly rejected. One side effect of the escalating battle of words between lawmakers and Internet users is that the cost of litigating over speech laws is increasing. Government lawyers are obliged to defend them, wasting millions of dollars that could be better spent doing just about anything else. To add insult to injury, in many cases the losing party pays the legal fees of the winning party, a bounty that encourages private citizens to challenge intentionally bad laws. Those who write and vote for legislation are rarely held accountable, leaving the taxpayers footing the bill for their folly.

Antispeech laws can also cause considerable collateral damage. In 2004, as part of the protracted COPA litigation, the ACLU argued that the law's goal of protecting children from harmful content could be served just as well with filtering technology. The government tried to prove otherwise. Justice Department lawyers ordered Google, AOL, Microsoft, and Yahoo to turn over a full week's worth of search data, which they argued would help them prove the ineffectiveness of filtering technology. All of the companies complied except for Google, which argued that the subpoena was hopelessly overbroad and threatened the company's trade secrets. Though the request did not include any data that could identify who had done the searches, Google complained that complying with the government's request would create a "perception" that it was willing to release private data. In 2007, the court agreed, and ruled that the company need not turn over any search data.

A more difficult class of free-speech problems on the Web has to do with the freedom of the press, another protection guaranteed in most democracies. In the pre-Internet days, it was easy to spot journalists—they were the men and women who in old movies wore a press card in their hat or, later, flashed laminated press passes. Journalists write about topics of interest to readers who buy their publications. But when every Web site can potentially reach every Internet user in the world, what does it mean to be a journalist? The answer matters. To ensure that democratic governments cannot silence their critics and cover up abuse, journalists are given special protection, insulating their speech not only from censorship but in many cases from private claims of defamation that might otherwise be actionable.

Problems are beginning to arise as bloggers claim privileges traditionally reserved exclusively for journalists. When enthusiastic bloggers in 2004 broke the news of products that Apple was planning to announce the following week, the company sued, claiming the information constituted trade secrets. In order to determine who had leaked the information, Apple demanded Apple fan sites reveal the identities of the bloggers. A California state judge initially agreed. The court of appeals, however, reversed that ruling, holding that the bloggers were journalists protected by a state shield law that allows reporters to keep their sources confidential.

Many states have similar shield laws, but the confidentiality privilege is not universal. After *New York Times* reporter Judith Miller was jailed for refusing to name Scooter Libby as her informant in the Valerie Plame Wilson CIA case, Congress considered a federal law that would protect reporters in similar situations nationwide. The effort failed, however, over concerns about extending the protection to online reporters. Since "journalist" was defined to include anyone who published an electronic periodical, lawmakers worried that criminals could claim protection under the law just by writing a blog.

A more troubling case from 2004 involved Diebold, the controversial manufacturer of electronic voting machines. Unknown persons somehow obtained an archive of 13,000 internal e-mails from Diebold employees that disclosed flaws in the company's equipment as well as efforts to cover them up. The archive was published on several Web sites, including one operated by the nonprofit Online Policy Group. Diebold demanded the owners of the sites remove the documents, on the theory that their unlicensed publication violated copyright law. OPG instead sued Diebold, claiming that the political nature of the materials and the group's motivation for republishing them trumped copyright. The court agreed and ordered Diebold to pay $5,000 in damages and $120,000 in attorneys' fees for abusing copyright law.

The Diebold case is a good example of the old legal adage that hard cases make bad law. Surely, some portions of Diebold's 13,000 messages were due a measure of copyright protection—enough, at least, to have insulated the company from a claim that they intentionally misrepresented their rights to OPG. The judge reasoned, however, that copyright didn't apply because OPG and the other sites were publishing the material to expose Diebold and not to make a profit. That's an attractive argument given the facts, but one with little support in law. The U.S. Supreme Court has held repeatedly that copyrights owners can sue an infringer even if the unauthorized copies make no money.

The more interesting question is why Diebold bothered. Their real objective, it's safe to say, was not to protect their copyrights. Diebold wasn't planning to publish the 13,000 e-mails or any part of them. They just wanted to keep embarrassing information from being disclosed. Once the archive had been posted and duplicated on multiple computers, however, the damage was done. All Diebold's lawyers achieved by threatening OPG was to generate even more negative publicity about the archive and its contents. Not only did the company expose their own dirty laundry, but the judgment against them now encourages future citizen journalists to take them on. Diebold's legal strategy backfired completely.

As these examples suggest, efforts to police Internet speech more vigorously than their real-world counterparts usually fail. Indeed, they have inadvertently galvanized a powerful and expanding opposition. That is not to say the matter is settled. There may be a strong argument, so far unarticulated, for regulating Internet speech. Moore's Law and Metcalfe's Law have created a digital marketplace of ideas in which everyone has a voice. Anonymous bloggers, cyberterrorists, online pornographers, and student journalists all take advantage of the falling price of technology to communicate, increasing the quantity, volume, and potential audience for new information. The result is a lot more speech. Some of it is good, but a lot of it is worthless. When everyone speaks at once the result is noise. Left to the Law of Disruption, the market for Internet speech is failing.

The Internet makes it cheap to produce and distribute speech, which means there is more of it. Free speech, then, may require more, not less, regulation if it is to remain in every sense free. This is no paradox; regulating online speech may simply be good information economics, improving the vitality of the market for all participants. Consider some of the examples we've just reviewed. Although sellers of printed media can restrict sales to adults, it is nearly impossible to keep kids from electronic porn. No one seriously doubts that adolescents can find ways around any filtering technology we put in front of them. If children are harmed by exposure to explicit imagery, the Internet has greatly increased the likelihood and degree of that harm. Online pornography, as government lawyers unsuccessfully argued, is in that sense more dangerous than printed pornography.

When journalists needed access to printing presses and distribution networks, likewise, those costs created a natural barrier that may have translated to higher-quality reporting. Blogging as a new means of communication might actually improve if fewer people did it, or did less of it, perhaps out of fear that careless words might lead to financial penalties. So perhaps bloggers, on the whole, don't deserve the same protection as print journalists. Posting the Diebold e-mail archive makes the point. How many people were likely to sift through 13,000 e-mails, most of which were irrelevant? The Online Policy Group didn't filter, analyze, or comment on the contents. They just posted them. We assume that if some information is good, more is better. But that's not necessarily so.

When the cost of speaking is zero, it is the forum, not the speaker, that needs protection. That, at least, is one argument for regulation. No legislator, however, has made it. Instead, regulators around the world have tried to use law like a bludgeon, censoring specific speech they simply don't like or want to appear not to like. Efforts to afford lesser status to online speech have so far been, at best, quixotic, suggesting that even if some kind of counterbalance is required, legislators in the physical world are unlikely to apply it objectively. Quite the opposite. That is why democratic governments grant their citizens such broad immunity in the first place.

Free speech, fueled by the Law of Disruption, is creating online chaos. If not traditional governments, who is better suited to protect the Internet from its own success? Who could determine just the right amount of control, and then apply it with the least-damaging side effects? There are other potential regulators for the marketplace of ideas. As we'll see later in this chapter, however, they may prove equally tone-deaf.

SEARCHING BITS, SEIZING INFORMATION

A second important protection citizens have from government is freedom from unreasonable search and seizure of their property. In the U.S. Constitution, that right is enshrined in the Fourth Amendment, enacted in response to warrantless searches by British agents in the run-up to the Revolutionary War. Over the past century, the U.S. Supreme Court has increasingly seen the Fourth Amendment as a source of protection for personal space—the right to a "zone of privacy" that governments can invade only with probable cause that evidence of a crime will be revealed. As we saw in the previous chapter,

Americans have little in the way of legal protection of their privacy from businesses and each other. The Fourth Amendment is an exception, albeit one that applies only to government.

Digital life has introduced new and thorny problems for Fourth Amendment law. Since the early part of the twentieth century, courts have struggled to extend the "zone of privacy" to intangible interests—a right to privacy, in other words, in one's information. But to "search" and "seize" implies real-world actions. People and places can be searched; property can be seized. Information, on the other hand, need not take physical form, and can be reproduced infinitely without damaging the original. Since copies of data may exist, however temporarily, on thousands of random computers, in what sense do netizens have "property" rights to their information? Does intercepting data constitute a search or a seizure or neither?

The law of electronic surveillance avoids these abstract questions by focusing instead on a suspect's expectations. Courts reviewing challenged investigations ask simply if the suspect believed the information acquired by the government was private data and whether his expectation of privacy was reasonable. It is not the actual search and seizure that the Fourth Amendment forbids, after all, but *unreasonable* search and seizure. So the legal analysis asks what, under the circumstances, is reasonable. If you are holding a loud conversation in a public place, it isn't reasonable for you to expect privacy, and the police can take advantage of whatever information they overhear. Most people assume, on the other hand, that data files stored on the hard drive of a home computer are private and cannot be copied without a warrant.

One problem with the "reasonable expectation" test is that as technology changes, so do user expectations. The faster the Law of Disruption accelerates, the more difficult it is for courts to keep pace. Once private telephones became common, for example, the Supreme Court required law enforcement agencies to follow special procedures for the search and seizure of conversations—that is, for wiretaps. Congress passed the first wiretap law, known as Title III, in 1968. As information technology has revolutionized communications and as user expectations have evolved, the courts and Congress have been forced to revise Title III repeatedly to keep it up to date.

In 1986, for example, the Electronic Communications Privacy Act amended Title III to include new protection for electronic communications, including e-mail and communications over cellular and other wireless technologies. A model of reasonable lawmaking, the ECPA ensured these new forms of communication were generally protected while closing a loophole for criminals who were using them to evade the police. (By 2005, 92 percent of wiretaps targeted cell phones.) As telephone service providers multiplied and networks moved from analog to digital, a 1994 revision required carriers to build in special access for investigators to get around new features such as call forwarding. Once a Title III warrant is issued, law enforcement agents can now simply log in to the suspect's network provider and receive real-time streams of network traffic.

Since 1968, Title III has maintained an uneasy truce between the rights of citizens to keep their communications private and the ability of law enforcement to maintain technological parity with criminals. As the digital age progresses, this balance is harder to maintain. With each cycle of Moore's Law, criminals discover new ways to use digital technology to improve the efficiency and secrecy of their operations, including encryption, anonymous e-mail resenders, and private telephone networks. During the 2008 terrorist attacks in Mumbai, for example, coconspirators used television reports of police activity to keep the gunmen at various sites informed, using Internet telephones that were hard to trace.

As criminals adopt new technologies, law enforcement agencies predictably call for new surveillance powers. China alone employs more than 30,000 "Internet police" to monitor online traffic, what is sometimes known as the "Great Firewall of China." The government apparently intercepts all Chinese-bound text messages and scans them for restricted words including *democracy*, *earthquake*, and *milk powder*. The words are removed from the messages, and a copy of the original along with identifying information is stored on the government's system. When Canadian human rights activists recently hacked into Chinese government networks they discovered a cluster of message-logging computers that had recorded more than a million censored messages.

Netizens, increasingly fearful that the arms race between law enforcement and criminals will claim their privacy rights as unintended victims, are caught in the middle. Those fears became palpable after the September 11, 2001, terrorist attacks and those that followed in Indonesia, London, and

Madrid. The world is now engaged in a war with no measurable objectives for winning, fought against an anonymous and technologically savvy enemy who recruits, trains, and plans assaults largely through international communication networks. Security and surveillance of all varieties are now global priorities, eroding privacy interests significantly.

The emphasis on security over privacy is likely to be felt for decades to come. Some of the loss has already been felt in the real world. To protect ourselves from future attacks, everyone can now expect more invasive surveillance of their activities, whether through massive networks of closed-circuit TV cameras in large cities or increased screening of people and luggage during air travel. New forms of identification are being developed, with a trend toward issuing a single national identity card in the United States, the so-called "RealID," which may include encrypted information and RFID tracking capabilities.

The erosion of privacy is even more severe online. Intelligence is seen as the most effective weapon in a war against terrorists. With or without authorization, law enforcement agencies around the world have been monitoring large quantities of the world's Internet data traffic. Title III has been extended to private networks and Internet phone companies, who must now insert government access points into their networks. (The FCC has proposed adding other providers of phone service, including universities and large corporations.) Because of difficulties in isolating electronic communications associated with a single IP address, investigators now demand the complete traffic of large segments of addresses, that is, of many users. Data-mining technology is applied after the fact to search the intercepted information for the relevant evidence.

Passed soon after 9/11, the USA Patriot Act went much further. The Patriot Act abandoned many of the hard-fought controls on electronic surveillance built into Title III. New "enhanced surveillance procedures" allow any judge to authorize electronic surveillance and lower the standard for warrants to seize voice mails. The FBI was given the power to conduct wiretaps without warrants and to issue so-called national security letters to gag network operators from revealing their forced cooperation. Under a 2006 extension, FBI officials were given the power to issue NSLs that silenced the recipient *forever*, backed up with a penalty of up to five years in prison.

Gone is even a hint of the Supreme Court's long-standing admonitions that search and seizure of information should be the investigatory tool of last resort.

Despite the relaxed rules, or perhaps inspired by them, the FBI acknowledged in 2007 that it had violated Title III and the Patriot Act repeatedly, illegally searching the telephone, Internet, and financial records of an unknown number of Americans. A Justice Department investigation found that from 2002 to 2005 the bureau had issued nearly 150,000 NSLs, a number the bureau had grossly underreported to Congress. Many of these letters violated even the relaxed requirements of the Patriot Act. The FBI habitually requested not only a suspect's data but also those of people with whom he maintained regular contact—his "community of interest," as the agency called it. "How could this happen?" FBI director Robert Mueller asked himself at the 2007 Senate hearings on the report. Mueller didn't offer an answer. Ultimately, a federal judge declared the FBI's use of NSLs unconstitutional on free-speech grounds, a decision that is still on appeal.

The National Security Agency, which gathers foreign intelligence, undertook an even more disturbing expansion of its electronic surveillance powers. Since the Constitution applies only within the U.S., foreign intelligence agencies are not required to operate within the limits of Title III. Instead, their information-gathering practices are held to a much more relaxed standard specified in the Foreign Intelligence Surveillance Act. FISA allows warrantless wiretaps anytime that intercepted communications do not include a U.S. citizen and when the communications are not conducted through U.S. networks. (The latter restriction was removed in 2008.)

Even these minimal requirements proved too restrictive for the agency. Concerned that U.S. operatives were organizing terrorist attacks electronically with overseas collaborators, President Bush authorized the NSA to bypass FISA and conduct warrantless electronic surveillance at will as long as one of the parties to the information exchange was believed to be outside the United States. According to a whistle-blower inside AT&T, the NSA built secret rooms at some of the company's busiest facilities where government operatives monitor network traffic directly. Many of the details of this story are still secret.

Even some of the president's staunchest allies found the NSA's plan, dubbed the Terrorist Surveillance Program, of dubious legality. Just before the program became public in 2005, senior officials in the Justice Department efused to reauthorize it. In a bizarre real-world game of cloak-and-dagger, residential aides, including future attorney general Alberto Gonzales, rushed o the hospital room of then attorney general John Ashcroft, who was seriusly ill, in hopes of getting him to overrule his staff. Justice Department offiials got wind of the end run and managed to get to Ashcroft first. Ashcroft, vho was barely able to speak from painkillers, sided with his staff.

Many top officials, including Ashcroft and FBI director Mueller, threatened o resign over the incident. President Bush agreed to stop bypassing the FISA procedure and seek a change in the law to allow the NSA more flexibility. Conress eventually granted his request, caving in on a further demand to grant ast and future immunity to phone companies who cooperated with the NSA ven when the law was not followed. Retroactive immunity (the companies ad already been sued by numerous public interest groups) held up the bill for nore than a year, during which time it isn't clear what procedure, if any, the NSA was following.

The NSA's machinations were both clumsy and dangerous. Still, I confess o having considerable sympathy for those trying to obtain actionable intelligence from online activity. Post-9/11 assessments revealed embarrassing noles in the technological capabilities of most intelligence agencies worldwide. (Admittedly, it also revealed repeated failures to act on intelligence that vas already collected.) Initially at least, the public demanded tougher meaures to avoid future attacks.

Keeping pace with international terror organizations and still following national laws, however, is increasingly difficult. For one thing, communicaions of all kinds are quickly migrating to the cheaper and more open archiecture of the Internet. An unintended consequence of this change is that the nationalities of those involved in intercepted communications are increasngly difficult to determine. E-mail addresses and instant-message IDs don't ell you the citizenship or even the location of the sender or receiver. Even elephone numbers don't necessarily reveal a physical location. Internet telehone services such as Skype give their customers U.S. phone numbers regardless of their actual location. Without knowing the nationality of a suspect, it is hard to know what rights she is entitled to.

The architecture of the Internet raises even more obstacles against effective surveillance. Traditional telephone calls take place over a dedicated circuit connecting the caller and the person being called, making wiretaps relatively easy to establish. Only the cooperation of the suspect's local ex change is required. The Internet, however, is a switched network that operate as a single global exchange. E-mails, voice, video, and data files—whatever i being sent is broken into small packets of data. Each packet follows its owr path between connected computers, largely determined by data traffic pat terns present at the time of the communication. Data may travel around th world even if its destination is local, crossing dozens of national border along the way. It is only on the receiving end that the packets are reassembled This design, the genius of the Internet, improves network efficiency. It alsc provides a significant advantage to anyone trying to hide his activities.

On the other hand, NSLs and warrantless wiretapping on the scale appar ently conducted by the NSA move us frighteningly close to the "general war rant" American colonists rejected in the Fourth Amendment. They wer right to revolt over the unchecked power of an executive to do what it wants whether in the name of orderly government, tax collection, or antiterrorism In trying to protect its citizens against future terror attacks, the secret opera tions of the U.S. government abandoned core principles of the Constitution Even with the best intentions, governments that operate in secrecy and with out judicial oversight quickly descend into totalitarianism. Only the inter vention of corporate whistle-blowers, conscientious government officials courts, and a free press brought the United States back from the brink of a different kind of terrorism.

Business owners may be entirely supportive of government efforts to im prove the technology of policing. A society governed by laws is efficient, and efficiency is good for business. At the same time, no one is immune from the pressures of anxious customers who worry that the information they provide will be quietly delivered to whichever regulator asks for it. Secret surveillance raises the level of customer paranoia, leading rational businesses to avoid countries whose practices are not transparent. Partly in response to the NSA program, companies and network operators are increasingly routing infor mation flow around U.S. networks, fearing that even transient communica tions might be subject to large-scale collection and mining operations by law enforcement agencies. But aside from using private networks and storing data offshore, routing transmissions to avoid some locations is as hard to do as forcing them through a particular network or node.

The real guarantor of privacy in our digital lives may not be the rule of law. The Fourth Amendment and its counterparts work in the physical world, after all, because tangible property cannot be searched and seized in secret. Information, however, can be intercepted and copied without anyone knowing it. You may never know when or by whom your privacy has been invaded. That is what makes electronic surveillance more dangerous than traditional investigations, as the Supreme Court realized as early as 1967.

In the uneasy balance between the right to privacy and the needs of law enforcement, the scales are increasingly held by the Law of Disruption. More devices, more users, more computing power: the sheer volume of information and the rapid evolution of how it can be exchanged have created an ocean of data. Much of it can be captured, deciphered, and analyzed only with great (that is, expensive) effort. Moore's Law lowers the costs to communicate, raising the costs for governments interested in the content of those communications. The kind of electronic surveillance performed by the Chinese government is outrageous in its scope, but only the clumsiness of its technical implementation exposed it. Even if governments want to know everything that happens in our digital lives, and even if the law allows them or is currently powerless to stop them, there isn't enough technology at their disposal to do it, or at least to do it secretly. So far.

SOCIAL CONTRACTS IN DIGITAL LIFE

If traditional governments can't or won't ensure civil rights in digital life, where else can netizens turn? One answer might be more organic forms of government, formed by the residents themselves. French philosopher Jean-Jacques Rousseau believed that governments represented an agreement among the citizens to be bound by the rule of law, or what Rousseau called "the social contract." On his view, the right to govern belongs to the citizens, who delegate some measure of their sovereignty to governments. Governments are a kind of collective-action organization, using their delegated powers to serve the people more efficiently than if every decision had to be put to a vote. Netizens, in theory, could form their own social contract and create governments that recognize the unique requirements for digital life, liberty, and the pursuit of happiness.

In some sense, a digital sovereign already exists. Internet standards, for example, are created by a unique and ruthlessly egalitarian social contract among software engineers who define and maintain the basic protocols. Since 1992, these standards have been maintained by the Internet Society, a nonprofit clearinghouse supported by corporations, government agencies, foundations, and individuals. ISOC engineering committees have brought the network from a simple experiment in data exchange to the engine of transformation it has become.

Right now, dozens of volunteers are meeting and deliberating virtually, enhancing old standards and adding new ones. Existing implementations are redesigned and redeployed in real time without end users ever knowing. Internet protocols are completely transparent and available for free to all users. No company or country owns the enabling software, and anyone can write applications that run on the Net simply by following the standards. Every user is treated equally, regardless of their location, age, or speed of their connection. The government of the Internet is truly democratic.

If Internet standards and information-exchange protocols form a kind of constitution for digital life, the more practical laws—the laws of contracts, the criminal code, the law of property—come from the application providers. Companies such as Microsoft, Google, Yahoo, and Facebook, whose software connects users to each other, determine what their customers can and cannot do in several ways. Most obviously, the features and functions of their programs—literally, the code—set the parameters for user behavior. I can send mail or chat through Gmail, create my own profile on Facebook, or post photo albums with Flickr. I'm limited first and foremost by the activities and features these services offer.

My behavior is also defined by legal documents, including license agreements for software products and "terms of service" for online services. (Those are the things you pretend to have read whenever you click "I Agree.") These documents define how I will or will not use an application. My Windows Vista license, for example, tells me that no matter what damage I suffer from errors in Microsoft's code, I can recover only "direct damages up to the amount you paid for the software." (Consumer protection laws may supersede that limitation, by the way.) The TOS I agreed to for Internet service from cable provider Comcast includes a promise that I will not "falsify, alter, or remove message headers" or "falsify references to Comcast or its network, by name or other identifier, in messages," on pain of having my service canceled. Adding all of these agreements together—and most people have agreed to hundreds of them—creates a body of law that governs digital life. As my examples suggest, however, there is nothing sophisticated or especially subtle about the rules created by the businesses that enforce them. Just as in the real world, most conflicts are resolved informally. Minor infractions are generally ignored. Only when a serious breach occurs does anyone go back to the documents themselves. Justice, when it's served, is usually summary.

Given the limited range of activities most Internet software supports, it's not surprising that nothing rising to a Bill of Rights or a Charter of Fundamental Rights has appeared. We can get a glimpse of the outlines of a real social contract for digital life by looking at more sophisticated online environments and how they are governed. Consider Linden Labs' popular Second Life. Second Life is a simulated online world, one of the most robust explorations to date of what a true digital life feels like. Much more than an information-sharing service, Second Life users create a visual avatar that can explore an interactive world that offers culture, commerce, games, and opportunities to interact in every conceivable way with the avatars of other users. Among other virtual goods, users can buy optional genitalia and other add-ons, including a "sex bed."

The laws of physics need not and do not apply. Your avatar can fly or teleport around the environment, and there's no need for clothing, food, or shelter, though all of these are available. If you like, you can acquire real estate, build houses, work, and buy and sell digital goods—all popular activities among Second Life regulars. Customers pay a monthly fee and are given (and can earn) an allowance of digital currency that can be used wherever barter isn't sufficient. The local currency can be converted back to U.S. dollars at online currency exchanges.

The Second Life environment has proven to be a rich source of not only new forms of interaction but also new kinds of problems on the border of physical and digital life. Relationships can go wrong, business transactions can fall through, neighbors can annoy each other—just like in the real world. When they do, the residents of Second Life inevitably look for the kind of collective-action solutions that the law represents. From that standpoint, perhaps unintentionally, Second Life is a sandbox for observing not only how people organize their lives in a new reality but also how they develop organic solutions to new forms of conflict.

By and large, Linden Labs has avoided the temptation to socially engineer user behavior, leaving a regulatory vacuum that the users are starting to fill themselves. Already, Second Life has formed its own Bar Association. There are banks and stock markets, so far unregulated by either digital agencies or their real-world counterparts. There are also thorny and so far untouched questions about rights to information products created using the environment. Can a user who creates a digital product—including sex toys, annoying sounds, dance steps, and yoga poses—take it with her to another environment? This is no small matter. Users spend an estimated $1.5 billion a year on virtual products, including licensed celebrity accessories such as Justin Timberlake's hat or Paris Hilton's pet Chihuahua.

Other online environments operate with a heavier hand. In the SIMS Online environment offered by gaming giant Electronic Arts, the TOS prohibited harassment, cheating, and obscenities. Peter Ludlow, a self-described muckraker and a philosophy professor in real life, published a digital newspaper called the *Alphaville Herald* to expose violations of those rules. Ludlow reported on players who took advantage of new participants and stole their simoleans (the local currency), teenagers who worked as online prostitutes, and other misconduct in what was supposed to be a family-friendly, even utopian, environment.

Ludlow also reported the failure of EA to enforce its own "law." In response, EA kicked Ludlow out of the game, citing Ludlow's own violation of the TOS in posting a link that explained the cheating he was complaining about. EA confiscated his online home and even his digital pets. Ludlow received no trial or other due process, nor was EA obliged to provide him any. In digital life, self-appointed regulators may choose not to enforce the law, or enforce it selectively to silence critics.

In the real world, citizens have the courts, legislators, and elections to address their grievances. In SIMS Online, the government is compressed into a single entity that answers to no one. Ultimately, if the citizens of Alphaville or any other digital community find the form of government created by the TOS too tyrannical, they can end their digital existence and go elsewhere—

indeed, with far more ease and far less bloodshed than it takes to break the social contract and start a new society in the physical world. In the interim, the gap between expectations and actual conduct in digital life teaches a great deal about what we take for granted about government.

"To me, it was clearly censorship," Ludlow complained. But in Alphaville, censorship is perfectly legal. Or rather, it was. EA disbanded all the communities in 2008 and shut the environment down for good.

FAST-FORWARD: THE BILL OF RIGHTS OF DISRUPTION

Digital life has the potential to create a global village that reflects the best characteristics of all its residents, translating the economic power of information into enhanced personal liberty. National and local governments, however, have proven themselves unwilling or unable to help the process. Indeed, nearly all of the examples we've seen point to an institutional bias by legislators against digital civil liberties. Panicked responses to external crises or just ignorance of the nature of digital life has led regulators worldwide to treat online activities as less deserving of basic protections.

Traditional governments have only the vaguest understanding of the information economy—how it operates technically, how it is used by its citizens, and how it is expanding and mutating under the Law of Disruption. Given the migration of so much economic, social, and political activity to digital life, it's understandable that governments believe they have a role to play in managing it. They want to protect their citizens. They also want to protect their turf. Even applying international law to an environment that exists outside the world of borders, however, is causing considerable friction of both the political and economic variety. But the migration to digital life can only be slowed. It can't be stopped.

This chapter looked at two areas of considerable conflict: free speech and electronic surveillance. Here there are two strong arguments in favor of government intervention: (1) in a digital world where talk is literally cheap, limiting free speech may be necessary to avoid anarchy; (2) crime is easier to commit and therefore requires more intrusive methods to deter and punish. In practice, governments have used these features of digital life as cover to suppress specific speech they don't like or expand the scope of surveillance to nearly boundless limits. The tendency to abuse these powers is precisely the reasons most social contracts severely limit the reach of elected officials in these sensitive areas.

The wrong kind of intervention is dangerous. Uncovering even wholesale violations of civil liberties can be difficult when police use the Internet to hide their activities, backed up with NSLs and other gag orders. But in its embryonic state, digital democracy immediately feels the effect of invasive laws. The trauma of too many restrictions enforced too soon can damage the shape of digital life far into the future. If governments fail to curb antisocial behaviors, on the other hand, the development of a robust digital life can be stunted just as severely. That balance is difficult enough to maintain in a world lawmakers inhabit. How are they to proceed in a place many of them have never visited?

Tensions between netizens and governments attempting to regulate them have, not surprisingly, increased, reflected not only in real-world litigation brought to protect digital rights but in acts of digital civil disobedience and outright revolt. John Perry Barlow's "Declaration of the Independence of Cyberspace" remains a powerful statement of the dangers of treating the Internet as a colony run by a distant king and an unrepresentative legislature. Here the digital natives don't have to fire weapons to expel a mad monarch. They can simply invent better technology.

Given the newness and fragility of digital life, online citizens need to apply real-world leverage to repel real-world governments. Today, netizens lobby against bad laws and bad judicial decisions through not-for-profit organizations including the EFF, the Center for Democracy and Technology (CDT), and ACLU. They define and operate their own quasi governments—the governments of open source, of peer to peer, of the blogosphere. They enforce behavioral mores against each other, though sometimes in abbreviated proceedings that trade due process for the hanging tree.

Businesses hoping to establish a long-lasting online presence must walk a fine line. Following the lead of their customers, they should demand an online environment that is as free as the freest society. Where companies must themselves take on the role of lawmaker and law enforcer, a minimalist approach is clearly best. Second Life is still in business; SIMS Online is not. The economics of information don't tolerate secret government, corruption, or laziness. The network simply routes around you.

Faced with the threat of more restrictive laws, industries often promise to self-regulate. This too can be dangerous. Over the years, comic book publishers, film studios, music labels, and video game companies have enacted varying forms of self-censorship, often imposing more limits on themselves and their consumers than would be allowed of governments under the First Amendment. Many of these efforts are considered in hindsight to have done more harm than good.

In a similar vein, leading Internet companies in 2008 waded into treacherous waters by signing on to the Global Network Initiative. The GNI is a self-regulatory charter calling on signatory companies and other organizations "to respect and protect the freedom of expression and privacy rights of their users." Despite the rhetoric, the GNI is far from an organic expression of higher aspirations. Lawmakers in the United States and elsewhere were already rattling their sabers about the cooperation of leading Internet companies including Yahoo, Google, and Microsoft with repressive governments. In China, in particular, the companies had agreed to release information identifying online dissidents and helped suppress online speech of which the government disapproved. Convened by the companies, the GNI was hastily drafted to head off pending legislation that would have limited how global companies could or could not do business in countries that significantly interfere with Internet speech.

The GNI seems unlikely to protect anything. Its formative documents are wordy, full of hedges and platitudes, fuzzy on implementation, and completely absent any enforcement mechanisms. It is reminiscent less of a Bill of Rights than of the notorious Sullivan Principles, which were drafted to provide cover for companies doing business with apartheid South Africa in the face of growing consumer protest. Its own author, the Reverend Leon Sullivan, ultimately rejected his creation as not going far enough. During the 1980s, as the regime showed little sign of reform, he came to see that engagement with the South African government under any terms was wrong, and called on companies to pull out of the country altogether. The same fate, I suspect, awaits the GNI.

The GNI's empty promises to one side, the simple truth is that governments and businesses consistently overlook the most important feature of digital life. We are not here simply to buy and sell, consume content, and pay our taxes. We're here to experience what it means to be citizens in a new world with new possibilities. As we relocate more of our personal and family life online, not to mention our business activities, the imperative to guarantee digital human rights will emerge. Information age Rousseaus, Mills, and Madisons will rise to the challenge, and global governments will agree to the digital equivalents of the Magna Carta, Declaration of Independence, and Universal Declaration of Human Rights.

Your digital self aspires to a better kind of civilization. Netizens will not accept a form of government that moves backward from the best that democratic societies enjoy today. Efforts to imprint more limited freedoms still suffered by much of the world's population will fail and bring their would-be enforcers down with them. Real-world institutions will either adapt or disappear. The Law of Disruption has no exceptions.

PUBLIC LIFE

LAW FOUR: INFRASTRUCTURE

Rules of the Road on the Information Highway

The information economy runs on a dynamic and rapidly changing infrastructure, one that has the remarkable property of operating even as it's being rebuilt. Governments, contrary to extremist libertarians in the blogosphere, play an important role here, such as defining the basic "rules of the road" that make it possible for innovation to blossom. As this chapter demonstrates, however, it's important for lobbyists and legislators to resist the ever-present temptation of more specific tinkering with the machinery. Regulatory corrections—outlawing Internet gambling, forcing access providers to abide by "neutrality" principles, special taxes—invariably fail, leaving behind legal time bombs that often go off in the hands of those who set them.

THE MAN BEHIND THE CURTAIN

Telephone customers had had enough.

By the end of the 1960s, AT&T was one of the most unpopular brands in the world. Over a one-hundred-year period, the phone giant had slowly but surely absorbed most local telephone companies and operated, from 1913, as a regulated monopoly. Through a combination of technological innovation and ruthless business practices, "Ma Bell" controlled everything having to do with phone service, including the wires and poles, local and long distance service, and the manufacture of "compatible" telephones that consumers were required to lease from AT&T's Western Electric subsidiary. A long-distance call from New York to Los Angeles cost 65 cents a minute. In some states, just getting a phone installed took months of waiting. As recently as 2006, an Ohio woman's daughter discovered her mother was still paying $30 a month to lease a black rotary-dial phone after forty-two years and over $14,000.

In 1974, the U.S. Justice Department finally bowed to consumer outrage and sued the company under federal antitrust laws. The verdict was obvious. The solution wasn't. The job of sorting through the mess fell on the shoulders of Harold H. Greene. A former Justice Department lawyer under Robert Kennedy, Greene was appointed a federal judge in 1978 and took over the AT&T case. The trial lasted for nearly a year; wrangling over the remedy another three years.

Finally, in 1982, Greene split the baby. First, he separated AT&T's long distance from its local phone service. Next, he divided AT&T's local phone service into seven regional companies, the "Baby Bells." Overseeing the complex terms of the agreement occupied much of Greene's time until 1996, when Congress finally took it away from him. By then, Greene had issued hundreds of opinions and orders, effectively running a multibillion-dollar industry from his chambers. The Communications Act of 1996, passed after years of negotiations between the swelling communications industry and Washington, promised to deregulate every aspect of the information infrastructure. Some senators predicted its passage would end the need for the FCC altogether.

The Law of Disruption, however, overruled everything. The World Wide Web, launched in 1993, signaled a rapid acceleration of the computing revolution. By 1996, the Internet had reached its tipping point. Data communications, which use the same infrastructure as voice, moved from businesses to consumers. New technologies, including fiber optics, cellular, broadband, and wireless communications, were waiting to meet new demand. The transformation from analog to digital led not only to the convergence of voice, data, and broadcast communications but to new combinations and new services as well.

Today, wired phone services have been eclipsed by wireless. Telephone, cable, and cellular providers offer voice and data, nearly all of which travels over the same infrastructure and increasingly uses the same network architecture—

the Internet. Western Electric is gone, replaced by global phone manufacturers that include Nokia, Eriksson, Samsung, and Motorola. In the United States, the competitive landscape is fragmented, including denationalized European phone companies offering cellular and wireless services, startups offering Internet telephony, and converged voice and data devices such as Google's Android, Apple's iPhone, and RIM's Blackberry. Web companies offer phone service, and phone companies offer data service. Cable and satellite companies offer everything.

Despite promises from Congress that the 1996 act would free the communications industry once and for all, the reality was far more modest. Though some restrictions were removed, phone companies still operate under a significant competitive handicap called common carrier rules, a holdover from the AT&T monopoly era. The rules require that phone companies open the pieces of their networks to competitors large and small, at rates set by the FCC. Common carriers must also charge "just and reasonable" rates to customers, design their systems to be easily interconnected with the systems of other carriers, and contribute to the Universal Service Fund, which subsidizes lower-income and rural customers who might otherwise not be served.

Competing lobbyists involved in negotiations over the 1996 act couldn't agree which of the new entrants in the communications industry should be subjected to common carrier rules. So Congress simply transplanted the distinction between phone companies and everybody else from the 1982 AT&T settlement. The definitions now hopelessly overlap, a problem that gets worse with every turn of Moore's Law. Left with no rational basis to apply the definitions, the FCC has decided that anyone who looked like a phone company in 1982 is still a common carrier, while companies who didn't look like a phone company in 1982 are free to compete without restriction. AT&T still operates as a common carrier. Cable, cellular, satellite, and wireless companies do not.

Under the lazy eye of the FCC, AT&T lost nearly 80 percent of its value between 1994 and 2004. The remnants were picked over by SBC, one of the former regional companies, which changed its name back to AT&T. The new version is a shadow of the original. It no longer has any monopolies, and competes fiercely in every local and national market. The research powerhouse, Bell Labs, is gone, as is end-user equipment manufacturing of any kind, or any hint of a computer business beyond basic Internet access. In 1982, AT&T was the largest company in the world. Today, despite the explosive growth of voice, data, and broadcast communications over the past twenty-five years, it is tenth. Meanwhile, the FCC's budget has grown from $200 million in 1996—the year it was supposedly made obsolete—to more than $300 million today.

The Law of Disruption transformed Judge Greene from Hercules to Sisyphus. Exhausted from his labors, Greene retired in 1998 and died two years later. His ghost still haunts us.

CURE FOR THE COMMON CARRIER

I was working in Europe when President Clinton signed the 1996 act, and I laughed when my European colleagues expressed shock that the new law completely and immediately deregulated the U.S. communications market. Even my client, a German communications start-up, couldn't imagine how its market could be deregulated without at least a five-year transition. The joke was on us. Within months, dozens of lawsuits were filed challenging the act and, later, testing the efforts of the FCC to implement it. Most of these lawsuits were initiated by the same industry leaders who had called for and endorsed the legislation up to the moment it became law.

Much of the trouble starts with the FCC itself. The commission, whose charter covers the radio, television, and telecommunication industries, was created in 1934. Communications then were rivalrous goods. Radio and later television required careful allocation of limited over-the-air spectrum; the communications infrastructure was dominated by the regulated monopoly of AT&T. Over the years, the agency created and later removed rules that closely controlled relationships between television networks and their affiliates, between producers of television programming and broadcasters, and between AT&T and its customers.

Today, the agency struggles to find an appropriate role for itself in an age where scarcity has been replaced by abundance. New infrastructures, including cable, satellite, cellular, and fiber-optic, have enormously expanded the capacity for communications. At the same time, the Law of Disruption has merged the technologies consumers use to enjoy their digital life.

Under the strain of constant litigation and rapid technological change, the FCC has performed poorly in the years since deregulation. Using its common carrier powers, the FCC jump-started competition after the 1996 act, often at the expense of AT&T and the regional operating companies. The FCC pointed with pride to the creation by 1999 of 250 new local phone companies, dozens of new equipment vendors, and more than 6,000 Internet service providers, all of whom could demand access to the equipment, lines, and other technology of incumbent phone companies. Every component of the phone network was unbundled, and the commission set low prices for competitors who wanted to lease the parts. Yet by 2000 the industry as a whole had entered a deep economic decline from which it has yet to emerge. Competition is good, but too many competitors without a profitable business model have badly damaged the industry.

The FCC's jurisdiction also includes television broadcasting. So, in theory, the agency has the power to ensure that as the digital revolution increasingly fuses together formerly separate activities, the transition goes smoothly for consumers. Instead, the commission continues to assume the broadcast industry structure of the 1970s is still in place. Broadcasters are subject to FCC decency rules, for example, leading to frequent fines against radio announcers who get too raunchy or the $550,000 levied against Fox for the accidental display of Janet Jackson's nipple during the 2004 Super Bowl halftime show. (An appeals court threw out the fines in 2009.)

Cable broadcasters and satellite radio, both more recent technologies for transmitting content, are exempt from these rules. Why? The agency's reasoning is that since broadcast television and radio are both free and sent through the airwaves, the likelihood that children might accidentally encounter indecent content is higher than for paid services that require special connections. Never mind the fact that nearly 60 percent of U.S. homes receive cable. The reality is that broadcasters are used to the rules, and the agency is used to applying them. Even as cable and satellite offer more explicit content without regulation, Congress increased the penalties for over-the-air broadcasters by a factor of ten.

More enlightened commissioners may someday bring the FCC into the twenty-first century, but there are other regulators to account for. The agency shares oversight with local authorities, for example, who have the power to grant franchises for new television services. Cable licensing has been a source of local graft for decades, and these are boom times for corruption. Since cable companies can now go into the phone business at will, phone companies have been trying to compete by offering television services. This means negotiating separate franchise agreements with as many as 30,000 municipal authorities.

Together, the myopia of the FCC and the provincialism of the local authorities have created a toxic environment in which consumers are usually the victims. Phone companies complain that city governments are holding their applications hostage, demanding the applicants fund everything from new street lighting to swimming pools, community centers, and other unrelated items in exchange for consideration of their licenses. Although the FCC cannot directly stop the practice, it did establish a "shot clock" rule in 2006 that required local authorities to decide petitions within 90 or 180 days. The new rule provoked outrage from local authorities and their partners in Congress, who unsuccessfully sued to have the rule overturned.

The entertainment industry, meanwhile, seems determined to use regulators as human shields in their efforts to thwart new customer demands. In response to industry hysteria over copyright abuse, for example, the FCC in 2003 passed industry-sponsored regulations that require manufacturers of digital TVs, computers, and other devices capable of receiving digital programming to support the so-called broadcast flag. The flag is a command sent from the broadcasting station to the home device receiving the signal (a set-top box, computer, DVR) that determines how the programming can be used. One command would limit recording and playback to a single device, prohibiting users from transferring a recording from a DVR to videotape, computer, or another DVR. Another might limit the quality of a recorded copy. Under the FCC's regulations, all device manufacturers were required to obey the flags.

In a stinging rebuke to the commission, the federal court of appeals in Washington threw out the regulations in 2005. "In the seven decades of its existence," the judges snarled, "the FCC has never before asserted such sweeping authority." Since the broadcast flag affected how digital programming was used after transmission was complete, the court held that the FCC had no authority to tell manufacturers or consumers what they could do with their copies. Mandating the design of televisions, the judges said, was no more in the FCC's power than regulating washing machines. Undeterred, the broadcasters tried to get Congress to mandate the flag in exchange for their cooperation with the conversion, in 2009, to all-digital broadcasts.

Still, the biggest problem for the postderegulation FCC continues to be the one we started with—making sense of common carrier rules and their application. Treating phone companies differently increasingly makes no sense. Every consumer knows that the cable infrastructure can carry television and data and that the phone network can transmit telephone calls as well as host Internet services. Even power lines and water pipes have been adapted to carry information. There is no rational way to distinguish what a company does based simply on the infrastructure technology it utilizes. Regardless of how it's transmitted, it's all information.

The FCC continues to insist, however, that there is some meaningful difference between telephone companies and computer companies or, to use the language of the 1996 act, between a "telecommunications service" and an "information service." The Law of Disruption has rendered these terms meaningless, as amply demonstrated by a 2005 case that pitted the cable industry against a Southern California ISP that calls itself Brand X Internet Services. Brand X used phone company equipment to offer high-speed Internet, but wanted to improve its transmission speeds by using the cable network. They argued that the local cable provider was a "telecommunications service" provider, too, subject to the same requirements of open access as the phone companies.

The FCC had consistently ruled that using the telephone network for Internet access was a "telecommunications service" and forced phone companies to lease their equipment to ISPs like Brand X. Here the FCC held that the very same service, offered through the cable system, was an "information service." The cable companies, in other words, were not common carriers and therefore not required to lease their network to Brand X on any terms, let alone at rates determined fair by the commission. The question for the U.S. Supreme Court was not whether phone companies were common carriers but why cable companies were not.

Just to understand how far the law has drifted away from reality, consider the definitions of the two kinds of service. Telecommunications, according to the 1996 act, are the "transmission, between or among points specified by the user, of information of the user's choosing, without change in the form or content of the information as sent and received." An information service, on the other hand, is one with "a capability for generating, acquiring, storing, transforming, processing, retrieving, utilizing, or making available information via telecommunications." These definitions are all that matter. And they are no help.

Perhaps there was once a meaningful difference. Back in the ancient world of the 1970s, completing a phone call was a well-understood transaction. The carrier simply moved the audio signal along from one point to another, performing no processing of any kind other than maintaining its integrity. Back then, data transmission was something else—something the FCC either didn't understand or didn't want to understand. In the early days, companies such as IBM, DEC, and Control Data bundled hardware, software, and phone lines to create private networks that sent data from one part of a company to another or to another company. These new services required a great deal of technical know-how, much of it draped in trade secrets.

With the advent of the Internet, the proprietary hardware, software, and data-exchange protocols have all disappeared. Most data transmission is now simply moving bits from one place to another, untouched, uninspected, and unmodified, just like a phone call. A user types the Internet address for Google, www.google.com, in a browser. Her ISP, using standard protocols, establishes a connection with the associated computer. Google then sends back the data that, when received by the user's computer, displays the familiar home page of the search giant. The ISP provides no services other than access and transmission.

In the Brand X case, the FCC searched high and low for a way to distinguish phone companies from everyone else. Cable companies, they told the Supreme Court, might not always relay bits to and from customers. They might modify the content, for example, by offering users a customized home page or providing location-specific advertising along with the Web site the user requested. (Phone companies offering Internet services can do the same, of course.) Since it was *possible* for the cable companies to modify the form or content, in other words, they were not providing a telecommunications service ("without modifying"). By process of elimination, cable companies must instead be providing an information service ("a capability for . . . transforming").

The FCC's argument sounds like the worst kind of pedantry, yet the Supreme Court bought it. The result surprised no one. Recognizing the inherent weakness courts have in understanding highly technical matters the agencies deal with, the Supreme Court in 1984 adopted the so-called Chevron Doctrine, which forbids judges from second-guessing most agency determinations. Since *Chevron*, federal courts generally uphold an agency's decisions regardless of the agency's motive. Any ambiguity in the law is resolved in favor of the agency. And there is always ambiguity in the law.

The FCC's nostalgic view of the industry increasingly threatens the health of the entire communications industry. Innovation continues to undermine the old rules, creating dangerous gaps that threaten new and valuable services. Since Brand X, for example, technology has emerged that is revolutionizing the transmission of phone calls. Using "Voice over Internet Protocol," phone calls can now be transmitted using the same packet-switching techniques the Internet uses for data. VoIP is a fast-growing alternative to traditional phone service, offered by start-ups such as Skype and Vonage as well as cable companies and ISPs who use the cable and DSL infrastructures to send and receive calls.

Information service providers, in other words, are rapidly absorbing the one activity that clearly distinguishes a telecommunications provider in the first place. In part, VoIP's success follows the Law of Disruption. As the reliability and back-end support of the Internet have improved, breaking calls into digital packets and routing them just as we do data have proven not only a more efficient use of bandwidth but also one that can deliver comparable quality and fidelity. VoIP proves that voice and data are technically if not legally indistinguishable. VoIP is also making headway, however, because as an information service it can avoid the common carrier rules.

VoIP providers, like most Internet services, offer their service for a monthly fee or bundle it in other services. In the case of Skype, computer-to-computer calls are unlimited and free. For consumers, phone calls are becoming just part of the mix of services they buy from ISPs, just as Brand X argued. Phone companies, already challenged to make money on wired local and long distance in the face of unlimited cellular plans, are now scrambling to make the transition to lower-cost VoIP as quickly as they can. The success of VoIP is encouraging traditional phone companies to change technologies, if only to remain competitive. The FCC's myopia may wind up putting the agency out of business.

The law of the FCC is quickly and inelegantly being eviscerated by the Law of Disruption. What's a regulator to do? Consumer groups have taken the position that the convergence of communication technologies means all bit transporters should be subject to common carrier rules. That's certainly one way to solve the problem. Here's another: just get rid of the rules. Eliminate the distinction between telephone and information services. Stop the lawsuits that plague the industry every time it invents new media, new protocols, and new infrastructure technologies. Cure the common carriers.

It's not unthinkable. Common carrier rules originated in the nineteenth century, initially applied to stagecoaches and steamships. The economic theory behind them is that the high cost of building a transportation infrastructure will create a "natural" monopoly for one or a few providers. In the absence of regulation, the theory goes, those providers will charge unfair prices for the use of their infrastructure, a problem the market can't fix.

The telephone industry in the days of AT&T's monopoly might have needed common carrier rules, but where's the risk now? Bits don't care how they get transported, or by whom. Interconnection is as easy as following Internet protocols—protocols that aren't owned by anybody. Bandwidth gets wider, networks grow faster, costs go down. Consumers around the world have multiple choices for how to transport their bits, including phone companies, cable companies, and cellular and wireless providers. Dominance by dial-up providers has already given way to broadband, and broadband will fall to fiber optic, WiMax, or whatever Moore's Law comes up with next. The justification for imposing common carrier rules on telecommunication services has disappeared. The market may not be perfectly competitive, but imposing regulation on one group and not the others is now more likely to cause rather than eliminate the imperfections.

AGAINST INTERNET FREEDOM

Even when regulators try to do the right thing, it often turns out wrong. Following the 1996 act, the number of phone companies swelled. That growth turned out to be a bubble, but the FCC benefited in the interim. More phone companies meant more money in the Universal Service Fund, to which common carriers are required to contribute part of their earnings, which in turn meant more money for the agency to spend even as its role was supposedly being reduced.

The agency uses the fund to subsidize customers who are either too poor or too remote to receive basic service. As the fund swelled, however, the FCC decided to spend some of the windfall on a new program to subsidize Internet access for schools and libraries. The E-Rate program offered grants for computers and software, and provided a subsidy of up to 90 percent for telecommunications and Internet service. E-Rate's yearly outlays rose to more than $2 billion.

Negligence and fraud followed the influx of new funding. Schools granted contracts to vendors without bids, and padded their grant proposals to include spending that had nothing to do with the program. Abuse of the E-Rate plan and poor oversight by the FCC have led to more than a dozen criminal prosecutions and several convictions. Computer maker NEC paid more than $35 million to settle charges it had rigged bids and bribed school officials in San Francisco. Another $8 million in equipment sold by SBC to Chicago schools was never deployed. In 2005, a congressional oversight committee found the program to be a disgrace, "completely [lacking] tangible measures of either effectiveness or impact." The plan was well intentioned, but the FCC had neither the staff nor the management skills to execute it professionally.

Still, no example demonstrates the temptation or the danger of tinkering with the machinery as much as the fight over "Net Neutrality." The issue first emerged in 2006, when phone companies suggested they might begin offering content providers such as Google and Yahoo a "premium" service. Where today data packets move through the Internet without regard for who sent them, a premium service would prioritize exchanges between paying content providers and their customers. Traffic from subscribers to the new service, in other words, would get special treatment.

A bomb had been dropped in the town square of digital life. Lobbyists, pundits, and industry leaders revved up their rhetorical engines, flinging metaphors and topping each other's hyperbole to the point that bloggers sounded measured by comparison. Net Neutrality advocates accused their opponents of discrimination and of conspiring to "strip the Internet of the First Amendment." Without it, the free market for information would become a "planned economy" like the failed Soviet system. Steve Forbes, a Net

Neutrality opponent, called it "an inexcusable barrier to the tradition of innovation at the heart of the Internet." Craigslist founder Craig Newmark countered, "It's just fairness. Americans want to play fair, work hard and get ahead. That's what net neutrality is about." New organizations supported by corporate money, with provocative names such as Hands Off the Internet and Save the Internet, took out TV ads to take their case directly to the people.

Before we can understand what Net Neutrality means or why it conjured up such strong emotions, we need to step back and understand its origins. The problem, according to Peter Christy of the Internet Research Group, goes back to the late 1980s. Cable TV companies, worried about future competition from broadcast satellite, invested heavily in the development of bidirectional, all-digital cable networks wired directly into the homes of subscribers. The hope was that these networks could serve customers with "interactive TV," but the service never caught on. Their investment, however, makes it possible for cable providers to support not only high-definition on-demand programming but also Internet and telephone service. There's plenty of bandwidth that is easy to separate. The network, by design, is already two-way.

Phone companies, including AT&T and Verizon aren't so lucky. In order to compete with cable, they need to offer the same "triple play" of phone, Internet, and high-definition digital programming. So far, partnerships with satellite providers such as Dish and DirecTV have filled the gap for television. But the copper infrastructure can't support customer demands for ever-faster Internet connections, especially as more consumers use the Web for video applications such as YouTube, Netflix, and Hulu. (As IRG's Christy says, "We finally figured out what people want to do with the Internet: watch TV!")

A very expensive arms race is now in progress. Phone companies have begun investing billions of dollars to deploy new services based on fiber-optic technology, including AT&T's U-verse and Verizon's FiOS, which is faster than cable. How will phone companies recover their investment in these new networks? One possibility is to pass the cost on to subscribers. But that would be like charging the first riders of the transcontinental railroad the full cost of the tracks. Phone company executives estimate that the true cost of the fiber network, if billed directly to consumers, would be about $560 a month, clearly a nonstarter no matter how wonderful the quality and speed. An alternative would be to charge users by the amount of bandwidth they use, similar to metered utilities such as electricity and water. "Power" users downloading enormous video files would pay more. Metering and billing, however, would become more complex and therefore more expensive.

Another option—the one that sparked the Net Neutrality fight—is to offer premium services to content providers. Today, when a user types a search into Google, the user's Internet provider simply sends the request across the internet and returns whatever data Google sends in reply. A premium service would allow ISPs to offer faster interactions for content providers who paid for it. Data going to and from customers would be checked and given priority if it involved a premium-content provider. The priority would not apply across the entire Internet but only to the part the ISP controls—that is, between their own equipment and that of their customers: the "last mile."

Web content providers today pay for outbound Internet service just as users do, but Internet routing algorithms don't give priority treatment to particular content. Once the packet enters the network, it moves through the public parts of the infrastructure following the same content-independent routing optimizations as every other packet. Sometimes the Internet is relatively slow, sometimes relatively fast. Transport speeds depend on traffic and temporary outages (as when major undersea cables were cut, severely limiting access for the Middle East and parts of Asia in early 2008), not on what is being transmitted. In effect, the Internet has always been managed as a highway without express or high-occupancy vehicle lanes. It has always been unmanaged or, to use the term that was applied in 2006, "neutral."

The last mile, on the other hand, has never been neutral. Television programming, which uses more bandwidth and requires stable speeds to keep programming from breaking up, already gets fast-lane treatment over phone calls. Phone calls, in turn, have priority over Internet traffic. Paying to gain access to a network's subscribers is also nothing new. It is at the core of how cable companies have made money all along—subscribers pay for access, and broadcasters pay to have their channels included. That's one reason Google has been investing heavily in new wireless infrastructure—to create its own network. Google hopes to cut the cable and phone companies out of the equation or at least improve the company's bargaining position.

What is new about premium services is the idea of offering priority to individual content providers instead of particular categories of content. That's where the trouble starts. Even as infrastructure providers look for ways to charge for high-bandwidth uses, information producers are experimenting with applications, including Hulu, YouTube, and iTunes, that deliver on demand content directly to consumers. These applications rely on increased bandwidth. If successful, they also strike at the heart of how access providers for television make money today. Instead of improving their economic position, investing in the infrastructure may actually cut access providers out of a very profitable loop.

The Net Neutrality fight was inevitable. ISPs want to defray the cost of their network investments by continuing to control the content available to their customers. Content providers want to use new technology to gain direct access to consumers. Many content companies, however, saw the idea of "premium" service as a back door to retaining control over programming. Net Neutrality is less a battle for the survival of the Internet and more the typical posturing of large businesses negotiating over wholesale pricing—pricing, by the way, for a service that isn't even being offered yet. So far, no provider is offering premium routing over its network. It's a hypothetical tempest in a microscopic teapot.

Or at least it seemed until content providers, for better or worse, accused the access providers of trying to destroy the Internet. The blogosphere lit up with outrage. Users who took full advantage of unlimited bandwidth plans were particularly agitated. Perhaps they feared the cost of premium service would be passed along to them. Maybe they were just uncomfortable with the idea that ISPs would know the contents of their packets (e.g., pornography, illegally downloaded movies, marathon World of Warcraft sessions?) Self-described "reluctant regulator" Lawrence Lessig, who had elsewhere called for the eradication of the FCC, weighed in on the side of the content providers. "Will we reinstate net neutrality and keep the Internet free?" he asked. "Or will we let it die at the hands of network owners itching to become content gatekeepers?" By May 2006, half a dozen bills had been introduced in Congress that would ban any prioritization.

Given the overblown rhetoric of both sides, it's hard not to see something disturbingly psychological at work here. A fight over local packet routing

urned into a war of pundits, with stakes no less than the salvation of demo-
ratic society. A person's stand on Net Neutrality became a kind of litmus
est, though what it tested wasn't entirely clear. When I published an antineu-
rality article on CNET's News.com Web site, I wasn't surprised to receive
lozens of negative responses from the site's tech-savvy readership (". . . *dis-*
•lays a shocking ignorance of history and a repellent prejudice towards big busi-
ness against the citizenry" and "*as a free American, I repudiate you*").

What did surprise me was the savagery of the replies, mostly attacks on
each other rather than me. Comments took the form of either hatred of
large corporations ("*Given their record, does the writer really think we are*
dumb enough to trust the telecoms?" or "*If it is corporate, it needs to die. If the*
Gov is the only sword long enough to kill it, the Gov should begin now") or ha-
red of the government ("*Given the choice, I trust the telcoms more. At least*
hey don't posess [sic] the legal right to violate my civil right" or "*Net Neutral-*
ty is just the opening shot in Net Regulation. We're idiots if we let it happen").
Opinions purportedly about neutrality struck me instead as being some-
hing far more primal, perhaps even Freudian. It was as if readers felt they
were being asked to choose between a smothering mother (government)
and a tyrannical father (business). Which do you fear least?

Most of the Net Neutrality froth ultimately dissipated. The FCC, the
FTC, the Justice Department, and the Bush White House sensibly recommended against legislating ahead of a problem that doesn't yet exist. None of
the Net Neutrality laws moved much beyond the initial stages, and the proposals went dormant. Throughout the first half of 2007, neutrality was dead.

Before a headstone could be placed, however, the issue roared back to life.
In October 2007, independent tests confirmed what a group of Comcast
users had been saying for months: the cable company was intentionally and
clumsily slowing their access to peer-to-peer applications, notably those
from BitTorrent. Designed to simplify large downloads, torrenting is a peer-
to-peer protocol that breaks large files into smaller pieces and stores them in
multiple locations. That way, downloads can proceed as multiple streams of
smaller file transfers.

Putting the files back together can place significant demands on network
resources, however. IRG's Peter Christy estimates that peer-to-peer users,
taking advantage of unlimited use contracts, hog as much as 80 percent of

available bandwidth. (Cable Internet is not dedicated to a single user the way a DSL line is. If your neighbors are downloading huge files, your connection will suffer.) Though torrenting is a favorite of those trading illegal copies of copyrighted movies and software, by 2007 the company that developed the technology began signing up movie studios to use the technology legally.

Comcast cagily denied blocking "access" to any site, but didn't deny that it slowed communications with high-volume applications, which its terms of service permitted them to do. Still, Net Neutrality advocates had found their smoking gun. The cable companies had implemented nonneutral technology, and used it to discriminate against a particular application. Worse, they had done so secretly. The froth rose again, and much of the proposed legislation was reintroduced. FCC chairman Kevin Martin, embarrassed by what appeared to be evidence the agency had fallen down on the job, announced in January 2008 that the FCC would review the practice.

The FCC convened raucous public hearings at both Harvard and Stanford law schools. Protesters, including a group of motorcycle-riding grandmothers, complained that Comcast was blocking precisely the kind of traffic—video— that it historically controlled. Internet pioneers criticized the particular engineering Comcast was using to slow high-volume traffic. Martin seemed to agree that the company at least needed to disclose more clearly how it was "shaping" Internet traffic.

Duly chastised, Comcast announced that it would stop singling out peer-to-peer traffic and switch to a more sophisticated network management model, this time targeting users who use the most bandwidth. During periods of high demand, the company said, the top 0.5 percent of users would be slowed to accommodate the other 99.5 percent. Comcast made peace with BitTorrent, and even called for the creation of a peer-to-peer user "bill of rights."

The commission, however, had held hearings. Some action, even modest, was required. In July, Chairman Martin proposed a diplomatic compromise: the FCC would uphold the complaints and order the company to make the changes it had already promised but refrain from levying any fine. Comcast is appealing anyway. Net Neutrality advocates claimed the incident proved the need for congressional action, while access providers argued that it proved the opposite—that the FCC had all the authority it needed.

Clearing away the rhetorical debris, the Net Neutrality controversy is simply a new round in two very old fights. One is about deregulation of the former telephone monopoly. Treating all packets identically, without inspecting or modifying them in any way, is precisely the way phone calls have historically been routed under common carrier rules. Imposing neutrality on Internet providers, in some sense, would treat everyone like a common carrier, just as Brand X had asked the FCC to do. But remember that the Supreme Court upheld the FCC's view that cable companies are *not* common carriers. Even if neutrality could be imposed on phone companies, cable and wireless providers would likely be exempt.

The Brand X case underscores the fact that telephone companies already operate at a significant regulatory disadvantage. Indeed, cellular companies providing wireless Internet are even less neutral than Comcast. Given limited bandwidth, wireless operators already impose significant restrictions on their users, including complete bans of file-sharing applications. It is at least a little disingenuous for Net Neutrality advocates to talk about level playing fields. Common carrier regulations increasingly determine who can and cannot make money in the information business, and how they can do so. Seen this way, Net Neutrality is just another version of the argument that's been going on since Judge Greene split the telecom baby back in 1982, praying that technology would keep the pieces apart.

Whether tiered pricing for network traffic would help or hurt communications companies, we should acknowledge that there's nothing "neutral" about the current legal rules. There's nothing rational about them either. There's a certain irony to the fact that Net Neutrality started over a fear of what AT&T and Verizon, both common carriers, might do with their fiber-optic networks. Those fears materialized, however, over something Comcast, an unregulated ISP, was already doing.

The second problem, the one that gives even proneutrality advocates pause, has to do with the appropriate role for government in regulating new technologies. Free-market types argue that neutrality laws are unnecessary. If neutrality is in fact what ordinary consumers want, then the market will provide it. Consumers will shun providers who unfairly "discriminate" against competing or nonpaying content providers under the guise of managing Internet traffic. Still, markets don't always work. If your choice for high-speed access is limited to one or two providers, as it is in many parts of the United States today, competition may not solve the problem. All the Net Neutrality advocates want is legislation that preserves the status quo—a protection against a potential, perhaps likely, future market failure.

On the surface, this sounds like a minimal intrusion on an otherwise well-functioning market, one unlikely to add new costs of its own to enforce. But how minimal would it be in practice? Consider one proposed law, the sanctimoniously named Internet Freedom Preservation Act. Under IFPA the definition of *neutrality* goes on for several hundred words, a toxic cocktail of legal and technical gibberish ("maintain the freedom to use for lawful purposes broadband telecommunications networks, including the Internet, without unreasonable interference from or discrimination by network operators," and so on). The definition is just the start. The IFPA's implementing rules are left to the discretion of the FCC, which has already flip-flopped in response to political pressure. And given the Chevron Doctrine, their interpretation of neutrality would be outside the review of federal courts.

Assuming neutrality was required, how would the FCC ensure broadband providers stay neutral? Would the commission set up compliance monitoring of network traffic? If so, where would the funding come from to hire the necessary technical staff? Under an earlier draft of the IFPA, any consumer would have the right to file a complaint with the commission, which the commission would have ninety days to review. (The current draft says nothing about enforcement, leaving the law toothless.) To investigate a complaint, the FCC would presumably have to intercept the network traffic of an ISP accused of nonneutral behavior, then seize and inspect the packets in question. The same civil liberties groups that were outraged by the NSA's antiterrorism surveillance don't seem to worry about giving the FCC power, in the name of investigating complaints, to look inside the contents of packets.

Whatever rules are enacted, the chances for over- and under-enforcement are high. The practice to be banned is largely theoretical and based on technology not yet developed. Neutrality rules would likely encourage inefficient workarounds. For one thing, it's already clear that network management requires nonneutral behavior. Some content should get higher (voice) or lower (file downloads) priority as a matter of optimization, and blanket bans on prioritizing may end up making a mess of traffic overall. The FCC lacks the engineering expertise to develop better practices, let alone the ability to write rules that can guess the right exceptions in advance. Institutionally, the commission has demonstrated it is better suited to looking for swear words and errant nipples on broadcast television than to policing Internet traffic patterns.

The problem with "simple" regulations is that they never are. This is especially true when the industry being regulated is in the midst of dramatic transformation. Maybe the Internet has worked so well because neutrality has been a persistent part of the architecture. It's also possible that it's worked so well because there has been minimal government regulation of its design and operation. Maybe both statements are true. More of the latter to shore up the former is a dangerous trade-off. The information highway to hell is surely paved with good intentions.

The Law of Disruption has already helped the Internet sidestep a barrage of efforts to micromanage it. Laws to ban indecent material, impose sales taxes on e-commerce, require "zoning" tags on Web sites, criminalize spam, prevent file sharing, and outlaw spyware have all been proposed with the same earnest arguments as Net Neutrality. Some of these laws have been overturned by the courts. Some died before being passed. The rest—well, the rest are effectively ignored, thanks to the Internet's ability to treat regulation as a network failure and reroute around the problem. Which is not to say there haven't been casualties, some of them innocent entrepreneurs, along the way.

FAST-FORWARD: CONTINUED DIVIDENDS, CONTINUED THREATS

The infrastructure of digital life is growing as fast as Moore's Law and Metcalfe's Law make possible. Today, more than 300 million homes worldwide have broadband access to information services, up from 0 homes in 2000, when the technology didn't exist. Britain has proposed to bring high-speed Internet service to every home by 2012. More than 500 million cellular customers, nearly half in Asia, are now connected to high-speed networks that offer video and Internet services in addition to phone. The number of computers connected to the Internet is more than 500 billion, with 3 million new Web sites added each month. As of March 1, 2009, the number of Internet users was 1,596,270,108—22 percent of the world's population.

Now for the bad news. Governments have scaled back dramatically or their investments in basic research, which funded most of the breakthrough in early Internet technology. Rollout of high-speed connections is slowing in part because the nearly 95 percent of the world's population withou them are poor or in remote locations. In the United States, the 2009 stimulus bill allocated more than $7 billion to encourage broadband deployment bu saddled much of that funding with undefined Net Neutrality requirements.

This chapter has explored the risks of overregulating the information highway. The solution, however, is not simply for governments to stay out Far from it. A healthy information infrastructure requires precisely the kind of oversight that lawmakers have historically provided, including:

- establishing the basic protocols and allocating sparse resources such as spectrum
- providing research and other incentives to nurture new technologies with high build-out and low operating costs
- intervening when markets fail and monopolistic practices harm consumers

What infrastructures do *not* benefit from, on the other hand, include:

- laws that are based on outdated understandings of how technology works and what users are doing with it
- provincial rules aimed at giving unearned advantage to a particular business, industry sector, or region
- laws that try to regulate the morality of consumers experimenting with a new environment

As the AT&T story suggests, leftover regulations and myopic regulators from a bygone era constrain the development for information products and services. Career legislators are simply out of touch with the latest uses of technology. California senator Diane Feinstein, who represents Silicon Valley, lobbied to ban laptops from the floor of the U.S. Senate as recently as 1998 (inkwells are still provided). Former Alaska senator Ted Stevens was mercilessly ridiculed for his 2007 description of the Internet as "a series of tubes"

"It's not something you just dump something on. It's not a truck"). His in-
coherence would have been funny were Stevens not the chairman of the committee that regulated the "tubes."

Technological ignorance is one reason lawmakers turn over the details of
regulating to agencies staffed by specialists. Regulatory agencies, however,
have limits of their own. Working with industry counterparts day in and day
out, the agencies develop a client relationship with the companies they are
supposed to be supervising. Instead of oversight, regulators become cheerleaders, a phenomenon economist George Stigler called "regulatory capture." Consumers, the real clients, are absent, save for the sometimes shrill
voice of public interest organizations and other nonprofits.

Regulatory capture can be dangerous. History shows that it creates an un-
healthy mutual dependency that metastasizes in the face of disruptive technologies. In the United States, railroads trained the ICC to manage rates in
ways that minimized competition, but when new modes of transport including trucking entered the picture, the industry no longer had the business skills
to respond. Communication firms should not use their intimacy with regulators to stack the deck against innovation. Nor should they cling desperately to
rules that give an advantage to themselves or harm a competitor when those
rules have clearly outlived their usefulness, or been made obsolete by new
technologies. Corrupting the system ultimately corrupts the perpetrator.

Regardless of motive, efforts to suspend the Law of Disruption have a
tendency of backfiring. Still, the temptation for regulators and even business
leaders who should know better can be irresistible. The best lawmakers, public interest groups, and angry mobs can find themselves agitating for that
one little fix, that one little correction, that one little step backward that will
calm things down or level the playing field. As they go through the motions
of legislating, the rules of the game have all changed or the game has ceased
to be played in the first place.

The mistake regulators and those who enable them continue to make is
trying to micromanage individual technologies or applications. Even when
these interventions seem like small adjustments to the clockwork of the Law
of Disruption, they cause expensive breakdowns. Even if a little rule change
for a small group of consumers seems like a fair and simple correction to a
gross injustice, interventions don't work. Individually, they quickly become

out-of-date, ready to spring back to life in some unexpected way, perhaps applied to some new technology that wasn't even on the drawing board when the rule was made. Failure to update the definition of "super-computer" in Department of Defense regulations, for example, meant that the Sony PlayStation was technically a "munition" requiring special export licenses to leave the United States.

At the same time, private infrastructure investments are expensive, risky and looked at suspiciously by public investors. Business users have a right to petition the government to underwrite, insure, or even subsidize the deployment of new infrastructure, even if they make no promises in return to operate those networks for the public good. The economics of information guarantee there are plenty of profits to be made, if only everyone has access.

For citizens, one universal benefit of digital life is that it dramatically reduces the costs of collective action. Where people were once entirely reliant on governments to redress problems that affected everyone a small amount, digital technology has created an alternative. Social networking, blogs, and even simple applications such as e-mail and instant messaging have made it possible for consumers to quickly form groups with shared values. That power has been unleashed to great effect in elections, lobbying, and protests. So far, at least, it is an alternative that has proven more responsive to its users.

That newfound power comes with an equally important responsibility to use it wisely. As the Net Neutrality saga suggests, regulators are not immune to pressure applied by residents of digital life. Infrastructure regulation has a long and twisted history. To understand the ramifications of even a small change in the rules requires considerable expertise not only in a wide body of law but also in the details of the technologies involved. Independent agencies were created for a very good reason—to insulate regulators from just such pressure. This chapter has reviewed a fraction of the competing interests involved in optimizing the value of the information infrastructure. The solutions may be simple, but understanding the problems is hard.

Getting consumers involved in the regulation of the technology they rely on is not inherently wrong. Still, content providers did a great disservice by reducing Net Neutrality to a sound bite, suggesting it was a problem about which the average consumer could easily form an opinion. Contrary to Craigslist's Craig Newmark, Net Neutrality is not "just" about "playing fair and getting ahead." It's about something much more complicated. Encouraging the mentality that complicated problems are black-and-white struggles between good and evil is ultimately unhelpful and likely to backfire. A dangerous precedent has been established. Digital democracy is one thing; digital mobs are another.

Just ask Google. In late 2008, the company admitted it had approached broadband providers about installing special Google servers within their networks to expedite downloading YouTube videos and other Google content. These servers, of course, would give Google's content a fast lane on the last mile. The company, which fought on the side of Net Neutrality advocates against access providers "playing favorites with particular applications or content providers," was predictably accused of treason. Google beat a hasty and awkward retreat. According to a company lawyer, the company was still behind Net Neutrality. It was simply offering to "colocate" its servers to reduce the access providers' bandwidth costs. The offers, he pointed out, "are nonexclusive, meaning any other entity could employ similar arrangements." Nonneutral side deals are apparently okay, so long as they are voluntary.

The bottom line is simple. Encouraging infrastructure is good; micromanaging it is bad. Nothing could be easier in principle or harder in practice. For now, regulators must work to eliminate as much of Judge Greene's handiwork as possible. They must at long last put to rest the common carrier rules, instead encouraging the deployment of new network technologies. Lawmakers must free the information economy to operate in an environment that makes its own regulations, where the Law of Disruption changes the rules as efficiently as it does the technologies to which they apply.

LAW FIVE: BUSINESS

All Regulation Is Local

Globalization has been turbocharged by the Internet. But merchants and consumers are learning to their peril that the easier it is to interact across borders, the more likely it is that provincial and often pointless local laws will rear up to interfere with trade. Sometimes, as with Microsoft and its worldwide antitrust problems, conflicting laws and uneven enforcement can come close to forcing a hard stop. We need a single uniform law of digital commerce. The building blocks for writing one are in place.

LAWS OF GENERAL APPLICABILITY

Roommates.com thought it was being helpful.

A popular Web-based service for listing and finding apartments in the United States and Canada, Roommates.com lists more than 100,000 available shared-living opportunities. Users with apartments to divide or those looking for a place to live each supply basic information about who they are and what they are looking for. Using a search function, potential roommates find each other on the site, review a detailed profile, and e-mail each other to work out specifics.

To register, you must indicate, among other characteristics, your age, gender, sexual orientation, whether you have kids or would live with someone else's, and your "level of cleanliness." It might seem obvious why an individual looking to share an apartment and sometimes even the same bedroom with an unrelated person might want to know these things up front. Still, fair-housing advocates in Southern California sued the company in 2006. Acknowledging these preferences, they argued, violates the federal Fair Housing Act as well as state and local ordinances. By collecting and listing that information, Roommates.com was complicit in the illegal discrimination of its users.

The company initially argued that even if their users were violating fair-housing laws, the Web site was not responsible. Under a 1996 law, Congress had provided online companies immunity for content posted by their users. In Chicago, in fact, an earlier case had dismissed claims against classified-ad site Craigslist for identical conduct by its users. Despite Craigslist ads that included captions like "No Minorities" and "No Children," the court found that Craigslist was not the "publisher" of its users' content and was therefore protected by the immunity law. Realistically, what other conclusion could the court reach? More than 30 million ads are posted to Craigslist every month. Despite its popularity, Craigslist is run by a staff of only thirty people. The immunity provision not only applied to Craigslist, the court concluded, but was also common sense.

Common sense, however, does not always carry the day in court. The federal court of appeals in the Roommates.com case reached the opposite conclusion just a few months later. Craigslist was not liable, but Roommates.com was. Why the different results? Users of Craigslist enter their entire classified ads as one block of text. Since the Roommates.com site is specifically addressed to finding someone to live with, however, it also asks the profile questions that help other users search for compatible living arrangements without having to read through thousands of essays. Because the preferences are given in drop-down menus and are required fields, the California court held that Roommates.com was not simply hosting content but helping to develop it. Craigslist was innocent, while Roommates.com was a full participant in thousands of potential housing-code violations. Immunity on the one hand and potentially fatal liability on the other rested on what appeared to be a trivial difference in Web site design.

The immunity law was designed to keep the federal courts out of the business of dictating how Web site operators design their sites and run their businesses. Though Congress has not repealed or otherwise watered down this important law, the California court refused to apply it. The Internet, the court noted, now has a "vast reach into the lives of millions." It no longer needs special protection. Just as local housing brokers can't discriminate on behalf of their clients, neither should Roommates.com be permitted to do so for their users. Immunity for the Web site, they concluded, would "give them an unfair advantage over their real-world counterparts, which must comply with laws of general applicability."

ROCKS AND SHOALS

As the Roommates.com case suggests, courts and legislators from the physical world are increasingly intervening in the business of digital life. That's a problem. The atmospheres of the two worlds are dramatically different, and the mismatch can lead to suffocation. Laws that deal with commercial transactions were written to reflect the tangible nature of business in the physical world. They assume an environment where the buyer and seller live in close proximity, where goods can be examined prior to purchase, and where service providers tailor their offerings to local conventions and practices. None of these assumptions applies online.

Local rules can also vary tremendously. Despite the creation of regional and continental "open markets" in the past twenty years, there are still significant differences in the laws of different geographies. Some are rooted in local culture, shared morality, or sometimes just accidents of history. Different countries—even neighboring cities and states—apply wildly different standards to the same commercial behavior. Yet the Internet is everywhere and nowhere at the same time, making it impossible to determine whose laws apply.

The obvious solution would be to establish a uniform code of Internet commerce, suited to the unique economics of digital life—a local ordinance determined by the Law of Disruption. Instead, provincial regulators from the physical world have tried to force-fit their own rules onto transactions both within and outside their borders. Even when local laws are virtually identical, some jurisdictions may choose not to enforce them. As the Roommates.com case suggests, judges may simply ignore the law, substituting their own policy for that of the legislature. The result is a crazy quilt of conflicting and often incompatible standards to which businesses around the world are being held. In the digital age, at least so far, businesses have to obey everyone's law.

Although there are more Internet-specific laws passed all the time, most of the important principles of online business have been developed through litigation. Most lawsuits, however, are initiated with the intention not of establishing future precedents but simply of doing damage to competitors. If your market share keeps slipping and you've lost the ability to innovate your way back to victory, Plan B is to sue your competitors. When you can't win through innovation, in other words, try litigation. Sometimes these cases hope to score only temporary benefit, or delay the release of a new technology for which one has no response. Sometimes it's just desperation—a Hail Mary pass to the courts when competing in the marketplace fails. These efforts almost never work. More likely, they make things worse for the failing company. The litigation further distracts them from the business of serving their customers, hastening their fall.

Consider a few early cases from the dawn of digital law, which amply demonstrate the futility of using the courts to regain a lost lead:

- After Borland introduced a more sophisticated spreadsheet program, Lotus sued, claiming that Borland's "1-2-3 compatibility mode" illegally cloned the structure of Lotus commands and menu structures.
- When game maker Accolade reverse engineered the protocols needed to make games for Sega's Genesis console without first obtaining a license, Sega charged that Accolade had violated their right to keep those requirements a secret.
- Once Apple found that the inferior Windows operating system was nonetheless winning customers, it sued Microsoft, arguing that despite a licensing agreement between the two companies, Windows had gone too far in borrowing the user interface embodied in early Macintosh computers.

In each case, the company doing the suing had once enjoyed a dominant position in its market—dominance that had been eroded by new products that users apparently liked better. Litigation was a last-ditch effort to hold on to what was left of the plaintiff's market share, or even somehow to turn back the clock. The plaintiff's strategy, in other words, was to stretch business law to protect elements of its software—a menu structure, a set of compatibility protocols, a design metaphor—that hadn't previously been thought protectable. Lotus, Sega, and Apple all lost their cases, and soon after they entered the darkest days of their corporate histories.

Today, there is plenty of evidence that the computer industry has learned othing from its own history. In the "live by the sword, die by the sword" tegory of ironic litigation, consider the fate of struggling hardware and ftware maker Sun Microsystems. In 2001, Sun accused Microsoft of abusg its license to distribute Java, Sun's standard for transmitting small proams embedded into Web sites. Three years later, Sun lost a suit brought by odak, which claimed Java violated patents the photo company had acuired from Wang Laboratories. Before the jury could decide how much Sun wed, the parties settled for close to $100 million. Kodak had asked for $1 llion, just as Sun had when it sued Microsoft.

Or consider an even more delicious irony: a lawsuit filed against the ecording Industry Association of America by P2P software vendor Altnet. he RIAA, until recently, was suing the teenage customers of its recording lal members for copyright violations, a last-ditch effort to save the hopelessly osolete system of reproducing music using expensive and now unnecessary ledia such as CDs. Altnet charged that the technology the RIAA is using to arch your kids' hard drives for infringing MP3s is itself an infringement of ltnet's patents. The RIAA may be committing the same piracy it has accused veryone else of. (The suit is ongoing.)

Regardless of the outcomes, these lawsuits result in precedents that everyne can come to regret, including the winners. Lotus's loss in the Borland se signaled the end of legal protection based on a program's user interface nd behaviors (its "look and feel"), leading to increased and dangerous reance on software patents to fend off competition. Unable to protect protools through the courts, likewise, the video game industry transformed into ne where console manufacturers own their own studios and cooperate with nly a few closely supervised outside developers. Consoles are now sold as oss leaders, while individual games are expensive, with little real competition mong titles. Apple's loss in its early Microsoft case has led to increasingly omplicated cross-licensing of technology among Silicon Valley companies, hich many believe has created a high barrier to new competitors for hardare, software, and applications.

Statutes represent a more carefully crafted set of policy decisions than ad oc lawsuits. As the Roommates.com case suggests, however, statutes may till fail to create a stable body of digital business law. The immunity law in he Roommates.com case, known as Section 230, was enacted in response to

problems encountered early in the formation of digital life by a compan
called Prodigy. Prodigy, a pre-Internet service offered by retailer Sears, Ro
buck & Company and IBM, was a private-information network for hom
computer users. Customers dialed into the service and paid the compan
based on how long they were connected. Prodigy offered a variety of onlin
services to its two million subscribers, including news, airline reservation
and a primitive form of e-mail.

One of Prodigy's most popular features was a series of online bullet
boards where users could share information on topics of mutual intere.
The most active board was a stock-trading discussion called "Money Talks
In 1995, anonymous posts to Money Talks claimed that criminal acts by
securities firm named Stratton-Oakmont were about to be exposed ar
urged users to avoid the company. The claim may have been false. (The con
pany had settled earlier charges with the Securities and Exchange Commi
sion without admitting guilt.) Stratton-Oakmont sued Prodigy, arguing the
were liable for defamation as a "publisher" of the damaging posts. A Ne
York State court agreed.

Prodigy, it's true, had provided some editorial guidance for its board
Automatic filters, for example, kept profanity off the site. Prodigy also use
volunteer monitors to spot-check the boards for inappropriate conten
These features, which distinguished Prodigy from its competitors, includin
CompuServe, which escaped liability in a similar case, seemed significant t
the court. Prodigy's partial review of user-generated content, the court hel
demonstrated "editorial control." Just like a newspaper, which selects, re
views, and edits all of its content, Prodigy was responsible for whatever i
users added to the site's bulletin boards—some 60,000 posts a day. Prodig
planned an appeal and began an investigation to determine if the posts wer
in fact accurate. Stratton quickly settled the case, dismissing its demand fc
$200 million in damages in exchange for a public apology.

Still, the Prodigy case sent shock waves through the nascent online ser
vices industry. Instead of encouraging self-regulation of the kind Prodigy wa
promoting, the decision was seen as creating a perverse incentive for compa
nies not to exercise any control and simply let all postings through. Congres
responded by amending U.S. communications law with Section 230, which
called "Protection for 'Good Samaritan' Blocking and Screening of Offensiv
Material." The law prohibits treating providers of any "interactive service" a

the publisher of content provided by users. It also prohibits lawsuits based on voluntary action taken by an interactive service to restrict offensive or objectionable material, even if the service doesn't do a perfect job. Congress not only refused to regulate Web content but also immunized Web sites from any state laws that might otherwise have been applied to fill the gap. As such, Section 230 is a kind of antilaw, a decision not to regulate.

In legal jargon, Section 230 provides a "safe harbor." It gives service providers the freedom to experiment with the optimal quality and quantity of editing, protecting users without stifling them. States and private litigants are barred from second-guessing these choices. Though headings and titles in laws have no legal significance, the use of the term *Good Samaritan* suggests Congress believed sites that policed content were acting in the best interests of all users, and ought to be encouraged to do so. "One of the specific purposes of this section," according to the House Conference Report, "is to overrule Stratton-Oakmont v. Prodigy and any other similar decisions which have treated such providers and users as publishers or speakers of content that is not their own because they have restricted access to objectionable material." The policy of the United States, according to the report, is "to preserve the vibrant and competitive free market that presently exists for the Internet and other interactive computer services, unfettered by Federal or State regulation."

In passing the immunity provision, Congress demonstrated unusual foresight. No other country provides similar immunity. Outside the United States, there are frequent lawsuits against Web sites for publishing untrue statements, even for content posted by anonymous third parties. Australia even extends the reach of its defamation laws worldwide. Lawsuits can be brought over content published and housed on computers located entirely outside the country, so long as the material is read by someone in Australia.

It might be a stretch—but not a big one—to say that the "unfettered" environment preserved by Section 230 has been responsible for the dominance of U.S. companies in the development of new forms of electronic communications. Blogging, Wikipedia, Twitter, and other collaborative technologies at the heart of social networking applications rely on user content for most if not all of their value. Forcing operators to police that content would deter many of these services from getting started in the first place.

As Internet technology has advanced, the open-ended definition of "interactive service" has been applied to all kinds of user-generated content.

Web sites, blogs, and online services that solicit customer comments and reviews—including Craigslist, AOL, and MySpace—have all benefited from immunity. Section 230's safe harbor has been extended to employers for the activities of employees on company computers, online auctioneers for the sale of a forged celebrity signature, and dating services for the posting of false information by members.

In the absence of Section 230, individual judges would have to decide when content does and does not deserve protection. In the earlier case involving Craigslist, for example, the appellate court was particularly concerned with how a lower court might fashion a remedy that would satisfy the housing advocates. Automatic filters would be of little use. Does "white" refer to the color of the room or the race of its occupant? Even if the site were to hire thousands of editors to review user content, what kind of information would they remove? One of the ads the housing advocates objected to described the neighborhood as having a "Catholic Church and beautiful Buddhist Temple within one block," which they claimed implied an illegal religious preference. Or did it just describe the area?

The Roommates.com case has set a disturbing precedent. The California court seemed confident that the Internet is "no longer a fragile new means of communication that could easily be smothered in its cradle by overzealous laws and regulations." Is that really true? Despite double-digit growth for more than ten years, e-commerce still accounts for well under 10 percent of retail activity. There isn't even a measurement for services of the kind Roommates.com provides.

Congress recognized the danger of regulating Internet content, the Craigslist court held. It's up to Congress to declare the danger over. Up until now, Section 230 preserved the most vibrant forms of digital life from regulatory second-guessing. But the safe harbor provided by Congress is now dotted with rocks and shoals. Whether new services will be able to avoid them remains to be seen.

TRUST AND ANTITRUST

The rapid commercialization of the Internet has made every business a global business, but few executives appreciate the sheer breadth of customs aws, and regulations that define local economies. Sometimes the differences are small but dangerous. Offering a discount or having a sale is illegal in Switzerland, even if the sale is on a U.S. Web site being accessed by a Swiss citizen. Sometimes, the disparities are large and potentially lethal. In the world's largest emerging markets, there is effectively no patent or copyright protection.

As high-technology companies including Intel, Google, Microsoft, and Yahoo have learned in the past ten years, regional regulators can take passionate interest in defining the emerging world of digital life. For the most part, these interventions come under the cover of what is known as antitrust law. Although antitrust law fell out of favor in the 1970s and 1980s, it came roaring back to life with the rise of the information economy. A closer look at the Microsoft case—clearly the most significant collision to date between the Law of Disruption and the law of competition—should give pause to any regulator considering similar action in the rapidly changing information economy.

The Justice Department, concerned with Microsoft's dominance in the PC operating system market, had been after the company since the early 1990s. Their theory wasn't that Windows was harming consumers. Though the company made spectacular profits, it plowed much of it back into research and development. Thanks to the Law of Disruption, Microsoft's dominance led not to higher prices and lower quality but to lower prices and higher quality. Indeed, it was the complaints not of consumers but of competitors, including Netscape, Oracle, Novell, Sun, and others who had failed to develop their own PC operating systems, that motivated the government throughout the case.

The most dangerous turn came in 1997, when the Department of Justice sued the company for a third time. On this go-round, the government's case was not about Windows but about Web browsers. The browser market was initially dominated by Netscape and its Navigator product, a commercialized though still free version of the Mosaic program that founder Marc Andreessen had helped developed as a student. The product was wildly successful, quickly capturing more than 90 percent of Web users and catapulting Netscape into an initial public offering that signaled the start of the Internet bubble.

Caught off guard by the sudden consumer interest in the Internet, Microsoft initially ignored it. Seeing its mistake, Microsoft also licensed the Mosaic code. In 1995, the company released the first version of its own browser, Internet Explorer, which it bundled into Windows 98 and subsequent versions of Windows. With Microsoft's backing, IE quickly dominated the browser market. As the suit was filed, IE was just about to overtake Navigator in market share. It eventually captured 95 percent of the users.

By integrating IE into Windows, according to the government's complaint, Microsoft had forced PC makers to make IE the primary Web browser for new computers. Though Navigator could still run under Windows, the government claimed Microsoft had interfered with Netscape's ability to compete fairly for (nonpaying) customers. In 2000, federal judge Thomas Penfield Jackson ruled that the company had violated antitrust law. He ordered Microsoft to split into two companies, one for Windows and one for applications, including IE, Office, and the Windows Media Player. Microsoft appealed, and Jackson agreed to hold off on his breakup order in the interim.

By 2001, there had been enough cloak-and-dagger in the litigation to generate several books and countless articles—all peppered with secret interviews with Judge Jackson during and after he ruled against Microsoft. Judge Jackson early on had tried to off-load the technical complexities of the case by appointing law professor Lawrence Lessig as a "special master." Lessig was quickly removed from the case, however, when Netscape released e-mails that Lessig had written to its legal counsel expressing dissatisfaction with his own use of IE. Later, Judge Jackson took the unprecedented step of asking federal appeals court judge Richard A. Posner, Lessig's onetime employer, to serve as mediator, which he did for nearly four months, ultimately without success.

Though the business press regularly assumed the case would ultimately be decided by the U.S. Supreme Court, the justices refused to hear it. The final word instead came from the federal court of appeals in Washington, D.C., whose decision ran to nearly one hundred single-spaced pages. The court upheld Jackson's findings that Microsoft had a monopoly on PC operating systems and had illegally leveraged that dominance to take market share from Netscape. But the judges reversed several of Jackson's key rulings, most important his order to break up the company. They sharply criticized Jackson's own behavior, and reassigned the case to another judge.

The parties soon reached a settlement. Microsoft agreed to separate its operating system products from so-called middleware products such as Web browsers, e-mail clients, and media players and agreed to make it easier for PC manufacturers to substitute non-Microsoft versions of these programs. Interfaces necessary to make other vendors' middleware work efficiently with Windows would also be published and licensed without charge to third-party developers. Private settlements were reached between Microsoft and nearly all of the companies pushing for antitrust action, many of whom had sued privately as well. Overall, the company paid more than $3 billion.

Microsoft's capitulations came as cold comfort to Netscape itself, which never actually developed a way to make money from its free software and was sold to AOL during the antitrust case. AOL and Microsoft settled Netscape's private antitrust lawsuit for $750 million, after which AOL licensed IE and shelved Navigator. Microsoft's other adversaries enjoyed an even more pyrrhic victory. On April 3, 2000, the day Jackson announced his rulings against Microsoft, the tech-heavy NASDAQ stock market crashed, losing 20 percent of its total value within a week. It never recovered, sitting now at roughly one-third of its worth the day before Jackson ruled. Few people remember that it was Jackson's decision in the Microsoft case that burst the Internet bubble once and for all.

Many of Microsoft's direst fears, brushed aside by the court of appeals, seem prescient and obvious seven years later. Consider just a few of the rejected arguments, taken from the first few pages of the court's opinion.

Relevant Market

In establishing that Microsoft had an illegal monopoly, Judge Jackson accepted the government's contention that the relevant market to consider was that for "Intel-compatible PC operating systems." Microsoft had argued that definition was far too narrow; indeed, it was recursive. Though there had been other operating systems in the PC market in the past, including IBM's OS/2, competitors had ceded this segment and moved on to other kinds of software. Microsoft argued that the relevant market should comprise all personal computers (including Apple, which still holds a 100 percent monopoly on operating systems for its computers), the growing server market where

UNIX and later Linux were popular, and the nascent market for smaller computing devices, such as cell phones and PDAs, where Microsoft had limited market share.

Today, Windows still dominates the "Intel-compatible" PC market, but that market constitutes a smaller piece of the overall computing industry all the time. Linux has expanded its push into server and even client uses. Microsoft controls only 13 percent of the operating systems market for smart phones. In the game-console market, the company launched its own product, the Xbox, in order to get a foot in the door. It has no presence on the millions of game consoles made by Nintendo and Sony, which use their own proprietary systems. Even in the browser market, though Netscape is long gone, an open-source version of the Mosaic-based browser called Firefox was launched in 2003. Today, Firefox has about 20 percent of the market—almost 40 percent in Europe. By early 2009 Internet Explorer had fallen to less than 70 percent of the browser market. Ten years into the fight, browsers are still 100 percent free.

Antitrust in the Software Industry

The appellate court went out of its way to dismiss what it called the "theoretical" question of whether antitrust should ever be applied to the information economy. In the software industry, the judges recognized, network effects often mean "one product or standard tends toward dominance." That dominance, however, may not require legal correction. Why not? The rapid cycling of innovation generated by the Law of Disruption means that dominance in emerging industries is unlikely to harm consumers. Market dominance, even monopoly, can prove transient as one standard is replaced by the next generation. In spreadsheet software, dominance rapidly moved from VisiCalc to Lotus 1-2-3 to Excel as better computers continued to raise user expectations of functionality.

Though the court quotes approvingly from several antitrust economists and legal scholars, ultimately it rejects the idea that software is different. "There is no consensus among commentators," the court notes, "on the question of whether, and to what extent, current monopolization doctrine should be amended to account for competition in technologically dynamic markets characterized by network effects."

The pace of change in digital life also left the court doubting its ability to correct anticompetitive behavior. From the time the government filed its lawsuit three years had passed before Judge Jackson issued his conclusions of law, perhaps a record for a complex antitrust proceeding. Still, it had been more than six years since the Justice Department began its investigation. "Six years," the court acknowledged, "seems like an eternity in the computer industry." Practical concerns with such a delay include difficulty fashioning a workable remedy. Oversight is also harder, given the likelihood that orders for companies to modify their conduct "may be unavailing in such cases, because innovation to a large degree has already rendered the anticompetitive conduct obsolete." Changes during and since the Microsoft case underscore the importance of that observation.

The Source of the Monopoly

The court also made short work of one of Microsoft's key arguments: that the monopoly was sanctioned by copyright. What competitors wanted was to alter the user interface presented to users when Windows starts up—removing some of Microsoft's icons, perhaps, or replacing some middleware components with alternatives supplied by the company's competitors. But that interface is protected, Microsoft argued, under copyright law. The anticompetitive behavior the government complained about, according to Microsoft, is nothing more than the rightful exercise of its legal rights. Allowing PC manufacturers to make changes to the software would, according to Microsoft, undermine "the principal value of Windows as a stable and consistent platform that supports a broad range of applications and that is familiar to users." Microsoft's refusal to allow the alterations did not violate the laws of competition. Rather, it was simply enforcing its copyrights.

The court, however, had none of this. The judges compared Microsoft's argument to the ridiculous analogy that having lawfully purchased a baseball bat, the owner can claim immunity from damages he may cause by bashing someone over the head with it. The problem is much more subtle than that, however, and as we'll see in later chapters, continues to be a source of tremendous confusion in the information economy.

Copyright is a government grant to the author, in this case the author of a software program, of the exclusive right to copy, use, or otherwise alter the work. It is, in other words, the grant of a monopoly. Here, Microsoft used its monopoly power to control a product that had, by operation of Metcalfe's Law, become the de facto standard for an important segment of the consumer computing industry. The very same government that granted the monopoly was now suing the company under antimonopoly laws. The same policies that favor the trust, in other words, also favor stopping the use of it through antitrust. Given that fundamental paradox, it's no surprise Judge Jackson crashed the stock market.

The Middleware Threat

One additional argument rejected by the court of appeals is worth revisiting. Microsoft argued that its decision to develop and promote IE was based on its fear that hardware and software vendors were increasingly bypassing Windows in favor of middleware. Middleware is software that sits between the operating system and user applications, and includes database management systems, browsers, and network management services. Middleware developers create different versions of their programs for different operating systems but present a standard interface to the applications and users that access them.

As a result, middleware makes it easier and cheaper for application developers to offer the same products on multiple computing environments (or "platforms," to use the technical term). Application developers no longer need to address the technical requirements of the underlying operating systems; middleware does that for them. An e-mail application that works through a Web browser, for example, doesn't need to include programming for Internet communications. The browser handles that function.

The features that make middleware attractive to application developers also make it less efficient than platform-specific operating systems, including Windows. That's why operating systems still exist—in general, they will perform the functions of middleware, but because they are specific to the underlying hardware, they use fewer computing resources. As Moore's Law continues to make computers that are faster, cheaper, and smaller, however, the technical disadvantages of middleware have largely disappeared. Even in 1995 when IE was first released, middleware, including Web browsers such

Navigator or platform-independent programming environments such as Java, was growing increasingly popular. Microsoft believed that if it did not respond aggressively to the middleware threat, application developers would continue to bypass Windows, turning the product into a commodity—a necessary but nonstrategic component of the hardware.

The court rejected the claim as speculative. Since 2001, however, Microsoft's fears have been borne out. Computing has increasingly migrated from the stand-alone PC to the Internet as a general-purpose network, where users make use of similar applications regardless of whether they are on their laptops, cell phones, PDAs, or game consoles. Web-based versions of most applications have become popular, including e-mail clients, word processors, and other office software, network management, file storage, and of course Web browsing.

In some sense the browser has replaced Windows as the principal interface with which users are most familiar. Indeed, Microsoft's chief competition today comes mostly from Google, a company that was only a gleam in its founders' eyes when the antitrust case began. Today, Google has expanded from a Web search tool (where it trashed, among others, Microsoft's offering) to a general-purpose provider of middleware, including a full suite of Web-based applications. In 2008, the company released Android, its first operating system, targeted not at PCs but the much larger cell phone market. Microsoft's aggressive push of IE, in retrospect, seems to have been a reasonable strategy to keep the company competitive.

CONTINUED INTERFERENCE

Microsoft's practices were causing little to no harm, a fact made clearer by events since the case was brought. The rejected arguments have turned into prophecies, underscoring the reality that in a business environment regulated by the Law of Disruption there is little need or use for legal controls like antitrust. But regulators still don't get it. Antitrust complaints and enforcement actions against information companies have expanded dramatically since the Microsoft case.

Indeed, even as the Justice Department was working out the details of a face-saving settlement with Microsoft, European regulators were ramping up their own antitrust action against the company. The European case dragged on even longer than the U.S. version. Though Microsoft privately settled with every company involved in both the U.S. and the European complaints by the end of 2004 (with the exception of the makers of RealMedia, with whom it later settled), European regulators persisted. Even as old rivals left the case new companies including security software giant McAfee and later Google took up the charge and pushed the EU to continue.

The European version of the case focused not on IE but on another piece of middleware, Windows Media Player, a program that plays music and video files. Competitors claimed that Media Player was unfairly bundled into the operating system, making it the de facto standard. The EU demanded Microsoft offer a version of Windows without Media Player, to disclose more of its programming interfaces, and give royalty-free use of some of its copyrights and patents to competing software companies. It also fined the company more than $600 million, a figure that ultimately rose to $1.3 billion. But with every turn of Moore's Law, the EU's complaints change. In the end, a case about Windows Media Player mutated into a plebiscite on the company's decision to create operating systems in the first place. In early 2009, for example, the EU filed new charges regarding the bundling of Windows and IE.

On paper, U.S. and European antitrust law and policy are largely the same. Yet even as U.S. regulators backed down, their European counterparts became more aggressive. By 2006, Microsoft found itself in a kind of best-of-times, worst-of-times world, with the United States agreeing the company was doing its best to comply while the European Commission continued to slap the company with larger fines and threatened new investigations.

After years of appeals and billions in fines, Microsoft and the EU seemed to reach a workable agreement in late 2007. By then, the key issue worrying European regulators was Microsoft's hostility to Linux, a rival operating system developed on the open-source model. Since 2000, Linux has captured 13 percent of the server market. Microsoft has come to see open source generally as the real threat behind the shift to Internet technologies. The company agreed to license even more of its core protocols to competitors, including Linux developers and vendors, and to drop its appeal of a key 2004 ruling still working its way through the European courts. Neelie Kroes, the chief European antitrust regulator, announced that "The major issues concerning compliance have been resolved." In 2009, the EU ended full-time monitoring of Microsoft's compliance.

Competitors and industry analysts, however, were less sanguine. Neither antitrust case had had much financial effect on Microsoft, nor have they altered the landscape of the ever-shifting software industry. Settling with Europe simply dissipated a cloud of uncertainty hanging over the company's future, uncertainty that was bothering stockholders. Microsoft had bigger problems to worry about. In the midst of the European settlement, Microsoft released Windows Vista, a major rewrite of the core operating system. Reflecting the changing business reality for the company, Vista has experienced slow acceptance even from the company's installed base of users.

In the end, the differences between Microsoft's problems in the United States and in Europe teach very little about antitrust but a lot about the politics of regulation. These cases were driven from the beginning by a fluid subset of Microsoft competitors, picked off one at a time by private settlements or by the market itself. Consumer interests were never seriously considered. When Microsoft offered versions of Windows without the components complained of, no one wanted them.

The only things left to explain the different outcomes in the United States and Europe were local interests lying just beneath the surface. In Europe, any distraction, fine, or operating constraint on Microsoft is seen as a victory for Linux, the open-source operating system that started life in Finland. In the midst of pursuing her antitrust case, Commissioner Kroes aggressively encouraged European governments to abandon Microsoft's "closed" technology for open-source alternatives.

Antitrust law continues to be used much as it was in the early twentieth century to fight popular, if economically ill-advised, crusades. Even as market conditions change and the company's PC dominance becomes less relevant, Microsoft is still seen as the evil empire. Open-source software poses the real threat to Microsoft's dominance. The legal maneuvering of its enemies has been a mere sideshow. Billions of dollars later, these actions have done little to nothing to shape the information economy, which continues to answer to only one real law—the Law of Disruption.

Having opened the Pandora's box, however, many of Microsoft's adversaries are now themselves being taunted by the same antitrust demons. Eyeing the enormous fines coughed up by Microsoft, regulators around the world have expanded their use of anticompetition laws to catch other prey. Chipmaker Intel, for one, has been plagued by complaints in several countries. Regulators in Europe and Japan have brought actions against the company's discounting policies. In 2008, South Korean regulators fined the company $25 million for rebates offered to local PC manufacturers and in 2009 the EU fined the company almost $1.5 billion. In the United States, New York attorney general Andrew Cuomo likewise opened a probe against the company's pricing practices in his state. These cases have all been brought or at least encouraged by its chief rival, Advanced Micro Devices.

Apple, which has so far steered clear of antitrust actions brought against its computer business, has recently found itself at odds with European regulators over the iPod music player. Initially, Apple sold music for the device in a proprietary format, and used anticopying technology known as "digital rights management." DRM limits the ability of users to transfer files to other devices or to other consumers, reducing the risk of illegal copying. French lawmakers, however, objected to the nonportability of the purchased songs, and in 2006 passed a law that required sellers of digital music to make their files playable on competing devices. The French minister of culture announced the establishment of "a new principle, interoperability, which makes France a pioneer country in Europe."

The law as written fell far short of that goal, however. During months of legislative negotiations, a series of compromises took most of the bite out of the bill before it was even passed. Under the law, Apple can avoid interoperability if the musicians licensing their songs to iTunes do not want their songs converted to other formats. Competing music-player manufacturers must also demonstrate to a new regulatory agency that their interoperable players do not infringe on Apple's patents, a difficult fact to prove. No matter. A month after the law was passed, France's highest court ruled much of it unconstitutional, an illegal imposition on Apple's legal rights under copyright and patent. So far, the law of trusts is winning over the law of antitrust.

The French law was only the opening salvo in an attack on Apple's "closed" architecture for the iPod. In 2007, EU commissioner Kroes formally charged the company with unfair trade practices over another feature of iTunes. Depending on which European country a consumer lived in, Apple harged different prices for songs. Apple responded by pointing out that these were restrictions imposed on the company by the four major record labels, but agreed to charge the same price to all European customers. It continues to negotiate with its suppliers over a single pan-European storefront.

The DRM matter, which Kroes also complained about, was left dangling. The labels had always allowed other retailers, including Amazon and Wal-Mart, to sell without the DRM but left the restriction on Apple out of concerns that iTunes' success had left them with little bargaining position. A decline in the pace of digital music sales may have convinced the labels that they were doing more harm to themselves than to Apple. While regulators dithered, the market solved the problem. In early 2009, Apple announced that it had convinced the labels to abandon DRM in exchange for Apple's agreement to change the pricing structure for songs from a single price of $0.99 each. Now, classic songs are sold for $0.69, while new releases will go for $1.29.

POSITIVE USES OF ANTICOMPETITION LAWS

In the transition to an information economy, there are productive uses, it should be said, for anticompetition laws. The operation of the Law of Disruption, as we have seen, tends to reveal gross inefficiencies in traditional ways of doing business. Left alone, it eventually eliminates excess fees, uncompetitive middlemen, and wasted transaction costs as business processes relocate online. For those whose livelihoods rely on the inefficiency, however, no price is too high to avoid modernization. When firmly entrenched businesses and cartels in the physical world use their dominance to avoid the ruthless efficiency of digital life, traditional law can and should be used to break the logjam.

Consider residential real estate. Operated by a cartel centered on the National Association of Realtors, the industry is notoriously inefficient. Home sellers traditionally pay brokers a 6 percent commission on the sale price of a home, a fee shared between the buyer's and seller's agents. Though agents claim to offer a range of value to home buyers and sellers, everyone knows the commission is paid largely for access to NAR members' central databases, the multiple listing service. The MLS systems are tightly controlled, accessible only to buyers and sellers represented by NAR members.

By 2005, modest cracks in the NAR monopoly had appeared. Online brokers, still fully licensed, offered a more efficient version of the buying and selling transaction using the Web and other information technology to create "officeless" agencies. Breaking with industry tradition, they offered customers a lower commission to reflect the low cost of the simplified process. Online brokers also allowed customers direct access to the MLS over the Web.

Anxiety over how the Internet would ultimately affect commissions led the NAR in 2003 to pass a bylaw that allowed members to block their listings from online agencies, either individually or as a group. Under pressure from the Justice Department, the NAR quickly agreed to modify the rule so that individual online agencies could not be singled out. The government sued anyway, claiming that even the revised rule discriminated against "brokers who use the Internet to more efficiently and cost-effectively serve home sellers and buyers."

Three years later, just as the case was about to go to trial, the NAR withdrew the rule. The Justice Department and the online agents hailed the capitulation as a major victory against an industry that had been uncompetitive for years. But traditional real estate agencies still don't get it. The NAR, which admitted no wrongdoing in the settlement, announced that the deal was unlikely to affect consumers. "The lawsuit," the agency's chief lawyer said, "never had anything to do with commission rates, or discount brokerages." Indeed, she said, the lawsuit was all a misunderstanding on the part of the government about how the NAR works. "This was a five-year education of the Department of Justice, unfortunately, and the real estate industry had to pay for that education." For all the real estate industry's talk of education, it's clear who didn't learn anything.

FAST-FORWARD: THE LAW MERCHANT OF DIGITAL LIFE

"All politics," Congressman Tip O'Neill once said, "is local." Apparently, so is the regulation of business in digital life. There are many more examples—more all the time—of efforts by legislatures, regulatory agencies, and the courts to modify the design of the business of digital life. Sometimes governments work in broad strokes, but more often they appear as gnats and mosquitoes buzzing around the building site, too small to do real harm individually but still annoying. A state court in Kentucky recently ordered Internet registrars to freeze the domains of more than one hundred gambling Web sites, threatening to have the sites removed altogether. Neither the companies nor their equipment—nor most of the registrars—are located in Kentucky. Most aren't even in the United States. Some of their users apparently are, however, and gambling, except for the sanctioned kind like horse racing, is illegal in Kentucky. On appeal, the judge's wildly overreaching orders were dissolved.

In digital life, inefficient business laws are treated the same way the Internet treats failed nodes in the network. Silently, quickly, commercial activities are rerouted to avoid them. The U.S. publishers of the Harry Potter books were regularly thwarted in their efforts to delay release of new volumes in the series in the United States, as they were contractually obliged to do. American readers simply ordered the books from Amazon in the UK. For transactions that don't require shipping in the first place (e.g., for "books" using Amazon's Kindle electronic reading device), artificial restrictions on time and place are impossible to enforce.

Still, the Law of Disruption isn't perfect. Its determination to avoid provincial regulations often leads to workarounds, such as physically relocating businesses (or at least their computers) to off-shore locations that otherwise add no value. Consumers and businesses alike need to understand the still potent reach of local laws, including those that define commerce and private conduct. Even if their enforcement makes little sense in digital life, there's too much at stake for local regulators to fold up their tents and go home. As citizens migrate more of their activities and assets to digital life, for one thing, there is less for regulators to do (and therefore to tax) in the physical world.

The alternative to global enforcement of local laws is not anarchy. As feudalism in the Middle Ages began to give way to an economy based on commerce, merchants faced a similar problem. There simply were no laws that dealt with new mercantile activities, and the medieval courts were hesitant to apply the laws they did have—laws created to address real estate, the defining element of feudal life—to new behaviors they considered beneath them.

In the absence of official statutes and courts, merchants devised their own codes of conduct, their own procedures, and even their own courts.

Merchants took their disputes to these new tribunals for quick resolution by more senior merchants—the experts in the field. The "law merchant," as it is known, grew up with the local markets, characterized by pragmatic rules of evidence, expedited trials, and immediate enforcement of remedies. Key commercial documents, including the bill of lading and the check, emerged from this marketplace of legal innovation. As commercial activity became central to modern life, the law merchant was eventually absorbed into English and later American common law, and embedded in the continental system of civil law enacted by Napoleon.

In the 1930s, in a quest for more predictable rules and less judicial discretion, independent legal organizations including the American Law Institute developed "uniform" laws that would regularize business practices throughout the United States. One of their most important creations was the Uniform Commercial Code, which devised a set of default rules for commercial transactions. The drafters of the UCC relied heavily on the law merchant, recognizing that its development by the people who needed it made it both elegant and efficient. Today, the UCC has been enacted through the United States and much of the rest of the world. Its adoption signaled the final victory of modern commercial law over the outdated rules and procedures of feudal society.

Businesses in the digital age need the modern equivalent of the law merchant—a law of digital business developed by those who are most immediately affected by it. Already there are early signs of progress in relaxed rules about digital "signatures" on documents, and in the expedited legal procedures of online arbitration and mediation. The growing standardization of Web site privacy policies and business practices supported by nonprofits such as the Better Business Bureau Online, TRUSTe, and arbitration service net-ARB are another positive sign. Antilaw including Section 230 is better still, creating a safe environment for businesses and consumers to work out the rules that best fit their needs in the new world. The Law of Disruption favors such organic development.

Microsoft may have borne the brunt of the first wave of antitrust enforcement actions, but governments around the world have since gone after other technology giants, including Intel, Yahoo, and eBay. Google increasingly finds itself in the precarious crosshairs of regulators who assume the ompany's success somehow proves it's breaking the law. Courts, regulators, nd legislators are all eager to make their mark in the law of digital life. As ae information economy continues to experience accelerated growth indexed to the Law of Disruption, consumers and businesses need to view local regulation, enforcement, and interpretation with increased concern and cepticism. We need to work with national governments, and with each ther, to make uniform business laws and regulatory practices a reality. We eed to speak with one voice in condemning the provincial behavior that is raped in the language of legal rhetoric, even when—especially when—the ictim happens to be a competitor.

LAW SIX: CRIME

Public Wrongs, Private Remedies

Crime is now a regular feature of the information economy, a sign of its growing maturity. But how can traditional law enforcement agencies find and bring to justice the miscreants who deal in spam, spyware, phishing, and other personal and property crimes if they don't understand the physics of information? They can't. This chapter explains why. It also explores the alternative: a growing economy of private enforcement through insurance, anticrime software and virtual posses. In digital life, crime is just another kind of information use. In this case, technology is being developed to stop rather than encourage it.

PROSECUTORIAL INDISCRETION

What did Lori Drew do?

The late-forties suburban St. Louis mother was apparently unhappy about the "mean" behavior of Megan Meier, a thirteen-year-old former friend of Drew's daughter Sarah. The Drews, along with Ashley Grills, the eighteen-year-old employee of Lori Drew's home business, hatched a plan. They created a fake MySpace profile for a bare-chested sixteen-year-old boy named "Josh," who would befriend Megan and encourage her to gossip about other girls. Then they would take printouts to Megan's mother to show her what the girl was up to.

Not only was the idea stupid, it wasn't even original—Sarah and Megan, back when they were friends, had done the same thing, creating a profile for a

167

boy who didn't exist as a way to talk to other boys. This time, however, the plan went awry. Megan became deeply infatuated with Josh. She pressed for his phone number. She wanted to meet him in person. The women behind his account looked for a way out. According to Grills, "We decided to be mean to her so she would leave him alone . . . and we could get rid of the page."

After deliberating on the easiest way to end an ill-conceived hoax that was going very wrong, Grills sent an instant message to Meier: "The world would be a better place without you." The consequences were tragic. Meier, who was being treated for depression, took the suggestion all too literally. After an argument with her parents, who had closely monitored the relationship with Josh from the beginning, Meier went to her room and hanged herself.

Media accounts of the teen's suicide and the subsequent revelation of who was behind "Josh" created a froth of outrage and hand-wringing. Commentators invented and then proclaimed an epidemic of "cyberbullying." When it became clear that the mother of one of Meier's former friends was involved, Drew herself was subjected to death threats and vandalism. A fake MySpace page for her husband was created. On cable news and the blogosphere, Drew was instantly convicted and sentenced to hell. ("Call me vindictive," a typical blog entry read, "but i hope that someone kills the woman who is responsible.")

In the midst of the media storm, state attorneys in Missouri announced there would be no prosecution of Drew for the simple reason that no criminal law had been broken. Federal prosecutors weren't so sure. They found a 1986 law, the Computer Fraud and Abuse Act, that set stiff penalties for breaking into and damaging computers. Drew was charged under the novel theory that since the MySpace terms of service agreement prohibits posting false information in one's profile, the creation of Josh violated Drew's contract. Hence, she "accessed" MySpace computers without "authorization." The creation of Josh, in other words, was a kind of hacking. The victim was not Meier (who with her parents' permission had also violated the TOS, which requires users to be at least fourteen years old). The victim was MySpace.

Although the jury ultimately refused to convict Drew on the felony charge, they did convict her of the lesser crime of unauthorized access. Valentina Kunasz, the jury's foreperson, made no apologies for the conviction. "It was so very childish; so very pathetic," she told reporters after the trial. "She could have done quite a few things to stop it, and she chose not to. And I think she got kind of a rise out of doing this to another person and that bothers me, it really irks me." Drew faces up to three years in prison and $300,000 in fines.

Legal scholars were generally in agreement that the prosecution was deeply flawed and will very likely be set aside or reversed on appeal. First, there were gaping holes in the government's case. For one thing, it was Grills, and not Drew, who set up the Josh account and therefore agreed to the TOS (Grills, testifying for the prosecution in exchange for immunity, admitted she never read the TOS). Drew herself was only occasionally involved in the hoax. By a weird twist of irony, one of the few times she communicated with Meier it turned out she was talking to Meier's mother, who told Josh he ought to be looking for friends his own age. The fateful message was sent by Grills without Drew's knowledge, and wasn't even sent through MySpace.

As a matter of public policy, the prosecution is even more disturbing. Even assuming Drew was bound by the TOS, these contracts are notoriously long and intentionally unreadable. Most of us, even lawyers, don't read them. Yet following the logic of the Drew prosecution, anyone who misrepresents some of their personal details on an online dating service has committed a federal crime. Anyone who gives a nonworking telephone number when signing up for a Web site has committed a federal crime. Indeed, after the verdict, one social network researcher was pained to admit, "We've been telling our kids to lie about ID information for a long time now."

The computer fraud law began as a protection against hackers targeting government computers. The law has never before been used in connection with the violation, willful or otherwise, of private terms of service. There's no reason to believe Congress intended to criminalize cyberbullying in 1986 or any other time. Supporters of the conviction argue that the real problem here was a hole in the law—the lack of a statute outlawing whatever it was Lori Drew had done.

But the decision of lawmakers not to criminalize a behavior is no reason to correct the problem in a way that undermines the very idea of law. People are often cruel to each other. Other children, adults, and even parents can and do humiliate children in the real world. No laws are broken. It's difficult to see how this case differs in any respect other than the use of a computer and the tragic outcome. If the conviction stands, it effectively gives every federal prosecutor a blank check to charge anyone they want with criminal behavior, subject only to their discretion of whether and when to use that power.

Some commentators, pleased with the result if not the process, argued that there was no cause for alarm. Prosecutors, they said, will only use this power in extreme cases. The Drew prosecution suggests precisely the opposite. For elected prosecutors, the real temptation is to exercise discretion not when the law would otherwise let a heinous crime slip through the cracks but when passions are high and the facts (at least the version presented by the media) are the most lurid—when, in other words, an angry mob demands it.

Perhaps there's another reason lawmakers hadn't criminalized bullying in the world of digital life. They don't need to. In 2008, a yearlong study commissioned by forty-nine state attorney generals to justify new protections found instead that the dangers to children living digital lives had been wildly overstated. When sexual predators or other abusers were successful, it was typically because the victims were already at risk due to poor home environments, substance abuse, and other real-world problems. Still, in the wake of the Drew case, Missouri hastily passed its own anti–cyber harassment law. It is now a crime in Missouri to send threatening messages or communications that cause emotional distress to the recipient. In the first three months of its enactment, local prosecutors charged seven people, including a nineteen-year-old boy who sent seventeen messages to his stepfather and a man protesting a proposed resort development.

THE RISE OF COMPUTER CRIME

The Lori Drew case suggests a growing problem in digital life. As more personal activity takes place online, crime is spreading. In some cases, including statutory rape and other forms of child abuse, the Internet lowers the transaction costs for perpetrators to find their victims. Other crimes are native to digital life, including stealing assets or damaging the victim's computer, without the need for any act by the criminal in the real world. Identity theft, spam-related fraud, and computer viruses all fall into this category.

A third category of criminal behavior, political crime or "cyberterrorism," has recently appeared. It perhaps presents the greatest risk. Here, the perpetrator intends to damage or destroy the infrastructure itself. The victim, in other words, is the network, or some part of it, perhaps belonging to an individual country. Though cyberterrorism has so far caused little damage, the most alarming feature of political crime online is the ease with which criminal enterprises, terrorist cells, gangs, and other new forms of organized crime can quickly and efficiently take shape. As with legal businesses, the low transaction costs of digital life allow cyberterrorists to communicate, plan, execute, and then disappear.

One thing should be made clear from the outset. Most crimes are easily solved, because most criminals are stupid. In part this is what defines those who commit crime in the first place—an inability to make rational economic choices. Criminals fail to factor in the cost of hiding their behavior or the penalties if caught. To them, stealing seems like a cheap or even free way to get what they want. This generalization is as true of Internet crime as it is of the more traditional kind. Cell phone thieves take their own pictures, unaware that the phone automatically uploads them to the carrier's server, where the real owner can access them and forward them along to the police. Carjackers send each other incriminating text messages, leading to capture. Though this chapter will focus for obvious reasons on the more sophisticated crimes and criminals, I don't want to suggest that there is a crisis. As we'll see, there's no need for panic.

Still, Internet-related crimes are clearly on the rise. Ten years ago, when I appeared on a technology talk show, one of the topics was Internet crime. At that point there was nothing to talk about. Given how few users there were and the minimal activities they engaged in, the likely benefit of engaging in cybercrime was very low. Early inhabitants of digital life were unlikely to have much money. No money, for the most part, meant no property crime. The early Internet attracted only the least-successful criminals. Most fraud at the time was the equivalent of ads in the back of old comic books selling x-ray glasses that didn't work or "sea monkeys" that were actually brine shrimp.

Increasingly, our robust digital life has made crime far more attractive. For one thing, there is more money to be had. The architecture of the Internet, moreover, makes it easier to avoid detection and capture, creating new headaches for law enforcement. Low transaction costs and the rapid evolution of software have become breeding grounds not just for new ideas and new ways of interacting. They have also bred new ways of destroying, stealing, and otherwise undermining the value of other people's information. Nigerian scammers, Russian mobsters, American Ponzi schemers—these and many more varieties of miscreant have taken up permanent residence in the ether.

Just today, I received a message at my university e-mail address from "Paul," whom I do not know, letting me know he had a new address at Yahoo.com. The text of his message was simple, if clumsy: "ATTN: Is my late father funds (US$28 Million) and 250k of Gold. I want to invest." Presumably, if I were to write back to Paul and let him know I was interested in helping him invest, the scam would begin in earnest. Following some now familiar patterns, Paul would seek to earn my trust by sharing bogus personal information about his father and appealing to my sense of decency or greed or both. Then he might ask for my bank account number in order to deposit his investment money, then use the information to make withdrawals from my account. Or he might send me a phony payment, asking that I forward part of it to a third party, leaving me holding the bag when his check bounces. Perhaps he'll ask me to wire money to him that he needs to get access to his late father's estate, with the promise of repayment and a generous gratuity for me.

As P. T. Barnum famously said, "There's a sucker born every minute." One would have to imagine a very stupid sucker who would fall for such a lame come-on. Still, given that the cost for Paul to send his message was immeasurably small no matter how many copies he sent, it takes only one idiot to make the crime profitable. Or even one nonidiot. You may be surprised to learn that some of the people who go for these scams don't seem to fit the profile. Some are educated, intelligent people, whose weakness may be a dormant gene that combines greed and gullibility that is somehow turned on by online con men, perhaps for the first and only time in their lives.

Economically speaking, the gap between actual and potential change created by the Law of Disruption represents inefficiency. And inefficiency in an economic system creates the opportunity for crime. If the likely benefit of breaking the law exceeds the penalty multiplied by the risk of getting caught, crime will occur. As the Law of Disruption accelerates, the attractiveness of crime—the likely benefit—increases. The rapidly changing information economy, consequently, will always be a magnet for criminals.

This equation also helps explain one of the reasons Internet crime is on the rise. Criminals have gotten smarter about using the most sophisticated technologies available to hide their identities, activities, and assets. They use technology to aim their behavior where the money is without having to be there themselves. Living off-shore, perhaps in jurisdictions with minimal law enforcement, criminals can both increase their benefits and lower the risk of getting caught. Whose police are best suited to investigate a crime—those of the victim or of the criminal? How do police in the United States even get hold of suspects in Nigeria? In most cases, coordinated efforts are needed, and coordination among law enforcement agencies, even within a single country, hardly ever happens. As a result, over the past decade the risk of getting caught has actually decreased.

For crimes that take place entirely online, enforcement has so far proven extremely expensive, if not impossible. The victims may be local, but the perpetrators are nowhere. Given the global nature of digital life, it isn't even clear whose law applies. There's an arms race going on between criminals and the police. The police are barely aware of where the battle line has been drawn or even who should be standing on it.

I live in a small unincorporated town in the hills east of San Francisco with a population of roughly 5,000. Crime is minimal, though not nonexistent. Every month, the local newspaper prints the highlights and lowlights from the police blotter. Mostly, the items deal with teen vandalism, property stolen from unlocked vehicles, and the occasional dispute over tree trimming and noise. Every now and then, the police get a call from a resident about a suspicious e-mail, an unauthorized Web purchase, or a virus that has damaged their computer.

Clearly, solving Internet crimes is not a job for the local police. What exactly can they do? Even in large cities, law enforcement agencies confess to being stymied. The London Metropolitan Police, which has established special "e-crime units," warned Parliament that they were unable to cope with the rise of Internet crime. Their investigators, they said, were overwhelmed by "the volume of offenses and the national and international nature of e-crime, sometimes involving hundreds or thousands of victims."

On the other hand, you can sympathize with my neighbors. Who else are they going to call?

CRIMES AGAINST INFORMATION

What happens when information itself is the focus of a crime? Information, as we have seen, does not behave like other kinds of property. Since information never gets used up, how can it be stolen? If sharing information only increases its value, how can data thefts be harmful or, indeed, thefts at all?

Since information can be used simultaneously by everyone without incurring transaction costs, why bother policing unauthorized access? Information crime, in some sense, sounds like an oxymoron.

Although information is, to recall the economic terms, a non-rivalrous good, it is still possible to reduce its value. This is where the focus on information crime begins. Misrepresenting information, for example, can make its true source seem less trustworthy. If I spread a lie that you are heavily in debt and unable to pay your bills, then creditors will incorrectly deem you a poor credit risk, raising the transaction cost for both you and them in negotiating the terms of future transactions. Worse, bad information seems to move more quickly and with less interference. As Mark Twain once said, "A lie can travel halfway around the world while the truth is still putting on its shoes."

Information crime takes many forms, with new ones appearing as digital life becomes more heavily populated. Identity thieves misrepresent who they are and in the process damage the data the world has about you, such as financial assets and credit scores. Spammers clog e-mail in-boxes with non-useful or fraudulent information, raising transaction costs for those trying to interact constructively. Large-scale data breaches, which may or may not lead to other information crimes, raise the general level of anxiety about the safety of digital life, another kind of transaction cost.

In 2004, information crime collided with anxiety over privacy. Journalists reported with increasing outrage a series of unrelated failures in data security by retailers, data brokers, government agencies, universities, and financial institutions. In the course of a few months, the most valuable personally identifiable information of millions of consumers, including credit card accounts and Social Security numbers, had potentially been exposed. An information crime spree, according to the media, was under way. Panic ensued.

Sometimes the thieves were sophisticated, intercepting the electronic signals of credit card swipes between stores and card-processing networks. In other cases, criminals simply posed as businesses and bought the information from data brokers, including ChoicePoint and LexisNexis. Often, those in charge of private information were negligent—leaving unencrypted data on laptop computers in unlocked cars, for example. In one case, Citigroup disclosed that backup tapes containing financial data of nearly four million customers of its loan business had been lost by UPS. The tapes literally fell off the back of a truck.

Some of the gaps in security revealed by these breaches are shocking. Few, however, actually led to information crimes. (According to payment industry analysts Javelin Strategy and Research, less than 1 percent of breach victims suffer any damage.) In some instances, backup tapes were simply misplaced. In cases where laptop computers are stolen, the thieves are usually after the hardware, not the data files. In many cases, consumers learned of the exposure not because any damage resulted but through mandatory disclosure laws on the books in California, New York, and other states.

Despite fines against some of the leading data brokers, a few criminal convictions, and dozens of proposed new data-protection and privacy laws, the security problems haven't gone away. In 2008, data breaches increased by 47 percent from the prior year, with another 35 million records potentially exposed. In one of the most serious breaches, credit card–transaction processing company CardSystems Solutions revealed in 2005 that its computer security had failed to repel hackers who gained access to as many as 40 million credit card accounts. Although the actual damage to consumers is unclear, the damage to CardSystems was fatal. Public outrage over the incident led Visa and American Express to expel the company from its networks, effectively shutting CardSystems down.

WHO STEALS MY PURSE

The principal concern with data breaches is that thieves will use PII to gain access to the assets of consumers, an information crime known as identity theft. "Who steals my purse steals trash," says Shakespeare's Iago, "but he that filches from me my good name / Robs me of that which not enriches him / And makes me poor indeed." These days, stealing someone's good name not only harms the victim but can enrich the criminal, so long as he also gets their good Social Security number, address, and possibly their bank account number along with it. The U.S. Federal Trade Commission reported in 2008 that for eight years in a row, identity theft was the most frequent category of fraud complaint received by the agency. Of nearly a million total complaints to the agency in 2007, 32 percent were related to identity theft.

The goal of an identity thief is to trade off the value of the victim's identity to increase his own assets. He may do so directly, by stealing them from the victim's accounts, or indirectly from banks and other creditors who may extend loans, credit cards, and cash to the thief, believing him to be the victim. In the commission of the crime, however, the victim's financial profile is damaged as well, giving him months or even years of unnecessary headaches to restore its accuracy. What makes identity theft a particularly dangerous crime is that it perpetrates this double harm.

Indeed, the myth about identity theft is that the harm to its victims comes from the direct loss of financial assets, when ID thieves either withdraw money from the victim's accounts or make unauthorized purchases with his credit cards. In fact, there is little to worry about on that front. Thanks to banking and consumer credit laws applicable in most of the world, banks are responsible when forged checks are honored or withdrawals are otherwise made without the true owner's permission. Credit card companies, likewise, are required by law to limit the liability of cardholders for unauthorized purchases to a minimal amount (as little as twenty-five dollars), and in most cases even these minimums are not enforced. Most credit card companies do not hold the victim liable for any of the losses.

The real harm from identity theft comes in the collateral damage. Once the identity thief's access has been cut off, the victim must restore the accuracy of his credit reports, credit scores, and financial history. This is where damage has been done, and often where the crime begins. Reporting services, department stores, lenders, and credit card issuers may be of little help in removing information that represents the activities not of the victim but of the thief acting under her name. Either through benign neglect, incompetence, or intentional obstruction, financial institutions may put up roadblocks that interfere with the victim's efforts to rehabilitate her information. Most consumers lack the sophistication to recognize the importance of correcting their profiles, let alone the skills to do it.

Consumers and lawmakers alike have called for new legislation to solve the identity theft crisis. Some proposals require tighter controls and better security by those who control PII. Others would shift the responsibility and cost of repairing a damaged reputation from the consumer to the entity that let the data escape in the first place. Still others require better cooperation from credit bureaus and other information brokers as consumers try to protect or restore their credit histories. Former National Security Council member Richard A. Clarke, for one, called on Congress in 2006 to come up with an identity-protection bill of rights.

But is law the answer? Identity theft and other forms of Internet fraud are already illegal, and there are a wide range of criminal laws that apply. New laws may not be necessary. Assuming they are, there are a number of factors that explain why, despite the hue and cry, no new legislation has actually passed. For one thing, regulators are some of the best customers of unregulated private data brokers. Federal law limits the collection and use of PII by government agencies, laws that don't apply to private companies. Agencies such as the Internal Revenue Service, Social Security Administration, and Department of Homeland Security (DHS) have used that fact to buy the data they cannot collect themselves from private brokers. Regulating the behavior of these companies might inadvertently close the loopholes. In the interests of national security and the U.S. Treasury, Congress prefers to do nothing here.

New laws may also have stalled because, despite the media hype, identity theft is not the epidemic it appears to be. Though much of the data about identity theft are incomplete, consider a few surprising facts that have emerged:

- According to the Federal Trade Commission, both the incidence and the costs of ID theft have declined from 2003 to 2007 by two-thirds. Large-scale data thefts led to ID-related fraud in less than .001 percent of cases (1 in 10,000). The declines can be attributed to more careful behavior by consumers and improved technology by financial services companies to anticipate unauthorized activities.
- Criminals use the Internet to gather information they need to steal identities less than 20 percent of the time. Thirty percent resulted from a lost or stolen credit card, and another 15 percent involved a friend or relative. The majority of ID theft results from stolen or discarded mail. A 2009 survey of identity theft victims by Javelin Research revealed that lost or stolen wallets accounted for almost half of all identity theft.
- A third of all ID thieves are insiders, including sales clerks at retail locations such as restaurants and gas stations, who are given the needed information by the consumer in the course of a normal transaction. In about a fifth of the insider cases, the ID thief is the employee of a

financial services company. In one notorious case, an American security consultant admitted to moonlighting as a famous hacker who stole hundreds of thousands of online bank passwords.

- More than half the victims of identity theft incur no out-of-pocket costs. On average, victims spend about $535, mostly on efforts to correct their credit history.

There is no crisis, in other words, or in any case no consumer crisis. ID theft is on the decline, and most of it has nothing to do with the Internet. Despite a string of embarrassing breaches of data security, thieves appeared uninterested in personal information. Although the problem of restoring the accuracy of one's information profile can be time-consuming and frustrating, few consumers lose real money to the thieves. The real losses are suffered by businesses that extend credit or otherwise engage with the identity thief, to the tune of nearly $50 billion in 2006. Still, that is a relatively modest cost. The financial services and retail industries, which continue to invest in new technologies to contain and minimize fraudulent transactions, are not calling for new legislation.

Even with a clearer understanding of the problem of identity theft, it is unlikely that any new law would actually solve it. Congress has a poor track record of legislating in a crisis, particularly when that crisis involves emerging technologies and industries that prefer to solve their own problems. What's the alternative? Here are four commonsense solutions that, taken together, would solve the identity theft problem, and do so in a cost-effective way. None requires new criminal laws or the creation of new regulatory systems.

1. *Self-regulation.* Companies that collect, store, or process consumer information must improve their data-handling practices. The International Standards Organization, for one, has published a "Code of Practice for Information Security Management." The code is filled with commonsense suggestions for reducing the risks of ID theft at a modest cost, including appropriate security checks before hiring new employees or contractors and the use of encryption for sensitive information. A pledge from a coalition of trade associations to beef up the standard and adopt it would go far toward quieting calls for legislation. But the promise must be kept.

2. *Market solutions.* Half a dozen major insurers already offer low-cost insurance and other forms of third-party protection against identity theft, some as cheap as twenty-five dollars a year. Credit agencies and data aggregators are also well suited to offer insurance. Start-ups including TrustedID and Lifelock offer more elaborate policies for around ten dollars per month, which include intensive monitoring of how and when a customer's information is being used. And widespread adoption of new insurance products would generate much more reliable data about the true scale of the problem.

3. *Targeted legislation.* Rather than setting and enforcing broad standards, Congress should consider more specific legislation that would slow the spread of identity theft and related crimes. Many consumer groups, for example, argue that the pervasive use of Social Security numbers as both a customer identifier and a means of authentication has made identity theft an easy crime to commit. Using the same number both to identify a customer and to validate her identity is sloppy security practice; it's also lazy software design. Replacing Social Security numbers with unique customer identifiers would be expensive but not as expensive as more sweeping proposals under consideration.

4. *Public education.* Although large-scale breaches grab the headlines, many victims of identity theft are themselves the source of the offending disclosure. Consumers who respond to online and off-line scams, or fail to shred identifying documents before disposing of them, account for a significant percentage of incidents. The occurrence and impact of fraud on consumers could be greatly reduced by educating consumers on what identity theft is, how they can prevent it, and their rights if it does happen. Unfortunately, the task of public education has been largely co-opted by antifraud service providers such as Freecreditreport.com (which, by the way, does not offer free credit reports). Some of these services use scare tactics to sign consumers up for services they don't need.

ATTACK OF THE ZOMBIES

If ID theft doesn't represent the Internet crime wave we've been led to believe, how about other forms of information crime? Perhaps the most serious are a collection of software viruses and other malicious code known generally as malware. Malware includes software that tracks a user's Internet activities and forwards the information to the software's providers. How that data is used varies from sending targeted banner ads to taking control of the user's computer to use as a "zombie" to send out spam or even more malware. Even at its most innocuous, malware can slow a user's computer or connection or aid illegal activities by helping hide the location of people committing other kinds of crime.

Malware is often installed without notice or with the notice buried deep in the TOS of another piece of software. Some malware is intentionally difficult to uninstall. One Russian-based enterprise, Bakasoftware, generates $5 million in annual revenues by installing itself on computers and then generating alarming pop-up messages warning the user that their system has been infected. The messages recommend paying the company $49.95 for software to clean up the infection. Other than the diagnostic software itself, however, there never was an infection. It's just automated blackmail. Microsoft reported nearly eight million similar infections from various forms of "scareware" during the last six months of 2008, an increase of nearly 50 percent over the prior six-month period.

Although I describe malware as a virus, that's not always an accurate description. Generally, we think of viruses as software that is installed on our computer without our knowledge, perhaps hidden in e-mail messages or downloaded when we visit a Web site. We also think of viruses as software that harms or damages the user's computer and files, either intentionally or as a side effect of its true purpose.

Some of the most insidious malware, however, is installed not furtively but rather with the user's full consent. Indeed, some of the most popular free software is or contains a kind of malware known as spyware. Many Internet companies that do not charge for their services rely on selling the data collected by spyware to finance their operations. Kazaa and Grokster, the peer-to-peer file-sharing services that were popular tools for trading music and other copyrighted material after the courts shut down Napster, included spyware that generated funding for the continued development of the network. Allowing the software to collect and use PII constituted a barter agreement between the developers and their users, who traded information instead of cash. The two services were ultimately shut down, but not for what the companies did to their users. No one, that is, objected to the spying. Indeed, the services were vigorously defended in file-sharing lawsuits brought by the entertainment industry by many of the same public interest groups that otherwise decry the kind of privacy invasions the spyware committed, including the Electronic Frontier Foundation and the ACLU.

The love-hate relationship both consumers and advertisers have with spyware makes it a particularly hard problem to solve with legislation. Perhaps that's why even though several antimalware laws have been proposed, none has been enacted. Take the 2004 "Securely Protect Yourself Against Cyber Trespass Act" (SPY ACT), a good example of bad legislation. The main problem the SPY ACT struggles with is defining exactly what it is trying to ban. The law lists several illegally "deceptive acts," including taking control of a user's computer, diverting the browser, delivering ads that users cannot turn off without closing the browser, and "modifying settings." Another section bans the collection of PII by logging keystrokes, or the collection of any information, without the user's consent.

The activities outlawed by the SPY ACT are intentionally vague. Its authors knew full well that malware and its uses are in only the early stages of gestation. The problem with vague definitions, however, is that they may cover both too much and too little. The Interactive Advertising Bureau, a trade group of nearly four hundred media and technology companies that generate 86 percent of online advertising, complained that the law would ban all data collection, including Java-based applications and other tools for collecting transaction data. Under the SPY ACT, users would have to "accept" (via a clumsy dialogue included in the law) all downloaded applications. That would mean regular interruption in the flow of most interactions, including the entry of shipping information on e-commerce sites or initiating a real-time chat session with a technical support representative. Real malware may evolve—indeed, in response to the law—to escape coverage, leaving productive practices unintentionally ensnared.

SPAM, SPAM, SPAM

Even criminal laws that are passed often have little or no effect on deterring information crimes. Consider the CAN-SPAM Act, a law passed in 2003 in response to alarming increases in unsolicited e-mail messages. Again, the law's chief weakness is defining what is being outlawed. CAN-SPAM first defines "commercial electronic mail messages" as e-mails whose primary purpose is "the commercial advertisement or promotion of a commercial product or service." The law, despite its name, does not ban commercial mail; indeed, senders are not even required to obtain a user's permission before sending them. Instead, the law puts the burden on consumers to tell the sender not to mail her any more commercial messages.

Unlike the "Do Not Call" list implemented to reduce telemarketing, consumers must opt out with each individual sender. Aside from the hassle of sending such opt-out messages, consumers are wise not to do so, as this simply verifies to the most unscrupulous spammers which e-mail addresses are actually working. And like the proposed SPY ACT, the spam law preempted more restrictive legislation under consideration or already passed by individual states. Given these sender-friendly provisions, critics refer to the law as the "You Can Spam" Act.

Most observers agree that CAN-SPAM has been a colossal failure. It has not reduced in the slightest the epidemic of unwanted commercial e-mails flooding the Internet. Nor has it reduced the danger posed by messages that represent phony or otherwise illegal commercial offers. On the FTC's own list of "How to 'Can' Unwanted Email," enforcement of the law barely registers, well below such unhelpful tips as "try not to display your email address in public." Nor is this a case where U.S. lawmakers fail because the problem they are trying to regulate is outside their jurisdiction. Nearly 30 percent of all spam and other malicious computer activity still originate in the United States.

The few convictions that prosecutors have won under CAN-SPAM all involve fraudulent business activities conducted through e-mail, that is, where the message's content is not only annoying but actually illegal. The Federal Trade Commission, however, fails to collect judgments levied against offenders. In the first criminal case, brought almost two years after the law was passed, the FTC sued a company that sold $230,000 worth of illegal diet patches through unsolicited e-mails. Despite winning a default judgment for the entire amount, the FTC stipulated a month later to a settlement in which the defendants admitted no guilt and paid a fine of $20,000. The defendants agreed to abide by CAN-SPAM in the future, which they were required to do all along.

I have some sympathy for the drafters of CAN-SPAM, but not for their creation. Consumers complain in the abstract about unwanted and un-solicited e-mails, but getting agreement on just what they want banned al-ways proves elusive. A message from a long-lost friend may be unsolicited, but it is not unwanted or commercial. A message announcing you've won a contest with a cash prize is commercial and unsolicited, but probably not unwanted. When I propose these hypothetical e-mail messages in class, stu-dents can never agree which ones are and are not spam.

The real problem is far more subtle. Advertisements for products and ser-vices one is interested in may not be unwelcome. As we saw earlier, however, the problem for most advertisers is that without collecting a great deal of PII it's difficult to predict what products we really want. Aside from offers that are inherently illegal (pharmaceuticals without a doctor's prescription, child pornography, pyramid and other fraudulent financial schemes), the kinds of e-mails that consumers want banned are largely indeterminate and subjective, based more on the reader's reaction to the message than the sender's intent.

Simply banning bulk mailings won't solve the problem, either. For one thing, such a ban is unconstitutional under the First Amendment, as at least one court has held. Antispam laws limited to *commercial* bulk mailings might pass muster, but despite what some of my students believe, commer-cial solicitations are not inherently worthless. "Bulk messages" appear on our television screens all the time, and no one seriously argues they should be made illegal. Perhaps consumers are just conditioned to accept them, in part because they have always been there, at least in the United States. TV com-mercials are generally well produced, entertaining in their own right, and well aimed at their target audiences, especially on special-interest cable chan-nels. More to the point, we understand implicitly that they underwrite or in some cases completely cover the cost of the programming they interrupt.

But in that sense, spam really is different. Spammers aren't underwriting any content we want to see, or at least not as directly as TV ads do. Worse, the architecture of the Internet makes spam essentially free to distribute to an infinite number of recipients, including those who have no interest what-soever in the message. Unlike direct mail, Internet "postage" is free. So a tiny response rate still generates a profit. Even when market research data are available that would help pinpoint interested customers, low-end spammers have no incentive to use it. They simply blanket the Internet, secure in the knowledge that their real audience will be among the recipients. Spammers need only a computer and a list of e-mail addresses, which can be purchased cheaply. In many cases, spam support software just guesses at thousands of variations of addresses, hoping that at least a few turn out to be valid.

The economics of spam are dangerous in another respect. According to Cisco's 2008 annual security report, 90 percent of all e-mails, or 200 billion messages a day, are spam. A more recent study from Microsoft puts the number closer to 100 percent. With no incentive to limit or target their mailings, spammers have taken over the Internet. Even as e-mail filters do a better job keeping spam out of your in-box, it's still out there, wasting bandwidth and threatening productive uses of the technology.

The sophistication of spammers has also grown. Increasingly, bulk e-mailers can hijack other computers to send out their messages, making detection more difficult. The external cost of spam is certainly in the billions of dollars, and at times has threatened to crash the Internet. Ironically, spammers themselves will be among the victims if the infrastructure becomes too choked with junk mail to be usable. But no individual spammer has an incentive to limit her output. Left uncontrolled, spam has the potential to destroy the infrastructure of digital life.

The solution may not be better laws but rather better defensive technology. Unfortunately, the diffusion of the harm makes it hard to coordinate the affected parties and encourage them to make the needed changes. Increasingly, the cost of spam is shifting from users (time plus the cost of spam-filtering software) to ISPs who manage the infrastructure (extra capacity, traffic management, and filtering software of their own). They, in turn, must rely on solutions from those, including Cisco, who sell routers and other network equipment as well as software companies, including Microsoft, Yahoo, and Google, who develop the operating systems and e-mail applications.

Address verification would go far toward ending spam. Microsoft, for one, has developed a protocol it calls "Sender ID," which, if made part of the basic architecture of the Internet, would stop spammers from hiding their true identity and location, an important factor in avoiding detection

and prosecution. To succeed, however, address verification requires the cooperation of several stakeholders, most of whom don't trust each other.
Other e-mail providers are concerned that a Microsoft-supplied solution
will give advantages to the company. Yahoo and others have offered competing standards. So far the Internet protocol committees involved have
endorsed none of the proposals. "The basic issue of security and trust," according to IRG's Peter Christy, "is an un-won war." For now, at least, the
bad guys are winning.

AN ARMS RACE TO THE BOTTOM

The Law of Disruption has initiated an arms race between those who use
technology productively and those who use it destructively. Even if we can
solve the problems of malware, spam, viruses, and the rest, a new generation
of malicious code is waiting in the wings. As we move more of our activities
to digital life, both the quantity and the quality of information crime are
sure to swell. Worldwide, information crime costs perhaps $100 billion a
year. Microsoft alone reported a 43 percent increase in malicious software
removed from Windows computers in the second half of 2008.

In the calculus of enforcement, the cost of information crime is falling.
According to Internet security company RSA, prices for e-mail lists, hosting
scams, and software for infecting computers have dropped as competition
heats up and new technology improves the productivity of the arms merchants. Today, 15,000 verified e-mail addresses may cost as little as $1,500;
scam-hosting services go for $80 a week. Trojan-horse software installers sell
for $600.

How might we do better in the fight against information crime? Legislation, we have seen, is unlikely to help. In the wake of the widely publicized
data breaches of 2004 and 2005, a deluge of proposed new laws and regulations were drafted. The Personal Data Privacy and Security Act, for example,
included extensive reforms for private data handling. The new law would increase penalties for identity theft, require disclosure of data breaches to all
those affected, and limit the government's ability to buy PII from private data
brokers. Its sponsor, Senator Patrick Leahy, described these reforms as "long
overdue." If so, they are even later now. As of 2009, the bill has gone nowhere.

When identifiable crimes do occur, prosecutors must spend their limited budgets on the most visible perpetrators, hoping that the capture and incarceration of the big fish will send a message to the guppies. The FTC has pursued this strategy in enforcing CAN-SPAM, but without success. Most of the little fish are still small enough to squeeze through whatever net the regulators design.

New regulations may also impose costs on people and businesses that are not doing anything wrong. When laws are vague about the conduct being outlawed, legislation may inadvertently deter productive behavior, imposing new costs for or simply frightening away those who engage in related, but legal, activity. After the accounting scandals at companies like Enron and WorldCom were revealed in 2001, for example, Congress passed a comprehensive reform known as the Sarbanes-Oxley Act, which requires all public companies to provide additional details in their financial statements. The act has cost billions of dollars in compliance for U.S. businesses, most of whom were not cooking their books. Most measures of the act's utility conclude it has completely failed to deter the destructive behavior it was meant to stop.

To fight information crime, we need solutions that will work instead of or in combination with new criminal laws. As with identity theft, self-regulation and public education can play a significant role in thwarting criminal activity. Unfortunately, those strategies do not lend themselves to dramatic rhetoric, and so do not satisfy the need for immediate gratification of lawmakers and the news media. So far, they have been underutilized weapons in the information crime arsenal.

Consumers and their advocates also need more and better technology. Most users already employ antimalware products, including e-mail filters, firewalls, and monitors that carefully control what new software can be installed on a home computer. Companies such as McAfee, Norton, and Microsoft (which builds some antivirus software directly into its products and sells others as add-ons) have developed an entire industry to combat malware. This automated law enforcement has proven far more effective at deterring and minimizing information crime than traditional policing. It's also made a profit—today, the market for protective software has grown to $15.1 billion a year worldwide. Industry analyst IDC expects it to reach $21 billion by 2011. In the arms race between good and evil in digital life, as in the real world, the arms merchants always win.

Information Crimes Against Humanity

There is one final category of computer crime to consider—cyberterrorism. Unlike other information criminals, cyberterrorists are not trying to profit from the information of others. Their goal, as in the physical world, is to make the world of digital life if not uninhabitable then at the very least considerably less appealing. Though the damage from terrorist attacks against the digital infrastructure may so far be minimal, it is without a doubt the area that security analysts, governments, and technology companies fear the most. The object of cyberterrorism is, after all, to destroy the Internet itself.

The open architecture and standards of the Internet leave it especially vulnerable to systemwide attacks, and the incidence of such crimes has been rising steadily in the past ten years. (The true extent is unknown. Most attacks against businesses and infrastructure providers are likely never reported.) In the early days, self-replicating software viruses and other automated attacks that crashed Web site host computers were largely the work of antisocial young programmers called hackers. In hacker communities, acts of digital vandalism are seen as rites of passage that establish technical prowess, earning new hackers no money but plenty of bragging rights at Internet security conferences.

Regardless of the motive of the perpetrator, these early forms of cyberterrorism still caused widespread outages and damaged individual computers and user files. In 2003, a series of viruses, such as Slammer, Lovesan, and Sobig, spread through self-replicating e-mails and unsecured software. They shut down computer systems of large businesses and individuals alike, costing billions of dollars in lost productivity. Law enforcement agents are still trying to track down the culprits. Two Americans and a Moroccan were initially charged, but so far only one suspect has been captured. Five years after the incidents, two Europeans were added to the list of coconspirators. Hacking is a global problem, it seems.

Not only are systematic attacks hard to deter or to punish, but they are also on the rise. In 2007, the U.S. Department of Homeland Security's cybersecurity chief, Greg Garcia, acknowledged that the number of reported attacks had increased 400 percent in the last three months of 2006 alone. "Make no mistake," Garcia said, "our networks and systems are vulnerable and they are exposed. Our adversaries are sophisticated, nimble, and organized, and they will stop at nothing to achieve their motives, which include economic gain . . . espionage, revenge and publicity."

Garcia's anxiety is understandable. The attacks of September 11, 2001, and the ongoing war on terror have greatly raised the risks and the stakes of cyberterror. Hacking has moved from the world of adolescent programmers to the shady underground of criminal gangs. In recent years, for example, Mexican drug cartels have begun using YouTube and blogs as part of their gang wars, posting ransom demands or videos of evidence that incriminates the other gangs. In 2008, rival cybergangs fighting for control of an online Ponzi scheme launched attacks against each other's computers, clogging not only their own servers but those of their respective service providers as well. When huge amounts of data are being hurled back and forth by competing hackers, it turns out, there's plenty of collateral damage. Although Internet backbone providers build in plenty of cushion, no one believes the Internet could survive a large-scale attack, what security analysts refer to as the "digital Pearl Harbor."

Beyond the criminal gangs, we've now seen the first signs of politically based attacks, if not from terrorists then at least from rival governments. In 2007, plans by the Estonian government to relocate the remains of Soviet soldiers from the country's capital led to days of rioting by Russian nationals and violent attacks at the Estonian embassy in Moscow. The attacks spilled over to the Internet, where coordinated strikes were launched against public and private Web sites in Estonia. It now appears the attacks were executed by "hacktivist" bloggers who posted instructions for jamming the Estonian sites and recruited others to join the mob. It is still not clear what if any role was played by the Russian government.

More ominous events took place in 2008, when security experts noticed similar attacks being launched against official Web sites of the government of Georgia. The hackers were traced to a U.S. computer that was quickly disabled. Weeks later, Russian forces entered and occupied the former Soviet republic, and the cyberattacks resumed. The second set of attacks came from a server based at a Russian telecommunications firm, suggesting the initial attack represented a trial run for a coordinated cyber- and conventional war.

The extent of Internet espionage may be more widespread. In March 2009, researchers at the University of Toronto discovered a vast computer spying operation, which they called GhostNet, that had stolen documents from computers in more than a hundred countries, many of them located in embassies and government offices. Most of the activities were traced to computers located in China, though there is no evidence that the Chinese government is responsible or even aware of the thefts.

Given the increasingly geopolitical nature of these attacks, one might think that here at last is a kind of Internet crime suited to government intervention. Maybe so, but most governments have proven inept at protecting even their own computers. In a 2006 report published by the Government Accountability Office, the Department of Homeland Security, whose job it is to protect national infrastructures from natural and terrorist catastrophes, was given a failing grade with regard to the Internet. A few highlights (or lowlights) from the report:

- Following the resignation of many of the agency's Internet security staff, Secretary Michael Chertoff created a high-ranking post of "assistant secretary for cybersecurity and telecommunications" to manage disparate and disorganized efforts. The assistant secretary's job included "identifying and assessing the vulnerability of critical telecommunications infrastructure and assets; providing timely, actionable and valuable threat information; and leading the national response to cyber and telecommunications attacks." A year later, the position had yet to be filled.
- The agency's National Cyber Response Coordination Group, the "primary entity responsible for coordinating governmentwide responses to cyber incidents," still hadn't decided what it was supposed to do. The group had also not identified the kinds of events that would trigger its activation.
- The DHS had begun several Internet-related initiatives, but had yet to finish any of them, or offer a timetable for when it might, or indicate how any of them fit together. As a result, the report concluded, "The nation is not prepared to effectively coordinate public/private plans for recovering from a major Internet disruption."

The DHS is not entirely to blame for its poor performance. The Internet is not like other national infrastructures. At its core, the Internet is a private infrastructure. Unlike highways, the Internet is not built and operated by government entities. Unlike public utilities, such as the power grid and the water supply, the Internet is not heavily supervised, inspected, or controlled by regulators. It owes its remarkable success to the fact that it is in some sense a reflection of market forces at their purest—it is an infrastructure of profoundly low, and always dropping, transaction costs.

Our best defense against a catastrophic loss of Internet access is the Internet itself, not a less supine DHS. The Internet's decentralized design, full of the kind of checks and balances that make democracies work, is far more capable of withstanding natural disaster or terrorist attacks than anything all the agencies, task forces, and public-private partnerships in Washington could ever come up with. Since 9/11, the Internet has withstood a Baltimore tunnel fire in 2001 that burned key fiber-optic cables, the destruction caused by Hurricane Katrina, and coordinated attacks from a variety of viruses. In all these instances there were local disruptions, but most Internet users weren't even aware of the damage. The DHS played no part in the recovery. Indeed, by 2008, frustration with the department's mishandling of cybersecurity led for calls to move that function directly to the White House, a topic that ignited an ugly turf war in the early days of the Obama administration.

But there's little need for a "national" strategy to protect the Internet. Today, we have a mostly functioning market of backbone providers, ISPs, and Internet security companies that work with corporate and private customers to eliminate the most obvious risks of failure and damage. Researchers at Stanford and other leading universities are working on next-generation Internet designs that will dramatically improve the security of the underlying network protocols (albeit with considerable loss of anonymity for users). We should not wait for the DHS to develop broad solutions to Internet security on both large and small scales. Nor should we appropriate more funds for the agency to pretend that's what it's doing.

FAST-FORWARD: THE TRILLION-DOLLAR PRIVATE ENFORCEMENT INDUSTRY

Digital crime is an arms race. So far, the criminals are clearly making better use of the Law of Disruption. The hackers, crackers, and phishers take full advantage of every new tool and improvement in networking or encryption technology. Criminals can hide themselves and their assets almost perfectly. The cost of committing crime is cheap—it costs nothing to send out millions of e-mails. Even if only one sucker takes the bait, the effort pays off.

Cybercriminals are often years ahead of local law enforcement. And local law enforcement, constrained by geographic as well as technological limits, is the only kind dealing with the problem so far. Enhanced penalties and specialized enforcement, preferably at the global level, might make a difference in the calculus of Internet crime. To be effective, these new agencies would require extensive powers to seize assets, extradite suspects, and impound enormous quantities of data just to investigate what might be criminal behavior. Well-founded fears of the abuse of such powers, even more pronounced in Europe than in the United States, make it unlikely that such agencies would ever be constituted or given the budgets they need. So even if law enforcement could compete with criminals, they won't.

Ending the scourge of Internet crimes, it turns out, is a job for the market and not the legal system. That, in any event, is the practical result of poorly written new laws, underfunded law enforcement, and intergovernmental turf battles. With no sheriff in town, the digital posse has organized itself. A new industry is emerging to provide technology, insurance, and other unique forms of protection against online crime. Businesses will eventually take the few simple steps needed to reduce today's biggest security risks. Though information crime will never be eliminated, enforcement technologies will ultimately make digital life easier to police than the physical one.

Private enforcement offers another advantage over public enforcement. The anticrime industry has a powerful financial incentive to get it right. Companies such as McAfee and Norton, which offer antivirus protection, make money only if they keep your computer from crashing. Likewise, consumers will pay for spam-blocking software only if it keeps spam out of their in-boxes. Prevention so far is also a high-profit business, encouraging future developments. Antivirus software still costs as much as $120 a year, despite substantial increases in the number of customers using it. Security software overall is projected to be a $100 billion market by 2010.

The market works, or works better—at least so far. But so far we are only talking about criminals who release viruses for antisocial reasons or promote scams for financial gain. Those who want to harm the information economy for political reasons are different. Unlike criminals, terrorists have no incentive to keep the system running at all. Since they are not in it for the money, they don't need to protect the infrastructure. Information terrorists will not hesitate to exercise their nuclear option, assuming they find one. So far they haven't, though the Internet's open architecture, in many respects its greatest strength, could prove its ultimate undoing. With the Law of Disruption, you never know.

INFORMATION LIFE

Law Seven: Copyright

Reset the Balance

Perhaps the most visible breakdowns in the economy of digital life center on the archaic law of copyright. Content producers are pursuing desperate measures to protect their right to define how, when, and by whom their ideas may be used. Consumers are fighting back with equal passion and, so far, greater success. This chapter explores the history of the copyright rebellion from its beginnings in the Enlightenment to the perfect storm of copyright abuse made both possible and inevitable by the Internet. I propose a radical but simple solution: reset the delicate balance between information producers and users, a balance ruined by decades of laws that have shrunk consumer rights to nothing. The fix is easy on paper, but requires a global act of common sense to achieve.

A Yawning Chasm

The two sides of the copyright debates aren't even speaking the same language.

Consider two articles published in the spring of 2007. The first, "A Great Idea Lives Forever—Shouldn't Its Copyright?" appeared as a *New York Times* op-ed from novelist Mark Helprin. Helprin argues that writers and artists are unfairly treated by copyright law. The owners of real estate and other physical property can rest comfortably in their graves knowing their descendants benefit in perpetuity from their bequests. Rights to literary works, on the other hand, expire a mere seventy years after the death of their creators.

After that, an author's work becomes free for anyone to do with as they please, a kind of literary purgatory known as the "public domain." "No good case exists for the inequality of real and intellectual property," Helprin concludes, "because no good case can exist for treating with special disfavor the work of the spirit and the mind."

In the second article, Chapman University law professor John Tehranian walks us through the seemingly innocent and mundane activities of a hypothetical law professor named "John," including replying to e-mails, teaching classes, doodling during a faculty meeting, and singing "Happy Birthday to You" at a dinner party. Applying current copyright law, the stunning conclusion is that the professor has committed multiple felonies. "All told," Tehranian concludes, John "has committed at least eighty-three acts of infringement and faces liability in the amount of $12.45 million (to say nothing of potential criminal charges)." At that pace, John's potential copyright violations leave him liable for more than $4.5 billion in damages each year.

Most of the violations John perpetrates are committed every day by nearly everyone. Replying to e-mail messages using the feature that includes the sender's message in the reply, for example, infringes the sender's copyright in the original. Doodling a cartoon that reminds John of Frank Gehry's design for the Bilbao art museum violates the architect's right to control "derivative" works. Despite being the most recognized song in the English language, "Happy Birthday to You" is still protected by copyright (currently owned by Warner Music) and will be until 2030 in the United States and 2016 in Europe. Singing it without paying a royalty constitutes an unlicensed public performance. Capturing the moment on a video cell phone is another violation.

Tehranian's story is one answer to Helprin's challenge. The seeming "inequality" between physical and so-called intellectual property is explained in part by the expansive protections afforded to information products during their brief period of ownership. There is no crime of "copying" my car; the FBI does not investigate someone writing a play "based on" the contents of my home. Though the vast majority of infringing behaviors are not prosecuted either by copyright owners or by the government, the fact remains that nearly every literate person in the world breaks the law on a daily basis. That they do so mostly without intending harm is irrelevant. Intent is not a requirement for a finding of infringement.

The enormous potential liability for "Professor John" suggests copyright is over- rather than underprotective. Since the 1970s, legislatures around the world have repeatedly and haphazardly expanded the penalties for infringement even as they extended the duration of copyright and made it easier for owners to sue even accidental infringers. The vast majority of useful copyrights, like Helprin's, have been assigned to large media companies, including publishers, music labels, and conglomerates such as Time-Warner, Viacom, Disney, and News Corporation. As the music industry's recently suspended campaign against file-sharing teenagers demonstrates, large media companies need only threaten litigation to win their case. When the defendants cannot afford to fight back, legal merits play no part in a lawsuit.

Today, enforcement of copyright is largely arbitrary and perhaps economically irrational. This, however, is no reason to abolish the system. Although Helprin doesn't make the point, the difficulty of detecting all the violations that occur and the expense of remedying them may be his best argument for more copyright protection. Why not compensate authors for unrecoverable losses by extending their control? Larger penalties, even when they can't be collected, can act as a deterrent. Longer terms would give authors and their families more time to sell licensed copies that might make up some of their injuries, if not sink the pirates who inflict them. Successive increases in copyright duration haven't kept entertainment from growing into one of the largest sectors in the information economy. Indeed, they may have helped. So why not extend copyright forever?

Here's why. Perpetual copyrights would generate both short-term and long-term harms, both of which can be demonstrated with a simple example. Let's say that copyright had been around in the time of William Shakespeare and that, as Helprin suggests, it treated original creations as the permanent possessions of their authors. Assume as well that Shakespeare, a notorious borrower of plots, characters, and stories, was not himself an infringer. Today, the rights to Shakespeare's plays would have descended some twenty generations. Assuming normal birthrates and that none of his progeny sold their rights, Shakespeare's copyrights might today be divided among some 1 million descendants. (Unlike physical property, which may be impossible to split more than a few ways, information ownership can be divided infinitely.)

Now suppose you wanted to produce *Romeo and Juliet* in modern attire and language. Not only would you have to pay a shared royalty to the 1 million owners, but you would also need their permission to adapt it. First you'd have to find them, verifying, perhaps through DNA testing, that they were in fact all Shakespeares. Then you'd have to convince them to approve your production. The contract might be short, but the signature pages would run into the thousands. The cost of negotiating—the transaction costs—would almost assuredly exceed the actual price the Shakespeares would charge.

Shakespeare is the easy case—his work has never gone out of fashion. Most literary works don't survive their authors, and are rarely bequeathed explicitly in trusts and wills. It is nearly impossible a few generations after the death of the author to determine who actually inherited rights that a literary revival might make valuable. Still, the potential for a long-lost relative to appear and make a claim would likely deter productive uses of what have, for practical purposes, become "orphaned" works.

That's the immediate danger. The long-term problem concerns the true nature of authorship. One reason information producers are not given unlimited protection is that there is little original about them. Shakespeare's practice of borrowing heavily from others was common practice, only slightly less explicit today. Most literary scholars believe there are only a few main themes to all of literature, and these originate in the myths, legends, and religious texts of ancient civilizations. At the most basic level of creativity, authors like Helprin borrow their words from the limited set that make up a language—each of which, at some point, was created by someone.

Copyright protection is limited, in part, because drawing the line between the particular expression of an idea (*Romeo and Juliet*) and the idea itself (love conquers all) is never easy. Change the staging, the characters' names, and the historical context, and *Romeo and Juliet* becomes *West Side Story*. What part of the musical borrows legally from the idea of the play (boy meets girl, boy loses girl, tragedy follows), and what part infringes on Shakespeare's interpretation of it? Judges, trained only generally on the law and armed simply with reasoning by analogy, blanch at the task. It requires at a minimum expertise in linguistics, semiotics, literary theory, history, and a dozen other fields in which no judge has likely had any training.

All of these problems explain why, contrary to the title of Helprin's article, governments never grant copyright to mere ideas or new words or phrases, no matter how novel or useful. You may be able to secure a patent on a new invention (the rules to basketball) or place modest limits on the

ommercial use of a phrase ("March Madness"), but you cannot copyright
ither. Copyright requires significant creativity. It grants rights only to those
vho transform an idea into a new and tangible expression. Books, music,
rchitectural designs, maps, software, and other creative artifacts are pro-
ected, but only to the extent that they display the novel vision of an original
nind at work.

Take another Shakespeare play, *The Winter's Tale*, in which a leading
haracter disappears for years, only to return transformed and redeemed.
Shakespeare took most of its elements from a story written thirty years ear-
er.) Three hundred and fifty years after the play was first produced, a mod-
rn novelist borrowed its basic elements for a book that was published to
ritical acclaim. Its title, *Winter's Tale*, begged comparison with Shakespeare.
Vo matter. Even if Shakespeare had a copyright, it would have long since ex-
ired. The novel's author didn't need the permission of any of the Bard's de-
cendants. Nor did he need to worry about being sued, rightly or wrongly,
or infringing on their rights.

That author was Mark Helprin.

AN ENLIGHTENED VIEW OF COPYRIGHT

t the accident-prone intersection of innovation and law, no broken light
as caused more collisions than copyright. Several books have been pub-
shed on obscure aspects of the problem—the fate of the public domain, the
conomics of collaborative technology, the dangers of closed standards, and
he risks of open ones. Even nonlawyers are passionate about the subject.
Judging from the comments posted to intellectual property blogs, the lack
f even a basic understanding of the law doesn't seem much of a handicap to
xpressing one's opinion.) From media company executives to ordinary
onsumers, everyone seems convinced they know just what to do. This chap-
er cuts through the misperceptions and blather. It also proposes meaningful
eform that could save the system.

Popular opinions, informed and otherwise, separate rather neatly into
wo opposing camps. One side, led by media conglomerates and their allies
n government, argues that digital technology has undermined copyright,
naking its enforcement nearly impossible. Content that once had to be
ransferred to expensive media and then distributed, retailed, and serviced

locally can now be effortlessly turned into bits. Like any other digital information, these bits can and are spread effortlessly, anonymously, and cheaply through the Internet. The fastest-growing categories of Internet traffic—file sharing, bit torrenting—represent the unwanted and unlicensed exchange of proprietary information. Owners make no money from the widespread trafficking of their property, and are powerless to stop it. Their information has been hijacked.

We live, according to the content-owner camp, in a world populated by modern-day pirates. The bandits are a mixed group, made up in the United States and Europe of nearly everyone under age 30 and, in the developing world, pretty much anyone with a computer. The thieves have grown up believing that content is and should be free. They download digital music, photographs, and software; they upload television shows and movies—all without making any effort to compensate the creators. They ignore their parents and Interpol warnings; they reject the very idea that what they do constitutes a crime. They scour the network plundering the riches of whomever they like without firing a single shot.

As soon as illegal businesses are closed, new ones pop up to replace them. Content owners managed to shut down companies like MP3.com, which allowed users to listen to albums they already owned on portable digital music players. File-sharing services including Napster, Grokster, and TorrentSpy have been disabled. Russia's entry into the World Trade Organization has been delayed in part by the country's refusal to stop a local Web site, AllOfMP3, which sold digital copies of any album for a dollar each. (AllOfMP3 was closed in 2007; TorrentSpy's appeal is pending.)

But staring down the jaws of civil and criminal enforcement, including individual lawsuits against thousands of file-sharing users, the pirates have nevertheless grown more numerous and more impudent. Peer-to-peer technology adapts instantly to avoid every court decision aimed at reining it in. The provocatively named Pirate Bay is flourishing despite the 2009 conviction on criminal charges of its principals. (The convictions are on appeal.) Despite a pending $1 billion lawsuit by entertainment giant Viacom, the video-sharing Web site YouTube continues to gain popularity with users who post both personal videos and unlicensed content taken from television and movies. Music sales have plummeted, DVD movie rentals are dying fast, and newspapers have all but given up. The parasitic behavior of consumers

ith too many computing cycles and too few morals, the argument goes,
reatens the creative enterprise itself. As media lawyer and former prosecu-
r Kenneth Starr told the U.S. Supreme Court in the Grokster case, file-
haring technologies "breed a culture of contempt for intellectual property,
nd for the rights of others generally."

At the other extreme, exemplified best by the work of Stanford law pro-
ssor Lawrence Lessig, copyright has become a totalitarian monarch no
nger deserving of respect or obedience. As digital technology eliminates
he need to reproduce creative artifacts in imperfect and intermediate me-
ia, creators and their audiences can connect to each other with almost no
ansaction costs or loss of fidelity.

Even more, the plasticity of digital life creates a unique opportunity for
veryone to be a creator, to collaborate, remix, enhance, and update each
ther's work for an audience of everyone. Applications such as Wikipedia,
lickr, and YouTube, where groups jointly create articles, photo galleries, and
hort films, represent the beginnings of a new kind of creation, perhaps even
truer form of egalitarian democracy—the ideal of the founding fathers
ealized in digital life.

The only crime being committed, according to this view, is the refusal of
he media companies and their lobbyist-influenced allies in legislatures to
mbrace the brave new world. Content owners, comfortable in the routines
nd habits of the analog world, have refused to offer their products legally or
t least at a fair price in the digital marketplace. Instead, they have perverted
opyright law to make felons of an entire generation of users—indeed, of
heir own children. They have only themselves to blame for rampant inno-
ation by customers to create the products and distribution channels con-
umers really want.

Worse, the content owners have corrupted the law in ways that inad-
ertently encourage more rebellion. Copyright law "reforms" and one-sided
ourt victories have eviscerated the concept of a limited or "fair use" of copy-
ighted materials that doesn't require permission or payment. Extensions to
he term of copyright, largely at the behest of the Walt Disney Company, have
ried up the main tributaries that feed the public domain. The 1998 Digital
Millennium Copyright Act (DMCA) criminalized the circumvention of tech-
ologies that limit how and by whom licensed digital copies can be enjoyed, a
iant step back in consumer rights. Even as digital technology has dramatically

reduced the potential cost of every aspect of the creative process, copyright law has been misused to inflate those costs artificially and destructively. This selfish and unnecessary increase in transaction costs constitutes a crime against economics, one that can't be forgiven or undone without scrapping the law and starting over.

Since governments of the analog world can't be expected or trusted, the rebels have formed their own social contract, fashioning new ways of protecting and sharing information. We stand on the verge of a new regime, a world not of copyright but of "copyleft." The Creative Commons license, for example, allows authors to grant all users the right to make productive uses of their creations without having to pay royalties or other fees. The "open-source" movement establishes a communal and virtual society of like-minded collaborators who can create software, documents, and other digital artifacts whose sum is greater than the parts donated by individual members.

The growing divide between copyright and copyleft is a classic battle inspired by the Law of Disruption. As the gap between what consumers can do and what information producers are comfortable with widens, relations between the two groups have turned very ugly very fast. Both sides are digging trenches for an extended fight. The owners have the law on their side, but consumers see that as a mere technicality.

Why shouldn't they? Since World War II, much of the world's most valuable information has been distributed without charge (television, radio) or for next to nothing (newspapers, magazines, paperback books). If a generation of young information users believes that content is free, it's largely because they've been conditioned to see it that way by media companies vying for their constant attention. But now that digital technology has made it possible for consumers to replicate and distribute perfect copies of everything without the ads that underwrite their distribution, producers are dusting off the legal catapults and battle-axes.

We stand on the brink. So let's take a step back. In some sense, the ongoing copyright war began in the seventeenth century, at the beginning of what is known as the Age of Enlightenment. The Enlightenment movement emphasized individual liberty through learning, an idea in stark contrast to the closed information architecture of the medieval Catholic Church. Enlightenment thinkers, including the authors of the U.S. Constitution, believed that widespread knowledge would give average people the ability to reason for themselves. These ideas fueled the gradual and sometimes violent transition from monarchy to democracy, sparking revolutionary wars in the New World and much of Europe.

The Enlightenment also changed the nature of publishing. In 1710, Parliament enacted "An Act for Encouragement of Learning, by Vesting the Copies of Printed Books in the Authors or Purchasers of Such Copies, during the Times therein Mentioned." The Statute of Anne, as it is known, turned what had been a monopoly by the Royal Stationer upside down. It gave the rights to authors, not printers, and limited the times for which those rights existed. It introduced the radical idea that a copyright was not simply the codification of some natural right the authors had as creators. Rather, it was a gift from the government given for the specific purpose of encouraging the spread of information. The grant, in other words, was given only to the extent necessary to meet an explicit economic goal—the encouragement of learning.

The U.S. Constitution adapted the Statute of Anne into a decidedly more democratic framework. Congress was given the power, if it deemed necessary, "To promote the Progress of Science and useful Arts, by securing for limited Times to Authors and Inventors the exclusive Right to their respective Writings and Discoveries." Under the current system, authors are instantly granted exclusive rights to their books, music, films, and maps from the moment of creation. The authors' monopoly includes the right to make and sell authorized copies, perform the work in public, and license "derivative" works, which are adaptations from one media to another. (For the book you are holding in your hands, I have assigned the rights to audio versions and translations into other languages to my publisher. My agent shrewdly kept the film rights for me.) Authors can enforce their own rights in civil actions or ask the government to do so in criminal prosecutions. Thanks to a treaty known as the Berne Convention, copyright laws are nearly uniform and reciprocal throughout the developed world.

The genius of copyright is that it is largely self-perpetuating, self-maintaining, and ruthlessly efficient. Legislators need not review applications for copyright, nor decide at what point each author must give them up. Authors and inventors are given economic incentives to create, but without the expense of government subsidies and the politics that might go with evaluating them. The possibility of criminal penalties for infringement deters most forms of cheating, keeping enforcement costs down.

But there's a paradox. Copyright achieves its Enlightenment goals of democratizing information by embracing a closed architecture. The exclusive rights encourage new production, but do so by giving the author monopoly power to control or even suppress her creations. How does information spread more freely—promoting arts and sciences—when authors are granted the power to micromanage it?

Several important limitations written directly into the U.S. Constitution help resolve this tension. The "limited Times" restriction, for example, emphasizes that the monopoly is given only as long as necessary to ensure a creator can earn back her investment plus a reasonable profit. During that period, the author can either sell her rights to a publisher or produce and sell authorized copies free of competitors who did not incur the author's development costs and who therefore could sell at a lower price. Once the author's investment is recovered, the exclusive rights—indeed, nearly all of the author's rights—vanish. At that point, the public becomes the owner of the work.

A second limitation on copyright is that it extends only to works that advance some social good—those that promote the progress of "Science and useful Arts." There is no copyright protection for ephemeral writings such as shopping lists, phone messages, and simple recipes. Recent copyright litigation included unsuccessful efforts to claim ownership of yoga poses and a 1970s dance step called the "Electric Slide." The audacious Web site Magnus-Opus invites users to check their touch-tone telephone number against its database of copyrighted melodies, which suspiciously includes every possible sequence. Once a user "tests" his number, he is offered a choice of paying a one hundred–dollar annual license fee or canceling his phone service! The company doesn't seem to have sued anyone yet, which is just as well.

Finally, only the author's unique expression (her "writings") is protected. Once written, the ideas themselves are free to be used by anyone, whether they've purchased a copy of the work or not. A famous nineteenth-century case, for example, denied the author of a new accounting methodology the right to sue readers who implemented the system without paying additional royalties. "The copyright of a book on bookkeeping," the U.S. Supreme Court held, "cannot secure the exclusive right to make, sell, and use account-books prepared upon the plan set forth in such book."

RESETTING THE BALANCE

Copyright balances incentives for authors to invest in new works against the Enlightenment goal of growing the public domain as quickly and cheaply as possible. Throughout the nineteenth century, the system performed brilliantly. The arts and sciences flourished, and piracy was minimal. The principal safeguard, however, was the market, not the law. Making unauthorized copies of books, sheet music, phonograph records, and movies required large capital investments in printing presses, disc stampers, dubbing equipment, as well as labor. Selling illegal copies meant hiring trucks to transport the copies and warehouses to store them. Copies had to be sold through established retailers. All of these activities were hard to conceal. Pirating was both expensive and risky, creating an effective deterrent.

Thanks to the Law of Disruption, a succession of low-cost copying technologies has put increasing pressure on the system. Player pianos, invented in the late 1800s, allowed anyone to perform even the most complicated works without buying or studying sheet music. Cheap photocopying let consumers make unauthorized copies of printed material by themselves. VCRs brought video-copying technology right into the living room. As technology got smaller, cheaper, and faster, the need for intermediaries, capital investment, factories, and retail distribution channels disappeared. The expense and risk of infringement evaporated. Detection and enforcement became correspondingly more expensive.

Then came the Internet, a costless and limitless copy machine. Once a single digital copy becomes available, any user can make any number of perfect duplicates. Moore's Law makes it possible to digitize more and more information and store it on an ever-expanding array of devices, including computers, cell phones, and music and movie players. As it does, Metcalfe's Law is there to help spread the bits around the world, with or without permission. Transaction costs are minimal. Anyone with a computer and an Internet connection can buy the latest Beyoncé CD and within minutes post its contents in digital form. Users from around the world can then help themselves to a free copy. Digital technology makes copying free, while the Internet acts as a channel for worldwide distribution, virtually invisible and anonymous. The cost and risk of infringement have all but disappeared.

Infringement, in economic terms, is like other information crimes. By undermining the author's exclusive right to sell copies, infringement reduces the opportunity for authors to recover their investment. In theory, rampant cheating by consumers makes authors less likely to undertake new works in the first place, which in turn reduces the production of valuable information ultimately headed for the public domain. If this book becomes available for illegal downloading, I'm likely to spend my time doing something other than writing books. My publisher may face more dire consequences. Like spam, piracy imposes costs on the system itself.

Infringement, however, can also effect a productive use of information. Sharing information with more people may increase its value, and may help the information reach markets the author might otherwise have ignored or charged too much to reach. A user who enjoys clips from *The Daily Show* on YouTube may become a regular viewer of the program. Illegally downloading a wide range of music may help a consumer decide which artists he likes best, leading to more rather than fewer real sales.

The need to balance productive uses against destructive ones has been forgotten in the escalating war between information producers and information users. With the invention of each new copying technology, legislatures have extended the duration of the monopoly (giving creators more time to recover costs) and beefed up the penalties for cheating (more deterrence against pirates). New kinds of works and new storage media, including music, choreography, TV broadcasts, opera performances, software, and semiconductor chip designs, have also been brought under copyright protection as they entered mainstream use.

These fixes have done little to reduce copyright violations. Like most attempts to slow down the Law of Disruption, they have instead made things worse. Enhanced penalties discourage productive practices, including criticism, parody, and simply making use of the ideas in a work. Extended terms mean new works are entering the public domain at a trickle. The concentration of rights in the hands of a few large corporations has led to one-sided legal battles, like those between the music industry and individual consumers, as well as vast expenditures on lobbying for even more advantages.

As new technologies for producing, distribution, marketing, and using information are invented and reach an eager market of information-hungry consumers, the copyright balance is constantly shifting. On the one hand, new technologies make it easier for "pirates" to violate the monopoly control given to the copyright owner. But those same technologies also lower development and production costs. Lower costs, at least in theory, make it easier for an author to turn a profit. One might think that less, not more, incentive would be needed to satisfy the real goal of the system.

It is now virtually impossible for average consumers to avoid violating copyright law on a daily basis. It's as if every time cars were made faster, speed limits were reduced to minimize the incidence of speeding. Copyright today is the equivalent of a five-mile-per-hour speed limit on the freeway. But laws that are impossible to obey lead rational citizens to give up trying. Getting caught is just a stroke of bad luck. A recent survey by the Pew Internet and American Life Project found that 72 percent of Americans ages 18 to 29 don't care whether the music they download onto their computers was copyrighted or not. Most of it is. A law that makes felons of everyone is no law at all.

Copyright law, however, need not be abandoned. I propose three modest reforms that, taken together, would bring the system into alignment with the realities of digital life: setting realistic time limits, restoring the concept of fair use, and undoing the damage caused by the Digital Millennium Copyright Act of 2000. Copyright law that is synchronized with rather than opposed to the Law of Disruption can work. When they are pitted against each other, however, it's already clear which one will win.

Set Realistic Time Limits

The term of "exclusive rights" granted by copyright has been extended eleven times in the past fifty years. In 1962, copyright lasted fifty-six years. Today, it spans the lifetime of the author plus an additional seventy years. One unfortunate and unintended consequence of these modifications is that the public domain is drying up. Thanks to the term extensions, no Disney cartoon has *ever* gone out of copyright protection. That's no coincidence. Disney is one of the most aggressive worldwide lobbyists for enhanced copyright protection.

Ironically or not, Disney itself relies heavily on the public domain for the stories and characters of its most successful products. *The Little Mermaid* is based on an 1837 Hans Christian Andersen story of the same name. *Snow

White was published by the Brothers Grimm in 1857. Rudyard Kipling's *Jungle Book* had just gone out of copyright when Disney began production. Disney paid no royalties to use any of these works. At the same time, the company vigorously pursues even modest borrowings of its own copyrighted works. Bounty-hunting lawyers are paid to turn in retail bakeries that include Mickey Mouse decorations on birthday cakes. Yet Mickey himself began life in a 1928 cartoon, *Steamboat Willie*, that was a parody of a Buster Keaton film.

The Constitution does not define an exact or even optimal length of time for copyright; it does not even require Congress to grant copyrights in the first place. The cavalier decision to continue extending them suggests lawmakers have forgotten the part about promoting science and the useful arts. Songwriter-turned-congressman Sonny Bono famously answered the Constitution's requirement that copyrights be granted only for "limited Times" by proposing "forever minus a day." "That's a limited time," he said, "isn't it?" He wasn't kidding, and neither are his colleagues. After Bono's death in 1998, Congress enacted the Sonny Bono Copyright Term Extension Act, which tacked another twenty years onto the term. It also made that extension retroactive to all works still under protection when the act was passed.

The CTEA's retroactive provision was especially outrageous. Eric Eldred, who publishes public domain works on the Internet, fought it all the way to the Supreme Court. Eldred argued that since incentives issued after publication did nothing to promote the aims of copyright, the retroactive provision was unconstitutional. The Court disagreed. It was up to Congress, the majority wrote, to determine the optimal term for copyrights, even for works that already exist. In his dissent, Justice Stephen Breyer pointed out that realistically, most copyrighted works have a life expectancy of fewer than ninety-five years. Citing data provided by a group of economists, including five Nobel Prize winners, Breyer noted that extending the term by twenty years meant that for more than 99.8 percent of all copyrights, the term is effectively perpetual. Since the Constitution allows Congress to grant copyright only for "limited Times," Breyer agreed with Eldred that the law was unconstitutional.

The retroactive extension for existing works, Breyer noted, harms more than just the public domain. The longer the term, the higher the transaction costs a potential user faces trying to locate the copyright owners. Many die without leaving their rights to anyone. "To extend that term, preventing works from the 1920's and 1930's from falling into the public domain,"

Breyer wrote in his dissent, "will dramatically increase the size of the costs just as—perversely—the likely benefits from protection diminish."

Even if the tiny percentage of works with residual value did fall out of copyright, the harm to current copyright owners would be much less dire than the CTEA's supporters claimed. Disney, for example, argued that in the absence of the CTEA the copyright for Mickey Mouse would expire. Not true. Only *Steamboat Willie* and a few other early cartoons would go into the public domain. Disney's copyright in later cartoons, drawings, and other uses of the character would remain. More to the point, the company's *trademark* in Mickey would be unaffected. Trademarks have no time limit. Assuming there was a market for public domain copies of *Steamboat Willie*, anyone making and selling them would be prohibited from using Disney's marks in packaging and promoting their product. Indeed, they would likely be required to disclaim any association with the company. Individual works would become the property of the public, but the company's truly valuable information products would remain securely in the vault.

Restore "Fair Use"

To stay with the Mickey Mouse theme, consider the long-running animated series *The Simpsons*. A recurring feature of the show is a cartoon within the cartoon, an ultraviolent cat and mouse series called *Itchy and Scratchy*. In a 1992 episode in which the duo get their own movie, a news show touting the film plays their very first black-and-white cartoon, a short called *Steamboat Itchy*. In plot, appearance, and music, *Steamboat Itchy* is essentially *Steamboat Willie*, except at the end of *The Simpsons*' version the mouse chops the cat into tiny pieces and shoves him in the locomotive's boiler.

Despite the obvious similarities between the two cartoons, the creators of *The Simpsons* didn't need permission from Disney to air their version. The reason is an exception built into copyright law known as "fair use." Fair use, which includes parodies, classroom copying, and short quotations in reviews and other criticism of the work, is the most important safety valve against abuse of the author's monopoly. It covers a variety of situations where the cost of negotiating a license would greatly exceed the value to the parties—situations, in other words, where the monopoly would create excessively high transaction costs.

Since the owner of a monopoly right doesn't have to license his work to anyone, without fair use it may be impossible to criticize the work effectively. Commentary, however, helps consumers sort their reading choices. It is, therefore, economically productive. Aside from the personal embarrassment of public criticism, even bad reviews may actually help the author sell his work. Without a fair-use exception, these productive uses might be forgone, undermining copyright's larger goals of public enlightenment. *Steamboat Itchy* lampoons both the Disney Company and its most beloved character. Had producers of *The Simpsons* asked, Disney may have refused permission to parody their cartoon, even though paying homage to it likely increased the value of the earlier work. Corporate executives don't take risks with the crown jewels.

Another fair use allows users to copy part or even all of a work under certain circumstances. You may legally record a television program as it is broadcast and play it later on a VCR or DVR. Under a 2004 FCC ruling, you may even share copies of digital TV programming recorded on your TiVo through the Internet, so long as the sharing is limited to ten or fewer other TiVo devices you own. Courts have held that software buyers can make backup copies of products they buy. Indeed, to view the pages of a Web site, users must of necessity make temporary copies of the text, graphics, and files from the host computers to their own, all of which are considered fair use. Fair use, in all of these examples, eliminates wasteful transaction costs.

The law of fair use, unfortunately, has failed to keep up with digital life. The reason has largely to do with a famous 1984 case that on the surface dramatically expanded consumer rights but in practice did the opposite. The case involved the Betamax, an early VCR produced by Sony. Initially released in 1975, the $3,000 device allowed users to automatically record television programs on tape as they were being aired. Once recorded, programs could be watched as often as and whenever the viewer wished.

Soon after the launch, Universal Studios and Walt Disney sued Sony, claiming the device was little more than an engine of theft for consumers to steal copyrighted content. Each recording by each customer was an illegal act. In producing and marketing Betamax, Sony was aiding and abetting widespread piracy. According to the studios, the only solution was to ban VCRs forever. But by the time the Supreme Court ultimately decided the case nine years later, VCRs had gone from expensive novelties to mainstream products. Ten percent of all American homes had one.

For complex litigation, nine years is relatively fast. For consumer electronics, nine years represents several cycles of Moore's Law. By the time the Betamax case was decided, Sony, along with competitors who had sprung up in the interim had sold millions of VCRs. The Supreme Court could hardly brand everyone who owned one as a felon and require them to surrender their machines and tapes to local authorities for destruction. Given the passage of time, the Court had little choice but to find a way to save the Betamax.

In the end, the Supreme Court sided with Sony. But rather than reject the studios' novel effort to hold Sony liable for the copyright violations of its customers, the Court declared that consumers weren't infringing in the first place. So long as the tape was used only by the consumer for later enjoyment, even the complete copying of a program was legal. Time shifting the program was a fair use.

Prior to the Betamax decision, no one imagined that unauthorized copying of entire programs by millions of users could be a fair use. But in the pre–cable TV age, broadcasters transmitted their programs to any TV set in range for no charge whatsoever. So what damage was done to the studios by a device that let the viewer watch the show sometime other than when it was transmitted? Time shifting, the Court said, caused no harm to the potential market for or value of the programs.

The shift in fair-use analysis from the degree of the copying to the economic harm it caused had unintended consequences. Rather than look at the amount of copying, courts after Betamax focus instead on the effect the use *may have* on the market for the work. Just a year later, for example, the Supreme Court upheld a finding of copyright infringement in a case that involved the autobiography of former president Gerald Ford. An early review in the *Nation* included a three-hundred-word quote from the five-hundred-page book. Those three hundred words explained Ford's decision to pardon his predecessor, Richard Nixon—the most important decision Ford had made in his entire life. By quoting them, the publisher argued, the market for the book had been severely damaged. The Court agreed.

Ironically, the Court's expansive reading of the fair-use exception in the Betamax decision opened the door to exceptions that have swallowed the rule.

The original reasons fair use was created have been forgotten. Content owners now simply argue that any copying negatively affects the potential market for the underlying work. In theory, it probably does. Media companies have argued successfully that even noncommercial uses, including Internet file sharing over peer-to-peer networks, damage the future market for their products and thus are never fair use. The music industry, for one, consistently argues that every illegal download is the equivalent of a lost sale, leading to damage estimates that reach millions of dollars for even a few songs. Of the RIAA's thousands of lawsuits, only one actually reached a verdict. A jury found a file-sharing user liable for $220,000 for posting twenty-four songs—$9,250 per song. In late 2008 Congress actually increased the penalties for infringement, and a 2009 retrial of the file-sharing case returned a verdict of nearly $2 milion for the same twenty-four songs.

Piracy may substitute for real purchases in some cases, but certainly not all of them. At the same time, widespread sharing accompanied by commentary and recommendations has positive value to the copyright holder. It's free publicity. Yet fair-use cases rarely weigh the productive aspects of sharing. Consider the experience of British comedy legends Monty Python, who recently posted their sketches on a dedicated YouTube channel. As the group explained their strategy, "We're letting you see absolutely everything for free. So there! But we want something in return. None of your driveling, mindless comments. Instead, we want you to click on the links, buy our movies & TV shows and soften our pain and disgust at being ripped off all these years." DVD sales on Amazon reportedly climbed 23,000 percent.

Years after the industry's victories against Napster and other P2P services, musicians have still received none of the nearly $400 million in damages paid to the labels, who claimed all along to be fighting solely on their behalf. Despite a nearly perfect record of wins for the industry in any case, the mass lawsuits did little to deter users determined to share their favorite songs. If anything, the evisceration of fair use as a safety valve has had the opposite effect. Young people are now united in their rejection of the industry's determination to continue selling music on overpriced CDs. (In the midst of the file-sharing wars, the industry settled price-fixing charges brought by U.S. and European regulators, paying nearly $200 million in fines.) In early 2009, the industry announced it was ending the mass litigation strategy, focusing instead on getting ISPs to do their policing for them. Meanwhile, a generation of consumers has been trained to ignore the law and the institutions that support it.

After years of expensive litigation aimed at disabling any digital distribution of music, the industry finally gave its tepid cooperation in the creation of legal forms of downloadable music. Apple launched the iPod and iTunes store in 2003. By early 2009, 6 billion legal downloads had been sold. Still, users and musicians are not satisfied that the industry has given them the kind of access to each other that they want and that the Internet makes possible. Increasingly, musicians are bypassing the notoriously corrupt system altogether and making direct contact with their audiences using MySpace and other media-rich Web sites. In one experiment, the popular band Radiohead allowed fans to download its 2007 album and pay whatever they wanted. Within a week, the band netted $10 million.

But the real danger to closing the fair-use safety valve is not to consumers but to content owners. The video rental and ownership business, "remastered" and limited-edition boxed sets, and direct-to-tape sequels were possible only because the studios lost the Betamax lawsuit. Media rentals and sales generate more revenue today than actual theatrical releases—revenue that the studios, had they won Betamax, never would have seen. In 1984, the year Michael Eisner took over as CEO of Disney, revenues were stagnant at $1.5 billion; the total value of the company was only $2 billion. Today, Disney, which now owns ABC and ESPN among other media properties, is worth $40 billion. VCRs didn't destroy the movie industry; VCRs saved the movie industry from itself. The Law of Disruption knows what it's doing, sometimes better than the companies it actually helps.

In the twenty years since the Betamax case, the law of fair use has become a mush. In spite of (or perhaps due to) the continued focus on abstract market effects, average citizens have developed a kind of urban legend about fair-use law, inventing rules that simply don't exist. My students and clients tell me with complete confidence that fair use allows you to play the first thirty seconds of any song, or that any copying is allowed as long as you don't charge for it. My academic colleagues are certain they are permitted to photocopy anything for classroom use, especially if they teach at public universities. All wrong. Despite what anyone else has told you, there are no "safe harbors" in fair use.

As the Law of Disruption has improved the speed and lowers the cost of digital distribution, the battle between content owners and their customers has moved from photographs (the earliest file-sharing litigation regularly featured *Playboy* as the plaintiff) to software and video games to music. It has now jumped, like a mutating virus, to television programs and full-length movies. Collateral damage to fair use has been devastating to both sides. Content owners believe fair use has been vanquished, while consumers believe that any use they can get away with is fair.

Fair use must be restored. Noncommercial uses, even those that might reduce the size of the commercial market, do more good than harm, both to the overall economy and perhaps even to copyright holders. Amending the law to make any noncommercial use a fair use would end most of the conflict between copyright owners and their customers. With that distinction in place, courts and law enforcement can focus their attention on true piracy. Meanwhile, content owners can begin the long public education process needed to rehabilitate those who will live the rest of their lives online.

Undo the Digital Millennium Copyright Act

The 1998 Digital Millennium Copyright Act was the first serious attempt by Congress to address the copyright implications of digital life. Two of its main provisions, however, have generated rather than reduced conflicts between information producers and users. The first involves a provision that immunizes ISPs from liability for the copyright violations of their customers. So long as the ISP responds to written demands to remove illegal files from its equipment, it cannot be sued for aiding and abetting. The so-called notice and takedown system, however, has proven controversial. ISPs regularly respond to takedown requests without evaluating whether there is actual legal merit to the complaint. (Copyright owners who act in bad faith can be fined, as we saw in the Diebold case, but such findings are rare.) Copyright owners may also subpoena ISPs to reveal the identities of the users they believe are violating their rights.

Some owners have abused the subpoena power to intimidate critics and citizen journalists. In a 2002 case, for example, Wal-Mart demanded Web site FatWallet.com identify an anonymous poster who revealed upcoming sale prices the retailer was planning, prices the company believed were its property. Price lists are unlikely to be protected under copyright law, however, and when a nonprofit law firm announced it would defend the site, Wal-Mart withdrew its demand.

A second provision of the DMCA, which prohibits circumvention of technologies designed to control access to copyrighted works, is even more contentious. These technologies, known as "digital rights management," limit the ways even lawful purchasers can use digital copies. DRM often denies purchasers the ability to resell their copies when they're done with them, a right the copyright act elsewhere ensures. Controversial features or even errors are cynically cited as copy-protection technology, stifling criticism of the quality of a work.

Copy protection may unintentionally frustrate even authorized uses of a product, disabling the application when users switch from one device to another. In one instance, Sony included copy-protection software on CDs that, when played on personal computers, opened dangerous security breaches in the Windows operating system. After public outcry, the CDs were recalled. Several other products, including Apple's iTunes and Intuit's TurboTax, have removed or relaxed DRM systems in the face of widespread unrest among their customers.

Anticircumvention also undermines the right of competitors to reverse engineer a competitor's product, even in situations where the law allows and encourages it. Consider the strange business of computer printer cartridges. The cost of cartridges, which can sell for as much if not more than the printer itself, is principally driven by the cost of the mechanism, not the ink. A growing market has emerged to recharge empty cartridges, allowing customers to reuse rather than replace them.

Printer manufacturers, however, would like to control as much of the recharging market as possible. So Lexmark, a leading manufacturer, tagged some of its cartridges with an access protection chip that disabled a customer's printer if it detected a cartridge recharged by someone other than Lexmark. These cartridges were sold at a discount to business customers, who agreed to return them after use to Lexmark. The "prebate" cartridges, as Lexmark called them, ensured that Lexmark would control at least some part of the recharge market for its printers.

A company called Static Control Components, however, developed a "Smartek" chip that mimicked the functions of Lexmark's lockout device. These chips were sold to third-party cartridge rechargers, making it possible to recharge the prebate cartridges without triggering the lockout. Users who sold their discounted cartridges to rechargers other than Lexmark were clearly violating their agreement with the company. But Lexmark, understandably, was not eager to sue its own customers. Instead, it claimed that SCC had violated the DMCA by marketing a product that circumvented the access protection chip. Under a long line of cases, courts had upheld the reverse engineering of products by competitors wishing to make replacement parts, supplies, and other add-ons. The court here sided with SCC. Lexmark was free to penalize customers who violated their user agreements or to cancel the discount program altogether. Lexmark could not, however, use the DMCA to enforce the prebate program.

Like most of the cases involving the DMCA, the Lexmark case demonstrates the danger of giving copyright owners new powers to limit the use of their content, especially when those limits are enforced by secret technologies. The natural tendency of digital information is to move through the network without constraints. Efforts to control or limit how users respond to content, whether it is to report on it, build on it, or simply pass their copies along to someone else, run contrary to the Law of Disruption. Markets resist. DRM introduces new transaction costs, adding little or no value in return.

Overall, the DMCA has done considerable damage to the balance between information producers and users. One proposed bill, the Digital Media Consumers Rights Act, would have gone far toward solving the worst offenses. It exempted researchers from the anticircumvention provisions and allowed consumers to bypass technological controls in order to fully exercise fair-use rights otherwise blocked by the technology. It also exempted anticircumvention technology that enabled noninfringing uses, such as the lawful resale of a product otherwise protected by DRM. The proposed law did nothing, however, to discourage content owners who abuse the notice-and-takedown provisions to intimidate ISPs and their users. In any event, the proposed "bill of rights" for digital media consumers was never passed. Instead, Congress has repeatedly increased the penalties for DMCA violations.

FAST-FORWARD: THE SHOULDERS OF GIANTS

Intellectual property is a fiction, if not an oxymoron. The fiction may have worked, but only because analog life required the transformation of information into physical artifacts. Since the cost of producing and distributing information fell so heavily on the physical copies, information industries organized their businesses around specific media formats. Newspapers focused on the paper, record companies on the records, and movie studios on the film. Applying the property metaphor to the underlying concepts and ideas that were the real source of value created some complications, but only at the margins. As Marshall McLuhan famously said, "The medium is the message."

Treating information as a kind of property just doesn't work anymore. In digital life, information need never take physical form. It is now a purely non-rivalrous good. As content owners have learned to their displeasure, it is nearly impossible to exclude users from accessing it, despite regular and reckless expansion of the author's exclusive rights and the penalties for infringing them. Increasingly, consumers will forgo owning copies of any kind, preferring always-on, on-demand access via the network. "For many people," as *Wired* magazine's Kevin Kelly writes, "this type of universal access is better than owning. No responsibility of care, backing up, sorting, cataloging, cleaning or storage."

Almost everyone agrees that the copyright system is broken. Users armed by the Law of Disruption with new technologies and new ways of interacting with information will continue to challenge it. It can be repaired, but only if the law takes a dramatically different form. It must grant far less protection for authors, including limits on the duration of their exclusive rights. There's no need to feel sorry for the creators. Exclusive rights were only a means to an end, a necessary evil to grow the public domain. All information products, even the most novel and brilliant ideas and expressions, borrow heavily from the cultural warehouse of an increasingly global community. Copyright starts with the understanding that civilization advances only when the intellectual creations of our predecessors are freely available—free in the sense of being both cheap and available with minimal transaction costs. As Sir Isaac Newton put it, "If I have seen further, it is only by standing on the shoulders of Giants."

Even in a world with relaxed copyright, there are still plenty of opportunities for creators to make a living in the digital age. A provocative 2007 study by law professors Kal Raustiala and Christopher Sprigman even found that the absence of copyright protection for clothing designs helps rather than harms the fashion industry. High-end designers rely on speedy obsolescence, so the rapid appearance of knockoffs signals to buyers that it's time to buy the newest lines. As financial writer James Surowiecki notes, "The absence of copyrights and patents also creates a more fertile ground for innovation, since designers are able to take other people's ideas in new directions."

A short period of exclusivity or something less than monopoly power can be enough for creators to recover their costs and make a profit. The Grateful Dead, a band popular with three generations of music fans, famously allowed and even assisted its audience in making and selling "bootleg" recordings of its concerts, providing direct access to the sound boards for better fidelity. The Dead were not philanthropists. They made their money not so much from recordings (though fans still bought plenty of them) as from concert ticket sales and a host of licensed merchandise, including clothing, bumper stickers, and other accessories. As comic book pioneer Stan Lee once told me with his usual candor, "In the digital age authors should be prepared to give away everything of value and make their money on the crap."

The losers in the transition from analog to digital information will be the middlemen who help transform and sell information in increasingly obsolete physical forms. This is not to say that all newspaper and book publishers are doomed. Nor does this suggest that record labels, film distributors, and mass media retailers will go the way of the dodo. The Law of Disruption always challenges the existing rules and profit allocations of industries, but in the end it creates more value than it destroys. Newspapers select, edit, and organize the day's news. Publishers and record labels establish brand identities that lower consumer search costs when choosing among thousands of possible titles. Film studios establish reputations for a certain level of production quality. These are the values that can and are translated into digital products and services.

The death of middlemen has been greatly exaggerated. To the extent that intermediaries add value, their expertise can be translated into similar roles in a digital society. They just have to do it. It's mostly too soon to say what some of these are and how they will make money for those involved, and I can sympathize with some amount of hesitancy by content owners to jump in with both feet. But my sympathy goes only so far. Media companies have shown a dangerous resistance to making the transition, preferring to spend their energy on doomed legal battles against the Law of Disruption. Perhaps the management of these companies knows everything in this chapter. Behind the scenes, they are quietly figuring out how to optimize digital technology for creation, distribution, and collaboration. All will be revealed in due time. Meanwhile, to preserve cash flow, they struggle to keep the lid on unruly user-generated innovations. That, at least, is one possibility.

Perhaps the most unstable explosive in the arsenal of the copyright owners is copy-protection technology. All DRM has done is to inspire more innovative technologies to break it. Apple's Steve Jobs, who finally found a way to make file sharing profitable through iTunes, has called on his content partners to abandon this losing arms race, not for the sake of consumers but for their own bottom lines. "If anything," he wrote in an open letter to music publishers, "the technical expertise and overhead required to create, operate and update a DRM system has limited the number of participants selling DRM protected music." Consensus is growing that he's right.

As the movie studios and other media combatants should have learned from the story of Betamax, preserving the industry in its predigital form is not only impossible but also a bad idea. For one thing, it foregoes vast amounts of new revenue in the name of preserving an inefficient status quo. Theatrical releases of movies are now little more than commercials for later releases to pay-per-view, special-edition media, and licensed products, where the real money is made. Most video game consoles are heavily subsidized to sell more games, and now the games are subsidized to sell related services, including new episodes, leagues, and multiplayer online environments.

Likewise, television network executives today can hardly believe that viewers are watching their programs and commercials when they are actually aired. So what? Television is stronger and more profitable than ever. Advertising sponsorship in the form of product placements has once again become part of the programming itself. In the digital age, advertisers can sponsor or even own an entire channel of relevant programming rather than lob an unrelated thirty seconds of commercials into the middle of a show.

The threats to traditional media from higher-bandwidth computer networks and new software applications such as YouTube, automated syndication, and other "mash-up" tools are more of the same. They allow consumers to remix information—some from public sources, some protected under copyright—to create new content and new forms of commentary. Yet information producers respond to them with the same shock and awe they did the VCR. These new digital collaborations cannot be stopped. Nor should media companies want to stop them. Information pirates start by slashing and burning. But new ways of commercializing and profiting from their innovations invariably float to the surface from the wreckage of their drunken sprees.

The Law of Disruption is clearly on the side of the rebels. The population cohort of those age 30 and under is remarkably homogenous in their attitudes toward information. Today's youth reject copyright when it stands in the way of what they know to be the best use of content. For them, sharing information is a way of bonding, much as their parents made "mix tapes" for each other in the 1960s. Unlike previous generations of users, moreover, this group does not have to overcome traditional economic obstacles to take collective action. They communicate with each other constantly, through their blogs, instant messaging clients, cell phones, Twitter feeds, and (when they have to) face-to-face. We can't lock up an entire generation, and that is the line they have drawn in the silicon. We adapt to their way of using information or we don't. Regardless, they will keep doing it.

Copyright is always a question of economics—of providing just the right incentives to encourage creative innovation, limiting transaction costs in the otherwise frictionless flow of information, and giving consumers just enough freedom to keep them from storming the Bastille. The solution to the copyleft rebellion is to just say no to the content owners—not only to stave off consumer revolt but for their own damned good.

We need to reset the scales so delicately balanced by the engineers of the Enlightenment. If the law of copyright doesn't adapt, the Law of Disruption stands ready to take over.

Law Eight: Patent

Virtual Machines Need Virtual Lubricants

This chapter reviews the sorry history of patent protection for computers and software, developed piecemeal and clumsily by judges reluctantly stepping in where patent offices and legislatures worldwide have abdicated. What no one seems to understand is that information technology is different. The combination of hardware and software creates devices that invent other devices, or what computer scientists call "virtual machines." Virtual machines require and deserve legal protection, but not the same kind given to bioengineered drugs or new chemical processes. A more limited kind of patent would protect inventors without stifling competition—the primary use of patents today.

Life and Death at the Patent Office

For most executives, patents are an exotic plant best handled by specialists. For others, they are a matter of life and death.

For the Canadian company Research in Motion, it was the latter. RIM became a technology giant in 2002 when it released the Blackberry, a device that offers telephone, mobile e-mail and other data services over cellular networks. The opportunity to be online no matter where you are attracted users already addicted to information; RIM's customers are so attached to the devices that they refer to them affectionately as "Crackberries." By 2005, more than 3 million Americans were hooked. Today, the company is valued at more than $30 billion.

Soon after the Blackberry was released, however, RIM was sued for patent infringement by a company called NTP, which claimed the Blackberry infringed on sixteen of its U.S. patents. NTP, however, does not offer a wireless e-mail service of its own. In fact, NTP does not offer any products or services. The company simply buys up patents and waits to see if other companies offer products or services that might infringe on them. They then offer to license their inventions after the fact. Failing a successful negotiation, they sue. NTP refers to itself as a patent holding company. The more descriptive, if less generous, term for such companies is "patent troll."

The patents in the RIM case covered the use of wireless technology to transmit e-mail messages to a mobile device. These include U.S. Patent Number 6,057,451, "Electronic Mail System with Radio Frequency Communications to Mobile Processors," filed in 1998. Patent 6,057,451 describes, in forty-four pages of complicated diagrams and convoluted text, a system for sending messages from one e-mail service to other services using a central distribution node. That description clearly covered RIM's service, as well as similar services by a growing number of its competitors. (Similar lawsuits brought by NTP against AT&T, Sprint Nextel, T-Mobile, Verizon Wireless, and others are still pending.)

In fact, RIM came up with the technology on its own without even being aware of the NTP patents. In patent law, however, independent invention is no defense. So when a Virginia jury found the NTP patents were valid, there was little doubt that they covered the Blackberry service. Consequently, the judge ordered RIM to pay $54 million in damages and enjoined them from selling or supporting its devices in the United States going forward. For the company, most of whose customers are in the United States, the injunction was a death sentence.

After a year of further legal maneuvers and on-again, off-again negotiations between RIM and NTP, the judge indicated the end of his patience. He ordered the Blackberry service to shut down. Lawyers from the Departments of Justice and Defense argued that the service, a favorite of federal employees, was crucial to national security, but the judge ignored them. In March 2006, just days before the order was to take effect, RIM and NTP reached an agreement. RIM agreed to pay NTP a little more than $600 million to settle all claims, one of the largest settlements in recent patent history.

Over half a billion dollars may seem a particularly outrageous amount for patents that NTP was not even using or planning to use. It's even more shocking considering the U.S. Patent Office reviewed the NTP patents during the RIM lawsuit and found nearly all of them had been improperly approved. So why did RIM pay? A final determination on the NTP patents, including appeals to the Patent Office, federal courts, and perhaps the U.S. Supreme Court, could still be years away. The judge refused to delay his injunction in the meantime, leaving RIM with no choice. Despite what are likely worthless patents, it could pay whatever amount NTP asked for or go out of business.

THE STRATEGY OF PATENTS

The patent system has been overwhelmed by the Law of Disruption. The accelerated pace of innovation in electronic commerce, mobile computing, and social networking has led to a tidal wave of patent applications. In many cases, the claimed "inventions" are so broadly described that they cover the most obvious uses imaginable. Patent examiners, unfamiliar with the basics of digital technology and the scientific literature that defines the art, don't know what to approve.

Examiners are overworked, and many have thrown in the towel. In the United States, examiners are compensated in part based on how many applications they complete. The U.S. Patent Office, funded by filing fees, has every incentive to approve applications and do so quickly. Approving patents takes less time than denying them. Today, 95 percent of all U.S. patent applications are approved, compared to fewer than 65 percent in Japan. In Europe, examiners staged a series of strikes to protest pressure from higher-ups to lower standards and approve more patents.

The Patent Office has effectively outsourced its duties to the market. The market, however, has few mechanisms for fixing mistakes. Applications are generally reviewed without input from competitors or other inventors who may hold better claims to the invention. Once approved, the only way to void a bad patent is to sue the holder. This means that lay juries are now absurdly tasked with evaluating the technical details of everything from computer services to bioengineered drugs. Even after lengthy trials, inappropriate patents may still be upheld. It's no surprise, then, that even after years of litigating and millions of dollars, companies often settle before a verdict is reached. Since judges routinely grant patent holders broad injunctions forbidding the continued use of infringing technologies, competitors are forced to pay anything the patent holder asks in order to stay in business. Adding insult to injury, defendants may spend millions licensing technology they know perfectly well to be worthless.

It's not even clear the patent system did much even when it was working smoothly. A study of innovation over a 150-year period by Harvard Business School professor Josh Lerner found that countries that introduced patent protection showed no gains in overall innovation over countries with weak or even no patent right. Despite increases in the United States to the scope and scale of patent protection, another recent study placed the United States last among forty countries in advances in innovation over the past decade. Adding these facts together, economists and legal scholars conclude the modern patent system does far less to encourage invention innovation than it does to squash it.

The temptation for most executives is simply to ignore the patent system, or to leave its arcane workings to company lawyers. These temptations must be resisted. There has been an explosion in patent grants—well over 100,000 a year in the United States alone. Courts have recently expanded the scope of patent law to include software and "business methods." Patent trolls like NTP buzz around the system like flies, buying up rights with the sole intention of using them to extract tribute from unsuspecting travelers on the road to innovation. As a result, new products and services increasingly infringe upon obscure and even dubious patents, often unknowingly. (Few patent cases allege intentional copying.) As the example of RIM suggests, executives adopting a head-in-the-sand strategy are courting disaster. Every executive, entrepreneur, and, increasingly, consumer needs at least a passing knowledge of patent law.

A patent is a set of exclusive rights granted to an inventor for a fixed period of time. In the United States and most European countries, a patent lasts twenty years. During the exclusive period, only the patent holder may make or use the invention or license others to do so. The patent holder gives up a great deal in exchange for these valuable rights. First, the application must fully disclose the specifics of the invention with enough detail that it can be reproduced by practitioners in his field of expertise. Once a patent expires, the invention becomes part of the public domain. It may then be used by anyone without paying any additional royalties to the inventor.

Patents give inventors time to recover the costs of their work, encouraging what might otherwise be risky investments. Pharmaceutical companies, for example, invest heavily to develop new drugs and rely on patents to be able to charge enough money for their products to earn back their investment. Once their exclusive rights expire, the invention becomes public property. Any manufacturer can duplicate the process and sell the same product. That's how generic versions of drugs can be identical to the original but still sell for much lower prices.

If that description sounds familiar, it should. Congress's patent jurisdiction comes from the same clause of the U.S. Constitution as the power to grant copyrights. Both systems have the same purpose—to encourage innovation. Both copyrights and patents grant a limited monopoly, during which time the owner can control the use of information. Both systems attempt to solve the same economic problem. As a non-rivalrous good, information is difficult to control once it is released to the market. Without protection, competitors could capitalize on the innovation and sell products and services more cheaply than the creator. That in turn would discourage socially beneficial investments.

There, however, the similarities between copyright and patent end. The most important difference between copyright and patent is the interests they protect. With copyright, recall, only the author's unique expression of a particular idea is covered. With patent, the invention itself is off-limits regardless of how other inventors try to duplicate it. Galvanized rubber, the telephone, Prozac—no matter how different the steps another inventor takes to reach the same result, he is forbidden during the patent period to exploit the fruits of his own labor. This is true even if the second inventor reached the same results without any knowledge of the first. Under current patent law, whoever first made the discovery is the inventor and the only one entitled to patent it.

These differences explain why patents are so much harder to secure than copyright. Patents encourage innovation, but they also constrain it. Knowing that another inventor is working on the same problem may put off others who, if they don't solve it first, will lose the value of all their work.

Protecting a basic invention, such as a drug, discourages others who may have come up with a cheaper version, or who could make a significant improvement to it.

For patents, the balancing act between incentives for inventors and protection of the public domain is taken seriously. Copyrights are granted automatically, without the need to file any paperwork. Patents, on the other hand, are granted only after considerable review and scrutiny. The duration of the patent period is also much shorter, giving inventors a limited window during which they can recover their investment. Indeed, one of the requirements for a patent is that the application fully disclose the discovery, so that once the patent expires any competitor can make free use of the documents submitted by the patentee to duplicate the invention.

To limit the damage that comes from giving such powerful monopolies, the patent application process discourages all but the most serious inventors. Applications must be prepared by specialized attorneys and may cost as much as $30,000. The filed applications are then reviewed by professionals in the field employed by the Patent Office, who apply a variety of tests to ensure the discovery qualifies for protection. The review may take years to complete. Competing inventors and others with an interest in the invention may file objections or even request the office reconsider patents after they have been granted.

There are other important conditions that must be satisfied before a patent is granted. Briefly, these include:

- *Patentable subject matter*—The patent must be for an invention such as the lightbulb or the cotton gin, not an abstract idea such as Einstein's equation "$E=MC^2$" or the discovery of a previously unknown plant or animal.
- *Utility*—The invention must do what it claims to do, and must have at least some beneficial use to society. One cannot patent a perpetual motion machine, since such machines do not work.
- *Novelty*—The invention must be new. The Patent Office searches through the relevant literature of the field, known in patent lingo as the "prior art," to ensure the invention has not already been used or described by someone else.

- *Nonobviousness*—The invention must be more than simply new; it must represent some kind of inventive breakthrough. If another inventor in the field would have considered the invention so obvious that he would not bother to patent it, the application will be denied.
- *Description and enablement*—The application must describe the invention in sufficient detail to allow other inventors in the same field to duplicate it once the patent expires. This requirement also ensures the patent does not cover more than the inventor actually created.

PATENT REFORM PENDING

Thanks to the Law of Disruption, the pace of innovation is accelerating. Constrained by the very human limits of the Patent Office staff, the system has reached a crisis point. Business leaders, legislators, and judges all agree that change is essential, but no one can agree on what to do. As Mark Twain once said, "Everyone talks about the weather, but nobody does anything about it."

In the past twenty years, there has been an explosion in the number of applications submitted to patent offices worldwide. Applications have doubled in the past ten years. The U.S. Patent Office alone has a backlog of more than 600,000 applications, many in fields related to digital life. The increased volume has led to the careless awarding of many wildly inappropriate patents. One estimate found that a company wanting to offer a new online product or service would need to first review more than 4,000 patents, many of them ridiculously broad. The existence of these bad patents adds uncertainty, risk, and transaction costs to the kind of innovation the system is supposed to encourage.

Even some of the principal beneficiaries of the current system, including senior executives at Amazon, IBM, Google, and Cisco Systems, are calling for change. Despite holding 10,000 patents itself, Microsoft is one of the loudest voices calling for an overhaul. The reason is obvious. From 2004 to 2007, the company spent $1.5 billion licensing other companies' patents. In 2007, the company was hit with an astonishing $1.5 billion verdict in a dispute with Alcatel-Lucent over rights to use the MP3 music-compression protocol, a verdict that was later overturned. Microsoft still faces a $512 million verdict for another piece of the same litigation. All told, the company spends nearly $100 million annually in legal fees to defend itself in patent-infringement lawsuits.

You'd think with that kind of consensus, patent reform would be easy. But the only thing that the parties can agree upon is that the current system doesn't work. In 2005, the European Parliament spent four years trying to unify Europe's discordant patent systems, which cost inventors ten times more in fees than their counterparts in the United States or Japan. Legislators couldn't agree whether or how to grant computer-related patents, however, and abandoned the effort. The EU revived the discussion in 2007, and managed to pass a patent revision law in 2008 that introduced what legislators admitted were "a considerable number of smaller amendments."

In the United States, Congress began deliberations on patent reform in 2005. If passed, the Patent Reform Act would make significant changes both to the process by which patents are awarded and to how courts deal with challenges to them. Competing lobbyists representing the two largest communities of innovators—information technology and biological technology—always manage a stalemate. Information technology companies want to limit damages; biotech companies do not. The effort has stalled every year. (The bill was reintroduced in early 2009.)

Still, no one imagines any version of patent reform under consideration would do anything but slow the system's accelerating race to disaster, especially as it applies to information technology. IT is different from more established fields. Unlike chemistry and manufacturing, prior art is not easily found in a few established journals but is instead scattered across Web sites, blogs, and other online publications. Until recently, Patent Office employees had minimal access to nonprint sources. After major court decisions opened the floodgates for patents on software and business processes, the Patent Office was overwhelmed with applications. Claims for basic inventions including video streaming, pop-up windows, and paying with a credit card online were granted. None of the proposed reforms do anything to fix these problems.

In the absence of meaningful reform from lawmakers, efforts to bring the patent system into better alignment with the realities of digital life have devolved into vigilante justice. In response to what it characterized as "crimes against the public domain," the Electronic Frontier Foundation launched a

Patent Busting Project to document and then challenge the most dangerous software and Internet-related patents. Its Web site displays a hit list of the most outrageous IT-related patents awarded (wanted for "willful ignorance of prior art" and "egregious displays of obviousness"), based on more than two hundred candidates submitted by outraged lawyers, researchers, and industry experts.

So far the project has managed to revoke one of its "ten most wanted," radio giant ClearChannel's patent for recording a concert and immediately posting it to a Web site for sale as a download. EFF discovered evidence that another company had invented the claimed technology a year before ClearChannel, defeating the company's claim of novelty. In 2006, the Patent Office canceled the application.

Five other offenders, including patents for online gaming and digital music encoding, are now being reexamined. Number one on the hit list, however, a patent that covers "the transmission and receipt of digital content via the Internet, cable, satellite and other means," is still on the books. Acacia Research, the holder of the patent, has threatened dozens of Web sites, claiming ownership of all streaming technology that delivers movies, documents, and other large files. EFF describes the patent as "laughably broad." "Broad is not necessarily bad," countered the company's general counsel.

A few superficial victories, however, can hardly stem the tide. Bad patents clog the system, frustrating innovation across the board. One 2001 study found that almost half of all granted patents that were litigated to a decisive conclusion were held to be invalid—that is, they should never have been awarded. Before 1982, 65 percent of all infringement cases litigated to the very end held the patents in question to be invalid. That year, in order to unify U.S. patent law, Congress channeled all patent appeals to a newly created court, the Federal Circuit. Although the FC has proven to be much friendlier to patent holders, a study of its first ten years of operation found that 33 percent of the time it too invalidated patents being asserted against an alleged infringer.

The slow pace of litigation is ill-matched in any event to solve problems of innovation developing at the speed of the Law of Disruption. Competitors are left with the expensive choice of paying royalties to an undeserving patent holder or spending perhaps millions to have the patent overturned by the Patent Office or by the courts. Since the 1980s, patent litigation has tripled. More than one hundred companies are involved in suits just for text-messaging patents. One estimate suggests patent lawsuits in the United States alone cost more than $2 billion a year. According to some studies, the expense of litigation in patent infringement cases now outweighs all the profits earned from valid patents. But to paraphrase a famous Chicago politician, the patent system ain't ready for reform yet.

POOLS AND TROLLS

In the face of potentially lethal patent lawsuits, businesses have developed a number of strategies to reduce their risks. To hedge the risks of patent abuse, leading companies in a variety of industries increasingly trade their collections of good and bad patents with each other, a maneuver known as cross-licensing. Samsung and Sony, for example, cross-licensed thousands of patents the two Asian companies hold, both to avoid future litigation against each other and to provide ammunition against other companies who sue either company. Microsoft has signed such deals with a dozen of its major competitors, including Sun, Nokia, and Apple, though notably not with Linux operating system vendors, including Red Hat, or more direct competitors such as Google and Oracle.

In a growing number of industries, multiple competitors have thrown all their patents for a particular technology into a common pool. Patent pools ward off lawsuits and limit the complexity of negotiating with multiple patent holders when new uses for existing technologies are developed. Pools generally offer access to all the patents in them using a single royalty schedule. Film and music industry companies created a DRM pool in 2005, for example. Cisco, Intel, Sprint Nextel, and other communication giants agreed to pool all their patents related to WiMax technology, a proposed standard for the next generation of wireless communications. The existence of the pool makes the standard more attractive to the industry, because royalty rates are known up front and the chance of patent litigation is reduced.

Patent pools improve economic efficiency by lowering transaction costs for everyone. They can also solve difficult bargaining problems. When two participants in a negotiation can deal only with each other, the likelihood of agreeing on a price is very slim. Why? The patent holder knows that the licensee cannot create his product without a license, but in many cases the licensee may be the only company interested in using the patent. If many individual patents are required, each owner may hold out for the top price, knowing that without his patent the entire venture will fail. Patent pools avoid some of the gridlock that might otherwise occur in these negotiations.

There's a fine line, however, between patent pooling and patent trolling. Trolls such as NTP buy up blocks of unused and often dubious patents and look for opportunities to extort value from them by suing companies that may or may not be infringing. In 2004, information technology companies were shocked to learn that a small software and consulting firm named DE Technologies had received a patent on "international commerce handled by computer," effectively covering all of electronic commerce. DE first sued Dell Computers, which sells its PCs and laptops almost exclusively online. (The two companies settled privately in 2007.) Other seemingly obvious patents involved in recent litigation include patents for digital distribution of audio and video (Apple, Google, and Napster were sued) and a patent granted to Singapore-based Creative Technology Ltd. for graphical user interfaces that allow users to play digital entertainment on portable devices (with Apple again in the crosshairs).

For patent trolls, getting the patents is the easy part. After that, they must clear several hurdles before they can extract payment from companies actively marketing products and services. The victims are likely to challenge the validity of the patents, both with the Patent Office and in court, and may assert patents of their own or those they have cross-licensed or pooled. Patent defendants may also claim "inequitable" behavior by the patent holder, including hiding known prior art, which can lead to the loss of the patent outright. In other cases, one side may simply have more money to spend on litigation than the other, winning a war not on the merits but by attrition.

The difference between a patent troll and a victimized entrepreneur is often in the eye of the beholder. Consider chip-design firm Rambus, which holds more than seven hundred patents (another five hundred are pending) for technologies that speed the performance of memory chips. Unlike patent holding companies such as NTP, Rambus engineers actually develop their own technology. But the company does not build its own chips, preferring to license their innovations to other chip makers, including Intel and Sony. Over the past ten years, however, the company has been increasingly focused on litigation against alleged infringers. Rambus claims it is protecting its assets from unlicensed use. Its adversaries say Rambus is an industry parasite. History will have to decide who is right.

Regardless of what you call it, one response to epidemic patent litigation has been the formation of defensive cartels, which buy up unused patents just to keep them out of the hands of trolls. One example is Allied Security Trust, whose members include Verizon, Google, and Hewlett-Packard. The trust, unlike a patent troll, does not assert its patents against other companies. Instead, it secures licenses for its members, and then "releases" the patents back to the market. Allied is run as a nonprofit, but venture capital–backed RPX Corp., another defensive cartel, charges membership fees based on the size of its subscribers. RPX's members receive full access to the patents RPX acquires. By late 2008, the start-up had already signed up fifteen members. "At thousands of members," according to the company's chief executive, "I think it's a game-changing business."

Patent trolls also plague open-source software developers, especially when patents are asserted against large numbers of users all sharing the same technology for core business activities. In response to proliferating lawsuits being brought against Linux users, the nonprofit Linux Defenders has adopted an aggressive response. Under a Patent Office program called "Peer-to-Patent," the group connects members of the Linux community to patent examiners, helping them identify prior art. The hope is that fewer bad patents will be issued in the first place. Linux Defenders also helps inventors publish their work to ensure that it becomes part of the public domain before nonparticipants apply for patents.

THE MIRACULOUS BIRTH AND UNHAPPY, SHORT LIFE OF BUSINESS PATENTS

Beyond these modest reforms by the affected industries, courts have also made efforts to better align patent law with the realities of digital life. Much of that activity centers on decisions by the U.S. Court of Appeals for the Federal Circuit. Like the FCC and other agencies, however, the court has adopted a client-service mentality, believing that its job is to serve its customers rather than interpret the law. Legal scholars believe the court has become the victim of "regulatory capture." The result has been a series of important precedents that have been widely criticized as too protective of patent holders.

The U.S. Supreme Court, in response, has begun to rein in the worst excesses of the FC's expansive view of patent law. Consider a recent case that pitted online marketplace eBay against MercExchange, a small patent holding company. MercExchange holds a number of patents it claims give the company ownership of the idea for online auctions although the company has never actually offered any auction services. After negotiations to sell the patents to eBay failed, MercExchange sued. In 2003 a jury found that some eBay features, including the "Buy It Now" option to end an auction early, infringed on the MercExchange patents, and MercExchange was awarded $35 million. The trial judge, however, refused to issue an injunction barring eBay from continuing to use the infringing features. Such injunctions had become standard practice in patent infringement cases, and MercExchange appealed the decision to the FC. The appellate court reversed, ordering the lower court judge to issue the injunction.

EBay appealed to the Supreme Court. Injunctions, the Court found, should not be issued every time there is a finding of infringement. Four of the justices were particularly critical of the practice when it was applied in favor of companies that don't make competing goods. If a plaintiff's business is simply to license its patents, they concluded, an injunction is not necessary. When "the threat of an injunction is employed simply for undue leverage" in negotiations over license fees, they wrote, money damages are all the patent holder should get.

The automatic rule, which the FC had endorsed, was a critical weapon for patent trolls seeking quick settlements. The grant of an injunction, as we saw in the Blackberry case, can be fatal regardless of the merits of the patents involved. Without the injunction, further litigation became less attractive to MercExchange. In early 2008, eBay purchased outright the three patents it was found to have infringed, and the parties settled privately. By 2007, a reexamination by the Patent Office found that every one of MercExchange's 265 auction patents were invalid on the grounds of obviousness. MercExchange is appealing.

A bigger patent issue has recently preoccupied the FC. To what extent, if any, do innovative new ways of doing business deserve patent protection?

This is a particularly important issue for entrepreneurs riding the curve of the Law of Disruption. Internet businesses, after all, often come to venture investors armed with little more than an idea. They promise to offer traditional products and services online, perhaps, or a new way to use new technology to strategically change the rules of an industry. Pets.com, eToys.com, and thousands of other early e-commerce Web sites, for example, sold items online that were traditionally purchased in big-box stores or specialty retailers. Banner ads, targeted marketing, social networking, animated Web sites—all of these innovations clearly built on the existing technology and traditional business methods, combined in clever and often compelling new ways made possible by advances in the development of digital life. Which of these innovations deserve patent protection?

Until recently, most patent scholars assumed the answer was none of the above. Although the Patent Act defines the subject matter of patents to be any new "process, machine, manufacture, or composition of matter," courts had long held that "process" in patent law didn't mean what it did in common usage. Abstract ideas and paper-and-pencil systems including business forms, algorithms, and other "mental steps" are all processes, but all were considered outside the scope of patent. That conclusion followed common sense. Some of the innovations we've just seen, including "selling goods over the Internet" or "converting recordings of live concerts for sale online," are likely, if patented, to severely restrict future innovation. Generic business ideas don't "do" anything concrete, the way a machine or a chemical process, the traditional domains of patent, does. Without being tied to anything specific, processes can potentially apply to anything, including technology on the near horizon.

Under this view, the Patent Office and the courts routinely rejected applications that claimed either methods of doing business or inventions that took the form of computer software. In the famous *Benson* case from 1972, for example, the Supreme Court rejected patent protection for a program that transformed binary-coded decimal numerals into pure binary code—converting the binary representation of a "1" next to "2" to "12" in binary. The program, critical to the efficient execution of nearly any computer, was described not as a program implemented in software but through the written description of the algorithm claimed by its inventor. The patent, if upheld, would have covered the algorithm's use on any "general purpose" computer.

Sensibly, the Court rejected the claim as too broadly defined. Since the algorithm had no practical use other than in computing, allowing the patent "would wholly pre-empt the mathematical formula and in practical effect would be a patent on the algorithm itself." The Court was concerned not only about the breadth of Benson's patent claim but also its implementation. The application described only what might be thought of as the "mental steps" a human being would use to solve the same problem.

Allowing patents that mimicked mental steps, the Court worried, would invite a raft of unsolvable institutional problems. Could a defendant be sued for thinking the algorithm? How would a patent examiner find "prior art" for a process that may have been used for generations but never written down? Although rarely expressed, such concerns can always be found lurking in the background of patent disputes involving information technology. It is one reason even average consumers react viscerally to the idea that a method or a program can be given protection. Had Benson's patent survived, it's hard to imagine the information revolution of the past thirty-five years taking place at all.

The Supreme Court did not go so far as to say software could never be patented, however. "It is said we freeze process patents to old technologies," the Court noted, "leaving no room for the revelations of the new, onrushing technology. Such is not our purpose." With the door to broader patent coverage cracked open, inventors looked for opportunities to force it all the way. In a 1981 case, for example, a well-known equation for determining the perfect temperature for curing rubber had been implemented in real-time sensors. When the sensors determined that the right temperature had been reached, the mold was opened automatically. Rather than requesting a patent on the equation, as Benson did, the inventor here claimed a patent on the implementation of the equation in hardware and software—the mold and the program that operated the sensor. In the Benson case, the transformation was abstract. Here, the invention used software to effect a physical transformation—opening the mold. With that difference, the Court held, the patent was valid.

But if software that caused a mold to open could be patented, what about software that merely changed the behavior of the computer itself—perhaps by changing the status of its circuitry, as all software does? In early computers, software turned on or off the vacuum tubes that represented the numbers in a calculation. Today, it effects billions of changes a second to the status of an individual circuit's "logic gates"—indeed, in computer jargon, opening and closing the gates. Benson hadn't addressed his claim to any particular computing environment. With that mistake corrected, what held back the deluge?

In 1998, the Federal Circuit gave a surprising answer. Nothing.

In the now infamous State Street case, Signature Financial Group claimed a system that automated a particular strategy for reducing risk in mutual funds. The system allowed the manager of a group of different funds to combine their assets into a single investment portfolio organized as a partnership. The system had two benefits. It reduced administrative overhead, and it allowed the funds to take advantage of tax benefits accorded to partnerships. Based on that description, the patent seems a likely candidate for rejection. The system made no change to any concrete thing in the physical world, and consisted mostly of mental steps. The assets were already being tracked by software. The additional programming to group them together was trivial.

The FC did not actually hold the patent valid. It did, however, reject the long-held belief that examiners should categorically reject all applications that claimed new business innovations, whether implemented in software or not. So long as such methods produced "useful, tangible, and concrete results," the court held, there was no reason to assume them unpatentable. The lower court was ordered to reconsider the patents under all the traditional tests. But the parties privately settled the case without any further proceedings.

If early cases had cracked open the dam that held back software and business-method patents, State Street was the tsunami that threw aside everything in its path. Not only did it clear away some of the old prejudices against software patents, but in a stroke it erased an even older rejection of patents for business methods. Such categorical exceptions, the State Street case held, had no basis in the patent law.

The response to the State Street case was immediate and dramatic. The Patent Office was flooded with business-method applications, from fewer than 1,000 in 1997 to more than 11,000 in 2007. With little guidance from the FC or the Supreme Court on how to evaluate them, examiners erred on the side of absurdity. Patents were granted for everything from "methods of training janitors to dust and vacuum using video displays" to "methods for enticing customers to order additional food at a fast food restaurant." Patents were allowed for encouraging cats to exercise using a laser pointer and for reserving office bathrooms. Inevitably, U.S. Patent No. 6049811 was granted—a patent on the method for obtaining a patent.

Not surprisingly, the most troubling business-method patent cases all involve digital life. Amazon.com, for example, was famously granted a patent for its "one-click" purchase feature, which allowed previously registered users to order individual items by simply clicking a single button on a screen. Traditional bookstore chain Barnes & Noble's Web site had a similar feature called "Express Lane." In 1999, as Barnes & Noble struggled to keep up with Amazon's rapid online growth, Amazon sued for patent infringement. A lower court quickly issued an injunction forbidding Barnes & Noble from using its Express Lane service. In 2001, however, the FC reversed, holding that the injunction should not have been granted. The appellate court agreed with Barnes & Noble that a pre-Internet online ordering system from CompuServe should have been considered as prior art that might invalidate the Amazon patent.

The parties settled without the patent ever being decisively tested. No matter. In the gaps created by the Law of Disruption, even a loss can be a win. All Amazon wanted in the first place was to cripple Barnes & Noble during the particularly important online holiday shopping season in 1999. The injunction did just that. The then start-up company was able to establish its dominance as the leading online bookstore, a wound from which Barnes & Noble never recovered. The injunction, wrongly granted as it turns out, put Barnes & Noble further behind Amazon.

Other business-method patents of dubious quality have likewise been used to gain a strategic advantage, perhaps unfairly. Playing the slow pace of litigation off the accelerating speed of digital life and its rapid evolution, patents can be more valuable as legal weapons than as protection for real innovation. Interim rulings, for example, supported TiVo's claim against other DVR manufacturers to technology that allows viewers to pause, fast-forward, or rewind television programs; Netflix's claim to the idea of online home video rentals against Blockbuster; and patents asserted by IBM against Amazon for core features of the concept of electronic commerce. Each win, even those later overturned, provided the patent holder with a valuable, sometimes priceless, bargaining chip: time.

That's the real problem with business-method patents. Most are unlikely to survive the drawn-out process, as long as ten years or more, of final determinations through the Patent Office and the courts. Tactical advantages are frequently the only value they provide. That value, however, is substantial. Although most of these cases end in private settlements, those accused of patent infringement often pay millions of dollars to make the lawsuits go away quickly, before injunctions shut down the whole business. Extracting such tribute can only encourage other "infringers" to cave in early and often.

Fortunately, the FC, perhaps in response to the criticism of the Supreme Court and others, seems to have regained its senses. Two recent cases in particular have dramatically scaled back the State Street decision. Several of the court's judges have now indicated they believe State Street—and business-method patents with it—should be relegated to the dustbin of history. The first case, from 2007, involved attorney Stephen W. Comiskey, author of a legal-career guide called *A Good Lawyer®: Secrets Good Lawyers (and Their Best Clients) Already Know*. Comiskey claimed a patent for his technique of managing the process of legal arbitrations, a claim the Patent Office rejected as obvious. Comiskey appealed, but the FC concluded that the patent examiner should never have reviewed the details of the claim in the first place. The arbitration system at issue depended "entirely on the use of mental processes," and was thus outside the scope of patent protection.

Comiskey had relied on the earlier ruling in State Street. But the State Street decision, the court reminded Comiskey, did not offer open-ended approval for such patents. All it did was erase the blanket prohibition against such patents. For business method claims to advance, inventors still needed something more—perhaps much more—than an abstract idea. The arbitration system Comiskey proposed did nothing. It did not make use of any machinery, nor did it effect the composition of matter in the physical world. It was merely the set of mental steps necessary to organize an efficient, well-run arbitration. Business methods, like any other patent, must describe an invention that effects some tangible change in the physical world. It must be "embodied in, operate on, [or] transform." It must, in other words, *do something*.

The Comiskey case was a shocking reversal by the FC, and its strong language raised serious doubts about the survival of any of more than 40,000 business-method patents applied for in the wake of the State Street case.

There was more to come. In late 2008, the court decided another business-method case involving Bernard Bilski, who claimed in 1997 to have invented a system for hedging the risks involved in commodities trading. Bilski's process was simple and, one might think, obvious. When a commodities trader makes a contract to sell goods at a fixed price in the future, he also executes a second set of hedging transactions that minimize the risk that the fixed price will prove too low. The patent claimed no calculations, nor did it make use of computers. On the surface, the process seemed to describe more or less what commodities traders had been doing for decades, dressed up in flowcharts and the elaborate language of patent applications.

After ten years, the Patent Office denied Bilski's patent. Bilski appealed to the FC, where something unusual happened. After a panel of three judges heard arguments, the full court decided on its own to rehear the case "en banc," meaning all twelve judges presided together. Such moves often signal that the court is considering a significant change in the law. That is precisely what happened. Bilski's claim, the full court concluded, was no good, but not because it was obvious. Bilski wanted a patent on a method of doing business, and business methods are outside the scope of patent protection. After ten years of flirting with broader rules for business-method patents, the court decided to call the whole thing off.

To be eligible for a patent, a majority of the court now agreed, a claimed process had to be implemented on a particular machine or transform some physical object from one state to another. The correct rule, in other words, was precisely the one announced in 1972 in the Benson case (the case where the Supreme Court rejected the binary-conversion algorithm). Business methods could not in most cases be patented. Several cases suggesting otherwise were now discredited or even overruled. From sacrilege to sanctity and now back again, business method patents had come full circle.

The Benson test, the court notes, isn't perfect. It's just the best one judges have to work with. "Future developments in technology and the sciences may present difficult challenges to the machine-or-transformation test," the FC admitted, "just as the widespread use of computers and the advent of the Internet has begun to challenge it in the past decade." Blurring the line between abstract ideas and the information technology that puts it into commercial use may lead Congress or the Supreme Court to ultimately decide "to alter or perhaps even set aside this test to accommodate emerging technologies." But for now, the war was over, and the FC was surrendering unconditionally.

The decision to reject business-method patents makes good sense. In the fast-moving world of digital commerce, entrepreneurs have all the incentives they need to experiment and invent. The Law of Disruption rapidly transforms ideas into applications. The cost of failure is, thanks to Moore's Law, relatively low. Investors are still eager to buy companies on the basis of little more than a good idea. If nothing else, separating the truly novel and inventive from the obvious and banal had proven far more work than the Patent Office and the courts could handle. Patents for business methods encouraged litigation, not innovation. The Law of Disruption had overcome the law of patents.

With business-method patents put to rest, the FC returned to the question of patents for software. Clearly, programs that merely implemented a business idea into a computer system were unpatentable. Comiskey's claimed system used the Internet to register participants and track the progress of an arbitration, but these trivial applications did not save his claim. The court had earlier held that using a computer to automate some or even all of an otherwise unpatentable business method does not satisfy the "machine or transformation" test. An inventor cannot save a business-method claim, in other words, by implementing it more or less arbitrarily in software.

Fair enough, but what about more elaborate uses of software? How about the touch-screen interface of the iPhone or the use of sensors to measure exercise performance on the Wii Fit? Does a claim that addresses itself to a specific technical environment satisfy the requirement of implementation on a particular "machine"? Likewise, does using software to change the appearance of information on a screen transform "matter" from one state to the other? From the standpoint of information technology, did the rejection of business methods really mean anything at all?

Unfortunately, the FC's answer in the Bilski case was no answer at all. "The raw materials of many information-age processes," the court wrote, "are electronically-manipulated data. Which, if any, of these processes qualify as a transformation or reduction of an article into a different state or thing constituting patent-eligible subject matter?" That's the right question, but the answer was a pure legal dodge. "Our case law has taken a measured approach to this question," the majority concluded, "and we see no reason here to expand the boundaries of what constitutes patent-eligible transformations of articles." In other words, read our cases, *other than those we've just overruled*, and you'll see what does and does not constitute patentable software.

The U.S. Supreme Court has agreed to review the Bilski case, but the real answer likely waits for another day and another case.

FAST-FORWARD: THE NEW PATENT SYSTEM

The reason that courts are unable to deal effectively with information technology has nothing to do with patent law. It has everything to do with the nature of computing. Under the Law of Disruption, computing technology evolves and mutates at a remarkable speed. Innovators spit out new products at an accelerated pace. The law—slow, methodical, and reactive—can't keep up. The Bilski decision was right to conclude that it's better for the court to do nothing and return patent law to where it was before the Internet. Artificially slowing innovation to the speed of lawsuits was just making things worse.

Here is what judges, lawmakers, and commentators all miss. Like the steam engine, computers are simply machines that make other machines. Just as steam drove the Industrial Revolution, the computer is driving the information revolution. Computing visionary Charles Babbage even described his late-nineteenth-century design as a general-purpose "analytical engine." On its own, a computer does nothing. Programmed through software, computers can perform an amazing range of activities, often simultaneously—calculating, animating, entertaining, conducting business transactions—all at a fraction of the transaction costs of the real-world counterparts of these same activities.

A computer is a fundamentally new kind of machine. One minute it's a word processor and the next a thermostat regulator; even better, sometimes it's both at the same time. The combination of general hardware and specific software turns the computer into a virtual machine. These are the features of computing technology that drive the creation of our new digital life.

Unfortunately, these features have confounded courts trying to decide whether or how to protect computing applications under patent law. Since their invention, computers have been programmed to perform thousands of useful, nonobvious, and novel tasks. Despite the exponential growth of the information economy, technology innovation does and will continue to need the kind of incentives that the patent process provides. Not to make a few individuals or corporations rich, but to get as many useful new inventions into the public domain as efficiently as possible. Judges are ill-equipped to decide which virtual machines deserve patent protection and which do not. After ten years of trying to tease out general rules from individual cases, the Federal Circuit simply gave up.

Trying to shoehorn software into the language of patent law leads time and again to linguistic mess. Patent expertise aside, federal judges struggle just to understand what software is and how it operates. The result is a dangerous gap between law and reality. Consider one of the Supreme Court's most recent patent decisions involving software. A special provision of the Patent Act extends what is otherwise U.S.-only protection to products made abroad when an infringer supplies "components" from the United States. AT&T claimed that its speech-compression patent was infringed upon by part of the Windows operating system, and sued Microsoft for damages based on the number of imported PCs on which Windows was preinstalled. Even though no physical component supplied from the United States was ever made part of a foreign PC, AT&T argued that software "in the abstract" should be considered a "component" under patent law. Not so, said the Court. Although Microsoft may send master disks to PC manufacturers outside the United States, those disks are like "blueprints," or "the notes of a symphony." They are instructions, not components in the conventional sense of the word. They are not "supplied" from the United States because they never become part of any product. The master disks are simply used to make copies of the software.

When legal rules confront revolutionary technology, reasoning by analogy just doesn't work. Software is not a blueprint, nor is it a musical score. Software is software, a unique, remarkable, new kind of thing that needs its own law, not clever (or not-so-clever) metaphors. As Brooks Adams said it so perfectly a hundred years ago, "You can no more reason from highway precedents to railway law than you can reason from the ox to the electric battery."

Courts are not designed to resolve the kind of mess that patent law has become. Unfortunately, legislators just look the other way. Terrified by America's unhinged experiment with business-method patents, the European Parliament spent years negotiating a directive that categorically rejected them from European patent systems. Bogged down in details, the EU gave up. Congress has failed for years to pass patent reform legislation. These were only superficial reforms, in any case. No one wants to touch the problem of the virtual machine.

The solution isn't to eliminate patent protection for information technology. It is to recognize, as elsewhere, that information is different. A piece of software might be developed in weeks and have a useful commercial life measured in months. It is not the same kind of invention as a bioengineered drug to treat Alzheimer's disease, which may cost a pharmaceutical company billions to get right. Today, both inventions get the same protection. Worse, software is protected both by patent (the invention) and by copyright (the particular expression in software code). A patent lasts twenty years, but copyright protection can last nearly a century.

What's needed instead is a specific form of patent protection that is far less generous and far more judiciously granted than in today's system. Virtual machines need virtual lubrication. To be patentable, innovations including software should be required to address a specific technological environment and result in a change to some physical matter beyond just the circuits of the computer itself. Amazon CEO Jeff Bezos has called for software patents that last only three to five years, a restriction he would make retroactive to existing grants. That's a good start. Once a patent expires, moreover, the former holders must be banned from extending their rights by claiming copyright in those programs. Following existing patent law, they should go into the public domain.

Beyond the "machine or transformation" test, each of the other requirements for patentability must be met. Today, the Patent Office routinely grants patents for software based on nothing more than a few flowcharts. Although this practice has yet to be challenged in court, it flies in the face of the requirement that a patentee fully disclose his invention. How can a patent leave out what might be millions of lines of code and still be duplicated once the patent expires? Only a patent office that doesn't understand IT could imagine the average programmer reproducing the code from flowcharts once the patent expires.

The incentives for patent trolls also need to be greatly reduced. For one thing, mandatory licensing should be required, eliminating the "life or death" litigation that nearly wiped out RIM. Both IBM and Microsoft have called for and implemented open licensing of their patents to any and all comers willing to pay predetermined royalty rates. This practice not only generates revenue but also limits the likelihood that either company will use their patents to stifle competition from smaller companies and start-ups. The cross-licensing and pooling of patents need to be evaluated much more carefully under antitrust principles than they currently are.

No one believes any of this is happening now. But until legislatures take over the job of patent reform from the courts and face head-on the special nature of IT, the complaints will just get louder. The costs for inventors, IT giants, and most of all the inhabitants of digital life will soar higher. Fortunately, the Law of Disruption generates so much excess social value that the waste associated with the current patent mess is more than outweighed by the benefits generated by the work of entrepreneurs and other innovators. So far, anyway.

In the end, virtual machine patents may prove to be more trouble than they are worth. After all, we got by without them just fine in the first fifty years of the computing revolution. For much of that time there wasn't even copyright protection for software. In the future, inventors can continue to rely on the short cycle times of the Law of Disruption to protect their up-front investments and earn back a return that encourages them to continue innovating. In the absence of meaningful reform, we'd be just as well off to have no software-related patents at all.

Maybe the market can solve this dilemma. Maybe the same entrepreneurs whose inventions shape digital life can innovate a better system of incentives and protections, maximizing our ability to take optimal advantage of the Law of Disruption. Maybe, in fact, there's already a better solution for dealing with software and the other technologies of the digital age. That, in any case, is the subject to which we now turn.

Law Nine: Software

Open Always Wins . . . Eventually

The law of software is full of surprises. At least four different systems—patents, copyright, licensing, and the barter economy of open source—apply to its creation and use. The last has been gaining in popularity, despite its reliance on platitudes from the consciousness-raising movements of the 1960s. At least online, communal collaboration actually works. In the past several years, open-source licensing has migrated from operating system and other basic software to applications, user-generated content, and even fields of science including biology and mathematics. A closer look at exactly how this parallel economy works reveals a surprising reliance on traditional property rights, suggesting that its proponents aren't quite ready to give up on capitalism after all.

The Nine Lives of a Lawsuit

There's a scourge running loose in the Linux community.

Linux, an operating system that competes with Microsoft's Windows and others, was launched in 1992 by Linus Torvalds. Rather than develop a commercial product, Torvalds created Linux on the "open source" model. Anyone may use Linux without paying a fee to Torvalds or anyone else. The one condition, however, is that users must donate any enhancements they make back to the core product. The approach has been wildly successful. Thousands of developers have contributed to the system, which now commands nearly 15 percent of the worldwide market for host computers.

Linux was designed to mimic an older operating system called UNIX, which was sold commercially by AT&T in the 1970s and later by IBM, Hewlett-Packard, and others. That's where the SCO Group comes in. SCO, which sold commercial versions of UNIX, acquired rights to the product from Novell, which had acquired them from AT&T. But UNIX has been rapidly losing customers to Linux. So in 2003, SCO launched a barrage of lawsuits, including one against IBM that sought $1 billion in damages. SCO claims that companies embracing Linux had previously sworn allegiance to UNIX. In making the switch to Linux, these companies violated contractual obligations made to SCO or its predecessors.

Since filing its initial suit, SCO has added additional defendants and spent at least $35 million on litigation. Even though the company has yet to prove its claims, SCO has also pressured hundreds of corporate Linux users to purchase "licenses" from them. These licenses would cover whatever interest SCO may or may not have in Linux—a kind of immunity in the event that SCO wins its case. The litigation has transformed SCO from a software company to an insurance firm, insurance being a nice way of describing what this really looks like: a protection racket.

The Byzantine litigation took a crucial turn in 2007, when a federal judge ruled that Novell and not SCO owns the UNIX source code. If this ruling stands (an appeal is still pending), SCO's copyright infringement claims against Linux developers and users will disappear and a significant legal cloud over the Linux pedigree will lift. The technology press and hundreds of bloggers were quick to seize the judge's 102-page opinion as a resolution of the four-year-old conflict. "The ruling," the *Wall Street Journal* proclaimed, "is a boon to the 'open source' software movement and to Linux."

Hardly. First of all, it's not a win. As we've seen throughout this book, interim rulings by lower courts are almost never the last word in lawsuits, especially complex, well-funded commercial disputes. Aspects of the case still have to be resolved by trial. Then there will be at least one if not two levels of appeals, which may lead to remands or outright reversal of some or all of the judge's rulings. In most cases, the parties reach a settlement before the litigation process ends. Although a favorable ruling from the trial judge certainly carries weight in the negotiations, it is no more definite than the first estimate you might get for a car repair or a kitchen remodel.

Within a month of the 2007 ruling, SCO declared bankruptcy, putting the litigation on hold. Again the press declared the end of the SCO threat. Again, they were premature. In early 2008, a private equity firm offered to buy up the remains of the company, which is to say the remains of the lawsuit, promising up to $100 million in new funding. The deal fell through, leaving SCO in bankruptcy court. In January 2009, the company, hanging on by a thread, filed a reorganization plan with the court. It is still seeking new funding.

Even if SCO finally dies or Novell's ownership of UNIX is ultimately affirmed, potential Linux users still have cause for concern. Novell supports Linux these days, but strategies change, companies merge, and assets can be sold. If Linux really does include large chunks of UNIX or other proprietary source code, copyright infringement claims might someday, like the phoenix, rise again.

THE CONTU CALAMITY

The real problem for Linux, of which the SCO litigation is only a symptom, is the absurd level of protection that copyright law affords to software. It may surprise you to learn that until 1976, there was no copyright for software at all. In a poorly reasoned shift, Congress that year extended to programmers the same rights previously given only to authors of books, music, and artwork. Among other protections, programmers enjoy the privileges we reviewed earlier, including the exclusive right to reproduce their code during their lifetime plus another seventy years. But in the fifty-year history of software, no program has ever lasted longer than a decade or two at the most. The commercial value of any code written thus far in software's short history will end long before the copyrights expire.

Among all the artifacts of digital life, software is unique. It is the basic building material through which new applications are created, making otherwise inert computer hardware do something other than hum. It is infinitely plastic, malleable, and adaptable to an amazing variety of tasks. It can control equipment, render three-dimensional movies in lifelike quality, and crunch its way through billions of calculations without getting bored. Software today is written in more than 2,500 different languages. Its versatility makes it perhaps the most important invention of the twentieth century.

Software is unique from a legal standpoint as well. It is the only form of creative expression to enjoy protection under both patent and copyright law. As we have seen, however, the scope and nature of patent protection for software are difficult to pin down. After the Bilski decision, it's not even clear how much longer patent offices will grant applications for software patents.

The history of software protection under copyright has proven even more awkward, starting with the decision to include it in the first place. In 1975, as Congress prepared for a massive rewrite of U.S. copyright law, a special commission was established to advise legislators on what to do about computers and computer software. By 1976, the Copyright Office was already allowing registrations for software. Two years later, the National Commission on New Technological Uses of Copyrighted Works, known as CONTU, finally published its report. CONTU recommended amendments to the law to make protection for software explicit, a change made soon after.

CONTU's recommendation was not unanimous. Commissioner John Hersey, a Pulitzer Prize–winning author and president of the Authors' League of America, filed a passionate dissent. Hersey believed analogizing computer code to other forms of literary expression was a bad idea. "Surely it is especially vital in a time of hurtling and insatiable technology," Hersey wrote, "that the nation's laws reflect, whenever possible, a distinction between the realm and responsibility of human beings and the realm and responsibility attributed to machines."

Hersey has a good point. Programming started out as a manual effort. Changing the wiring of early computers was the only way to change their behavior. Early software was "written" on punch cards in a highly cryptic code, which essentially instructed the computer to turn on or off individual registers. Then as now, software controls the arithmetic, which is all computer hardware actually does. By 1970, software had evolved as an intermediate layer between users and computer hardware (a role that has dramatically expanded in the thirty years since CONTU). High-level programming languages including FORTRAN and COBOL were making programs easier to write, read, and especially to maintain.

Even in high-level languages, programs are unreadable except to software engineers, but the process still offered enough similarities to composing in a natural language to suggest the connection between literary works and software. The CONTU committee emphasized those similarities in its recommendations. Hersey agreed that this version of software—what is known as the source code—was entitled to copyright protection. Source code cannot be understood by hardware, however, and must be translated by other programs into the precise instruction sequence that the computer executes—the "object code." Once translated into machine instructions, Hersey believed, protection should end. A program, "once it enters a computer and is activated, does not communicate information of its own, intelligible to a human being. . . . The mature program is purely and simply a mechanical substitute for human labor."

It is not clear what problem CONTU's majority thought it was solving. Prior to CONTU, software manufacturers protected their work using the law of trade secrets, a technique that, as Hersey reminded the commission, had worked just fine. Users were generally not shown the source code at all, and had to agree not to disclose anything they learned about how the software behaved or was written. In the early days, most computer users were large businesses who leased their equipment and the software to operate it. Only a few vendors, notably IBM, offered both. Antitrust proceedings against IBM, however, led to more competition in the commercial software market. Independent software companies, many writing business applications for accounting and manufacturing systems, were growing.

Other developments were changing information technology even more dramatically. Moore's Law was beginning to bring the cost of computing within range of small businesses and, after that, consumers. Systems that largely produced printed output were increasingly becoming interactive, accepting user input and displaying rather than printing the results of their operation. As CONTU noted, software was poised to explode in both the things it could do and the number of companies developing it.

In the midst of a rapidly evolving new industry and at the urging of CONTU, Congress acted rashly. Software was granted the full protection of copyright. One immediate result was that judges found themselves being asked to decide cases in which developers of one program accused the authors of another of infringing on their code. But what did it mean to copy the "expression" in a piece of software? In the classic infringement case, the author is principally concerned with ensuring that her choice of words, characters, names, and other features of the writing has not been copied or closely imitated. In 2002, for example, the estate of novelist Margaret Mitchell sued the author of *The Wind Done Gone*, a reinterpretation of Mitchell's classic, *Gone with the Wind*, told from the viewpoint of one of Scarlett O'Hara's slaves. The second book was clearly a different work, but the estate claimed it had borrowed too many original elements from the Mitchell book. (The parties settled after a court refused to enjoin publication of *The Wind Done Gone*.)

If software protection relied solely on a similar kind of line-by-line comparison, copyright protection would have meant nothing. In most software litigation, the alleged infringer has likely never seen the source or even the object code the first programmer wrote and has made no effort to duplicate it. The second piece of software likely reads nothing like the first, and may even have been written in a different language. So early software copyright cases instead focused on whether the second program too closely duplicated the inputs and outputs of the first. Rather than protect the structure and literary elements of a program, in other words, software developers argued that copyright really protected the way their software behaved.

In business, however, software behavior is largely dictated by functional requirements defined by users. In a much criticized early decision from 1986, a federal court was asked to find infringement in a program that automated the administration of a dental office. The author of the second program had helped develop the original product, then decided to write his own. The structure, sequence, and organization of the two programs, according to expert testimony, were substantially similar, as were many of the displays presented to users. Although the second was written from scratch in a different programming language, the owner of the original claimed the new version infringed on her copyright. The court agreed. The basic idea for the program (the "plot," as it were) was "the efficient management of a dental laboratory." Since countless variations could be designed, any copying beyond the basic idea counted toward infringement.

This early case was immediately criticized, and today has been soundly rejected. It is too generous to the copyright holder, and comes close to protecting not the expression (the source code) of the original system but most of its underlying ideas. The judge's characterization of the program was at far too high a level to be meaningful. Under the reasoning of the dental office case, a judge might have said the idea for *Gone with the Wind* was the period just before and after the Civil War. Any book covering the same ground would necessarily share many elements with Mitchell's book, but no court would have used that starting point to determine copyright infringement.

Finding a workable test to determine what elements of a program did deserve protection proved difficult. In another famous case, the makers of Lotus 1-2-3, the leading spreadsheet software for the first generation of personal computers, sued Borland, who marketed a newer product called Quattro. Quattro introduced significant improvements in the spreadsheet interface that looked and acted very different from 1-2-3. To make it easier for Lotus users to make the transition, however, Quattro offered an "emulation mode" in which the familiar hierarchy of menus, submenus, and individual commands from 1-2-3 could be used instead of the new ones Borland had developed.

Lotus quickly lost market share to the new program and sued Borland in 1990, charging that the emulation of 1-2-3 menus and commands infringed Lotus's copyright. After years of back-and-forth litigation, Borland won. The 1-2-3 menu system, the appellate court held, was simply a "method of operation," like the buttons on a VCR. Even in an original work, such utilitarian elements are not protected by copyright. Lotus's loss signaled the end of a string of lawsuits in which developers tried to use copyright to protect user behavior or the "look and feel" of their programs. Menus, commands, and other features of popular software, most legal scholars now believe, are not part of the protectable expression of a computer program, particularly when asserted to make an older product incompatible with new ones. Following the Lotus decision, software companies moved increasingly toward protection through patent law, which, though shorter in duration, protects more elements of the program.

Although copyright law has proven of little use to protect software vendors from competing products, it has a played a somewhat more productive role in curbing outright theft. Cheap media including disks and CDs have made widespread illegal copying of software easy. Wholesale copying is clearly illegal under copyright. Most of the illegal copies sold, however, originate in Asia. Governments there have been ambivalent at best about enforcing international copyright treaties. In early 2009, the Chinese government notably prosecuted twelve members of a counterfeiting ring that had global sales of $2 billion, mostly of Microsoft products.

The other major source of illegal copying is enabled by the Internet, where file-sharing users trade software much as they do music and other content. Unlike entertainment companies, however, software vendors have been reluctant to sue individual users. In part, software changes so quickly that old versions of software aren't worth much. Margins on software, moreover, are apparently high enough that large business customers underwrite those who don't pay.

Software piracy is a serious problem, but hardly enough to threaten the industry's survival. A few years ago, Bill Gates told a group of my students that less than one-tenth of 1 percent of the copies of his Windows operating system in China were legal copies. He hoped to get that number up to 1 percent in the next ten years. Despite the wholesale theft of its software, Microsoft is still one of the most successful companies in the world.

Software vendors also seem to realize that those doing the copying probably can't afford the real thing. Getting young users hooked on products, even if they haven't paid for them, can generate significant value when those users are in positions to influence the software purchases of their future employers. Increasingly, students get cheap or free software anyway. Given the lack of marginal cost to vendors for the pirated copies, the cost of curbing piracy for the most part exceeds any benefits.

New methods of software distribution have succeeded much better than copyright law to reduce what was certainly rampant illegal copying. Customer service, upgrades, updates, and other necessary extensions to commercial software products are now distributed almost exclusively online. These frequent points of reconnection give vendors the opportunity to verify that each user has a legal copy of the product. Customers aren't required to participate in these services, but often find the usefulness of their "free" copies greatly limited without them.

As digital life develops, CONTU's infatuation with the metaphor of software as a form of written expression looks increasingly naive. Software has evolved away from novel-length programs toward smaller reusable modules known as objects. At the same time, operating systems, database management systems, and other middleware now provide many of the functions that used to be included, often repetitiously, by individual programs. Web site developers, for example, increasingly rely on interactive development tools such as Sun Microsystem's Java and Microsoft's .NET environment, which are built on the object model. The structure and design of new applications are largely dictated by the technical requirements of these sophisticated environments, leaving less room for the unique expression of individual programmers.

More sophisticated software now gives users the tools to "write" their own applications graphically. Many video game companies provide customers the ability to write their own levels and extensions. One recent release, Little Big Planet, is essentially a sandbox filled with tools for users to develop their own games. Programming is done entirely by dragging and dropping items onto a blank canvas and then assigning behaviors to the items as they interact with each other. At the end, the user's work is translated to a program, much as a word processor saves documents in encoded files. No "programming" takes place at all.

These improvements signal the next stage of realism for digital life. They also suggest that upcoming legal battles over copyright will challenge courts in new ways to determine what elements do and do not deserve protection. Are programs "written" using graphical interfaces the work of the user or of the tool's vendor? Are new elements created by users within virtual environments including Second Life a kind of joint work in which both have ownership interests? As the Law of Disruption continues to take software further away from the simple world of CONTU, the fiction that programs are like anything else under copyright law becomes harder to maintain.

THE PATH TO OPEN SOURCE

If not through copyright, how else can software developers protect their ability to make a profit? According to a growing number of vendors, the answer, oddly enough, is to give the code away. Since the mid-1980s, a movement with political as well as business aspirations has pushed for unrestricted access to software. The movement goes under different names with slightly different philosophies, including copyleft, the free software movement, Creative Commons, and open source. Economically, these developers seek to maximize the non-rivalrous nature of software. Information, as we have seen, wants to be free. So why introduce either law or technology to try to stop it?

Richard Stallman, one of the long-standing leaders of the movement, was an early software pioneer at the Massachusetts Institute of Technology in the 1970s. Back then, it was common practice for commercial software to be

delivered with the source code intact, with users encouraged to modify programs for their specific needs. That practice, unfortunately, also allowed
them to reproduce and redistribute programs, leading commercial vendors
either to restrict access to the source code or to introduce technology that
would limit the ability of users to copy it.

At the same time, a great deal of software was developed under a nonprofit model, either at research universities or with funding from government agencies. Their developers, including Stallman, saw this as a more
efficient approach, and looked for ways to institutionalize it as an alternative
to commercial software products sold as individual copies. In 1989, Stallman
wrote a new operating system he made available for free—a program that
later formed the basis for Linux. Stallman also drafted a document known as
the General Public License. Under the GPL, users are free to use the accompanying software in any way they wish, including modifying and reproducing it. The only restriction is that they may not sell the software, even to
charge for the modifications they make to it. In that way, even as the software is improved by its users, the enhanced product remains free, encouraging more users to make more improvements. The GPL is still the model for
most open-source development.

Open source turns the traditional assumptions of the copyright model
on their head. Instead of one developer licensing the code to individual customers, the users themselves develop the product over time. The original developer charges nothing, encouraging future users to rewrite whatever parts
of the program they like and to freely distribute their new versions.

Open source has succeeded by taking advantage of the very feature of the
information economy that makes it so disruptive in the first place—its ruthless efficiency. Millions of users can jointly build and distribute a product,
executing hundreds of complicated business transactions along the way. By
keeping money out of the equation, they can do it all without any negotiation, overhead, or lawyers. Absent the kind of transaction costs associated
with a commercial transaction, open-source software follows more closely
the curve of Metcalfe's Law, quickly reaching its tipping point and maximizing network effects.

Thousands of developers have contributed improvements to Linux, for
example, making it a fully functional system capable of competing against

Windows. In Europe, many national governments have adopted Linux as their operating system of choice. UK-based Canonical Systems offers a desktop version known as Ubuntu, complete with the familiar Windows-like user interface. Ubuntu has more than 10 million users, including about half of Google's employees. In Spain, there are 200,000 users in the public school system, and another 80,000 in the French National Assembly and military police. With revenue of only $30 million a year, Canonical is hardly a speck on Microsoft's windshield. But then the company launched Ubuntu only four years ago.

The open-source approach clearly meets its philosophical objectives. But absent fees for the software, however, how do its developers pay their bills, let alone make any profit? Some Linux developers are supported by universities and government grants, as Stallman was when he wrote the predecessor system. Other Linux developers treat the product as a kind of loss leader, selling ancillary products and services to support it. The GPL license, for example, disclaims all warranties for products distributed with it, so commercial Linux providers often act as a kind of insurer. Red Hat, a Linux company that began in 1993, charges nothing for the software itself. Instead, it makes money from training, support, and customizing Linux for large enterprises. With proprietary software, warranties are bundled into the price of the program.

IBM, in particular, invests heavily in Linux, contributing the time of its engineers to its continued development. The company has even offered free access to more than five hundred of its software patents to other open-source developers, and donated significant amounts of code to foundations promoting open source. In exchange for giving up control of the software, IBM is able to sell more hardware to run Linux, as well as services to support its installation and operation.

There's more to open source than simply an alternate way of making money with software. As John Markoff documents in his 2005 book *What the Dormouse Said*, the early computer culture was heavily connected with the counterculture movement of the 1960s. Silicon Valley's proximity to San Francisco's Haight-Ashbury, ground zero for the counterculture, led to a fusion of technology and ideology. Computing pioneers including Doug Engelbart, for example, were among those who participated in government-sponsored experiments with LSD. (Engelbart, among other things, invented the first computing mouse and a prototype of the World Wide Web, all in the 1960s.) Giving software away was part of the same mentality that also believed in free love, free drugs, and freedom of expression.

The tension between free software and commercial vendors, a familiar feature of today's polarized software industry, was there from the beginning. Foreshadowing a long and still unresolved conflict, Markoff includes an open letter from a young Bill Gates complaining that personal computer hobbyists were using early Microsoft products without paying for them. "Hardware must be paid for," he laments, "but software is something to share."

The link between the open-source movement and an antiestablishment political philosophy continues to this day. In coining the phrase Web 2.0 to refer to collaborative environments such as Wikipedia and social networking sites including Facebook and MySpace, computer book publisher Tim O'Reilly distinguished the new generation of Web companies by their appeal to community and openness. "The Internet today is so much an echo of what we were talking about at Esalen in the '70s—except we didn't know it would be technology-mediated."

O'Reilly is referring to the Esalen Institute, a New Age retreat on the Big Sur coast where guests pay to attend courses on everything from Gestalt psychology and spiritual massage to the semiotics of golf. What O'Reilly and others "talked about" there in the 1970s was a broad agenda for social change based on consciousness raising, communal living, and other elements of the counterculture. Forty years later social networking is spreading the word, ironically using technologies that were once viewed as tools of the establishment.

Those altruistic properties of open source may actually be a source of sustainable business advantage. Google's early success resulted in part from the ability of Web sites to easily incorporate related ads served by Google on their pages, generating income for both companies. Google now offers all of its software tools and gadgets using the same open architecture. Web sites and application developers can embed Google products, including search functions, maps, and photos and YouTube videos, sometimes referred to as "mash-ups." Flickrvision, for example, combines photographs from Flickr with maps from Google to show recently uploaded pictures from around the world on a real-time map. Extending Google's reach beyond its own Web sites expands the visibility of Google's sponsored ads, the company's main source of income.

Following Google's lead, a number of Web-based software companies have moved toward an open model, expanding their potential development team to include all of a product's customers. In 2008, Yahoo opened its search technology, long its prized proprietary asset, allowing users to customize Yahoo search results. Facebook likewise open-sourced much of its software, giving users the same tools to develop new applications that Facebook itself uses. Within its first year of operating on an open architecture, users developed 24,000 new applications, or about 65 a day. Some of these new user-written applications attract millions of users in less than a week.

The move from closed to open can also extend the life of commercial software products. Salesforce.com, which offers Web-based tools for managing customer relationships, allows users to enhance its products under a semi-open-source license. Users at Thomson Financial and Dow Jones used that feature to tailor the product to the financial services industry, making the product more attractive to other companies. CEO Marc Benioff believes open access to his company's software is key in its success over the closed architecture of rivals such as Siebel systems. A closed system is a product, but an open one becomes a platform for new development by users. Platform operators give up a great deal of control, but the improvements to their products that result generate network effects that much faster. "The killer apps of the Internet," Benioff says, "are becoming platforms that are creating communities of innovation."

As an alternative model for protecting software innovations, the low transaction costs of open source relative to copyright are attractive. So is its lack of reliance on heavy-handed law enforcement and expensive litigation. Unfortunately, the open-source model has significant drawbacks. There are, besides GPL, dozens of variations on open-source licensing, many with significant differences. There is no uniform open-source contract, leading to confusion and uncertainty among users. Even within the GPL community, tensions recently arose over a proposed new version of the license, in development since 2006. Early drafts included controversial provisions waiving software patent claims that GPL users might have against users who violate the license. An outright ban on using any form of DRM was also included but later removed based on criticism from Linus Torvalds.

Open-source software has also faced significant challenges from copyright holders claiming that some of the code being dedicated to public use has been illegally appropriated from commercial products. Software patents are also an issue. Microsoft claims that Linux violates hundreds of its patents, and is encouraging open-source distributors to buy licenses to those patents. In 2007, Novell agreed under pressure from Microsoft to trade royalties from its Linux business for a promise by Redmond not to sue Novell's Linux customers.

Microsoft is encouraging other Linux distributors to follow Novell's lead. The licensing carrot, on the other hand, comes with a nearby stick. In early 2009, the company filed its first patent lawsuit against a Linux developer, car navigation maker TomTom. Microsoft charged that TomTom's version of the core Linux system, known as the "kernel," infringes on three of its software patents. Asked by a reporter if the suit suggests a new tack in Microsoft's legal strategy toward Linux, a company lawyer glibly replied, "Our position is and has been that we believe licensing is the right way to approach and resolve these things." The suit was quickly settled for an undisclosed sum.

OPEN ALWAYS WINS

The legal status of the open-source licenses themselves has remained largely untested. In 2006, a would-be operating systems developer sued IBM, claiming that the Linux GPL violated antitrust laws and constituted a conspiracy. Prohibiting users from charging for products distributed under it, the suit argued, amounted to an illegal restraint on trade that made it impossible for others to compete. The court of appeals rejected the claim.

A case decided by the Federal Circuit in 2008 posed a more direct challenge. The developer of free software used by model railroad buffs to control trains using personal computers sued a competitor who sold a similar program. Though the original software was distributed for free, the accompanying license prohibited commercial redistribution. The second developer admitted to reusing code from the first without complying with the terms of the license, but argued that by granting free licenses the original program had waived any copyright. The FC disagreed. Just because the original developer was not charging for his program did not mean he had not waived rights to enforce his copyright, which attached to his program as soon as he wrote it. "Copyright holders who engage in open source licensing," the court said, "have the right to control the modification and distribution of copyrighted material." Courts must enforce these preferences. "The choice to exact consideration in the form of compliance with the open source requirements of disclosure and explanation of changes rather than as a dollar-denominated fee," the court reasoned, "is entitled to no less legal recognition."

These early decisions are encouraging signs for open-source developers. They also underscore what might be the greatest weakness of the GPL and its variations. Despite the implicit and often explicit rejection of the copyright system, open-source licenses are useful only as long as copyright exists. To see why, consider a hypothetical example. Let's say that you take the core Linux system (known as the "kernel") and develop some new uses for it. Instead of distributing your code for free, however, you decide to charge your users. Any preceding developer can theoretically sue you for copyright infringement.

Why? The developers of the code you started with still own the rights to that software, including the right to modify it. Open-source licenses waive those rights, but they do not give them up altogether. So long as subsequent users continue to replicate the waiver, there's no problem. If you violate the license, you forfeit your free use of the software and the privilege of redistributing it. Under the GPL, all the copyrights of all the authors who came before you are revived, making your use of the source code a straightforward act of infringement.

The open-source movement, it turns out, has built its utopian village on the crumbling foundations of the old capitalist fortress. That's not a criticism. It's just the Law of Disruption in action. The information economy has the potential to operate without transaction costs, producing and distributing true non-rivalrous goods. Still, we humans aren't quite ready to give up the property rights that have defined our existence for the past thousand years, especially when those property rights help generate income in clearly understood ways.

At the very least, we don't yet trust each other enough. We're happy to experiment with more efficient models of information creation, but only if everyone else does the same. In the meantime, the old system is always waiting in the background in case it's needed. Even at Esalen, disputes over who actually owned the land on which the institute was built ended only when a flying boulder mysteriously killed one of the founders.

The open-source movement, for all its faults, has tapped into a crucial truth about digital life. Closed systems, whether those of computer software or governments operating in secret, are constantly fighting the natural tendency of information to spread. Open systems, on the other hand, work with, not against, Metcalfe's Law. Most of the standards, protocols, file formats, and compression software that make up the Internet are open source. It is a least common denominator standard, simple enough to be used by even the lowliest device. Cell phones, PDAs, video game consoles, and RFID tags can all be full participants in the network.

A standard controlled by one manufacturer or supplier gives the owner the ability to charge more for his product or service than a competitor, a strong incentive to keep that standard closed. But information, like water, flows along the path of least resistance. It may take some time, but every closed standard faces constant erosion from a growing body of its users and their pent-up demand for more freedom. Over time, consumers force the closed standard open, little by little and in a hundred different ways. In the end, the Law of Disruption won't tolerate the inefficiency of closed standards. *Open always wins; closed always loses.*

Nothing else can explain how the Internet triumphed, without trying, over proprietary network architectures promoted heavily by IBM, DEC, and other computer manufacturers. Or consider Microsoft, which famously dismissed the World Wide Web as a toy. Once the company woke up to the reality of digital life, however, it found itself forced to embrace the playbook of its enemy. Internet Explorer, Microsoft's browser, is still free, as are most of Microsoft's Web-based products. Even so, it has been unable to fend off competition in Internet search from Yahoo and Google.

Even what appear to be exceptions to this rule take on new meaning under closer scrutiny. In the 1980s, for example, Sony bet heavily on Betamax, its proprietary VCR standard. Though it won a decisive courtroom win against entertainment companies who wanted to ban the device, it was a pyrrhic victory. Even as the litigation proceeded, VHS, a competing and arguably weaker standard, was stealing market share from Sony. VHS was licensed to a large group of manufacturers, and together they caught the Metcalfe curve. Beta was effectively dead within a few years of the Supreme Court decision that saved it. Sony won the battle but lost the war.

Sony turned the tables in 2008, however, winning a rematch over high-definition DVD standards. Sony pushed its proprietary Blu-ray system, which was initially both expensive and fragile. Again the closed standard was challenged by a consortium of competitors, who offered the cheaper HD-DVD system. HD was endorsed by major movie studios, and Microsoft included HD support in its Xbox game consoles. By contrast, Sony simply included Blu-ray players in its PlayStation game consoles at no additional charge, putting millions of units in place. In 2008, support for HD-DVD dried up, and the standard died. The closed standard won.

Or did it? As with Betamax, Sony may have lined up its troops on the wrong front. Increasingly, consumers simply download content without the cost and inconvenience of any media. Apple's iTunes store offers a growing library of current and older movie titles. Cable and telephone companies are using higher-bandwidth technologies to provide on-demand entertainment, including high-definition movies. In 2007, DVD sales declined for the first year since the medium was introduced. Further drops are expected in coming years. Within days of declaring the high-definition DVD war over, analysts were already writing eulogies for Blu-ray. The real competition for Blu-ray was not the competing standards; it was and remains the Internet, the most open standard of all. "The window of opportunity for DVD and Blu-Ray is longer than most people think," according to Netflix CEO Reed Hastings. "But it's not going to last forever."

What about the Windows operating system, which also seems to defy the open rule? In the 1980s, PC manufacturers assumed they could distinguish themselves from competitors by the quality of their hardware, and let Microsoft include DOS (the predecessor to Windows) on every machine they sold. Today, despite inroads by Linux and Apple (which is equally closed, but beloved by its small user base), Windows remains the dominant operating system. The company has weathered ferocious consumer backlash and catastrophic antitrust losses in the United States, Europe, and parts of Asia. Yet it still controls over 90 percent of the PC market, a de facto closed standard.

Well, maybe not. As noted earlier, the vast majority of users in some countries, including China, use unlicensed copies of Windows. In some of its fastest-growing markets, Windows is effectively an open system. More to the point, why define the relevant market as personal computers? Since the initial explosion of PCs in the 1980s, computing has spread far beyond the stand-alone computer. There are fewer than a billion PCs in the world but more than 3 billion cell phones, PDAs, game consoles, digital cameras, set-top boxes, and in-car systems. All of these computing markets are expanding much faster than PCs. Microsoft plays a role in most of these markets, but by and large it's a minor player. In the coming generation of RFID-enabled products, the next trillion computing devices will need very little in the way of an operating system.

LICENSE TO INNOVATE

As some of the examples in this chapter already suggest, technical improvements in Internet and Web technology are creating new ways of designing and deploying software. In the development of a more robust digital life, software is evolving from a singular act of creative expression to an act of continuous collaboration. Along the way, the nature of software is changing dramatically. The struggle between closed and open software may be resolved not by the law of copyright and patent but by the Law of Disruption.

The next generation of software deployment, already in its early stages, goes by many names, including cloud computing, Web services, virtualization, utility computing, and "software as a service." There are differences between these models, but all coalesce around the same basic premise. As software is written with standard interfaces, it becomes easier to host the programs and much of the processing of customer data on the software vendor's own equipment. Companies who once made and sold packaged software are becoming service providers, using the Web to process user data dynamically in real time. In that transition, the importance of software as a product protected by copyright and patent is fading.

The transition to SaaS is the natural by-product of the continued operation of Moore's Law and Metcalfe's Law. As computers and networks become more powerful, major software applications, including operating systems and antivirus and graphics programs, must be continually revised and enhanced. Keeping the software on a remote, centrally hosted computer greatly simplifies the process of updating, repairing, and otherwise revising the application. Users may still purchase copies of these programs on CD, but the short life span of each version turns the transaction from a sale to a subscription.

Consumers have long understood the convenience and appeal of SaaS. Instead of downloading software from Google, users type their search directly into a Web browser whenever they need it. Rather than purchasing auction software from eBay, sellers and buyers conduct transactions through the company's servers, paying not for the software but for the use of eBay's marketplace. Amazon, Yahoo, the *New York Times*, and millions of blogs allow their content to be embedded in the Web sites of others using real-time syndication software. Few software products come with user manuals, even in digital form, offering help as an online service. All of these examples allow users to reduce their search costs for information products. In effect, they allow users to customize the environment in which they experience digital life.

More sophisticated uses of SaaS for business-to-business transactions have been around for decades. But the continued operation of the Law of Disruption has now made "utility" computing both reliable and cost-effective. Users of Salesforce.com need not download or run the company's software. Users of Intuit's popular tax preparation program, TurboTax, can prepare their returns entirely online. Microsoft has developed Web-based versions of its popular Office applications.

The appeal of SaaS to vendors is obvious. Instead of preparing and distributing millions of media copies of software, users connect to the vendor through their Web browsers and interact with software maintained on the developer's computers. Since users never take possession of the software, even in digital form, concerns about illegal reproduction or counterfeiting are greatly reduced.

The move to SaaS transforms the relationship between vendor and user from one of sales to service. Instead of buying a program, you subscribe to a service. In many cases, even the services are free, supported by advertising or other transaction fees. Google charges nothing; the iTunes store charges for whatever content a user decides to download. For business applications, subscriptions may be based on the number of users, the volume of data processed, or annual fees based on the size of the company.

In legal terms, the shift from product to service changes the transaction from a sale to a license. A license is a limited privilege to use someone else's property in a particular way. As citizens, a license is the grant of some intangible right by a government—the right to drive a car, the right to keep a pet, run a business, get married, and so on. James Bond's fictional "license to kill" is a special privilege to violate a variety of criminal laws without fear of prosecution. But many licenses are issued by private parties. A ticket to see a movie is a license, as is a hotel room, a lift pass at a ski resort, or a parking sticker at a private lot. Digital life is made up of a variety of licenses, including terms of service for the use of Web sites, private information, and for trademarks, patents, and copyrighted products.

Moving software from product to service has significant legal consequences. Products are governed by the law of sales, where consumers have won many hard-fought protections under the law of sales. The UCC and many supplemental state laws, for example, entitle buyers to warranties on the products they purchase. There are also provisions that protect them from damage caused by defective products and built-in procedures for returning faulty goods or otherwise canceling a sale.

The law of licenses, however, is not well codified, and is generally interpreted under judge-made principles of contract law. There are no built-in protections. Software vendors can and do write whatever terms they want. These terms often contradict long-established principles of the UCC or other applicable laws. Under copyright, the purchaser of a copy has the right to resell her copy at any price she wants. Many software licenses and the DRM technologies that enforce them, however, make it difficult if not impossible for licensees to transfer their rights to another user. In many cases courts have upheld these terms despite the conflict with other law.

Ironically, the groups responsible for the UCC foresaw these problems early in the development of digital life. A new law, the Uniform Computer Information Transactions Act, was drafted specifically to establish standard terms for software and other information goods. UCITA, however, was perceived as being heavily biased in favor of sellers. It assigned liability to vendors whose products damaged the data of users, for example, but allowed vendors to avoid that liability simply by declaiming it in a shrink-wrap license. Only two states ever passed the bill, and its proponents have now given up the fight. Yet most shrink-wrap licenses, in the absence of UCITA, are even more one-sided than the proposed law would have permitted.

As software migrates from physical media to Web-based usage, even the shrink-wrap license has more or less disappeared. It has been replaced by terms of service agreements discussed earlier. Digital life is increasingly governed by hundreds of these documents. Emboldened by court decisions enforcing a variety of one-sided TOS, lawyers are now including pretty much every disclaimer they can think of. In many cases, simply using a Web site binds you to follow the TOS, usually a long document written in dense legal terminology. As corporate lawyers find terms they like, they attach them to their own TOS, making the documents even longer and less likely to be coherent, even to other lawyers.

This might seem to be the makings for a crisis. In fact, there's little practical difference between the sale of a software product and a TOS agreement to use it as a service. Lawyers write ridiculous license agreements. They also write ridiculous sales contracts. These documents matter only at the margins, when something goes very wrong or when buyer and seller definitively end their relationship. As we have seen repeatedly, the cost of enforcing an agreement through lawsuits is high, and the end result may be difficult to predict. Even if vendors usually win, the chance of a catastrophic loss may be too dangerous to risk. For the most part, the behavior of competitors and the interests of good customer relations set the "real" rules followed by both sides.

FAST-FORWARD: THE ECONOMY OF PERPETUAL VALUE

Software products are moving to SaaS largely for business reasons. The legal advantages and disadvantages, like most collisions with the Law of Disruption, are an unintended side effect. In this case, however, the natural evolution of digital life seems to be giving software and other information producers even more control over their creations at the expense of consumers. That at least is the view of an increasingly vocal group of law professors, not-for-profit advocacy groups, and bloggers. Today, software vendors can pick and choose among the various bodies of law that protect their interests. Copyright may offer the best remedies, or patent the most protection, or licensing the greatest flexibility. When in doubt, vendors simply assert all of them.

The more software migrates to the service model, however, the clearer it becomes that software is not the kind of information product that deserves or requires the same protections as literary works, on the one hand, or new inventions, on the other. Just as it has been from the beginning of the information revolution, software simply automates processes and methods. The techniques, algorithms, and formula may need protection as trade secrets, but the code is increasingly utilitarian. As John Hersey put it in his dissent to the CONTU report, software "utters work. Work is its only utterance and its only purpose."

Information products and services, which will grow from software to a category that includes some aspects of all human activity, have already proven they operate best in an environment suited to their uniquely plastic and adaptable form. Though property rights form the background for mass collaboration, the need for and ability to determine who actually contributed what will fade. Excess value provided by information's inexhaustible economic properties makes it possible for everyone using it to profit in their own way, regardless of what they contribute. As more real-world products and services evolve to include information components (smart appliances, digital money, RFID-enabled consumer goods), every industry will find itself with a bigger pie to divide.

Open standards already underlie key information services, from Web sites to digital devices to business transactions. Soon, you will be able to move your personal information and your digital self from one activity to another. All your various devices will know who you are and what you want from them. Companies that today rely on locking customers in to a particular network or particular interface will need to adapt to a world of rapid improvements, low customer loyalty, and the ever-present threat of start-up competitors. Whether applied to technical standards, software, or forms of government, open always wins. Sometimes it just takes a little longer.

Consider once again social networking site Facebook. In early 2009, the company tried to modify their terms of service agreement, a modification we reviewed at the beginning of the book. Facebook, which manages a great deal of information provided by users, wanted a license *from the users* describing how that data could be used by the site. The change was modest enough. The terms proposed were relatively straightforward, even boilerplate. But some Facebook users actually read the text. An abundance of legal jargon scared them, and they quickly organized a very embarrassing and very public revolt.

Within days, Facebook not only backed down but announced a dramatic change in the law of software. Henceforth, the company promised, the terms of service would be an open-source document, developed in collaboration with the user community. The users, in other words, will dictate terms, rather than the other way around. For companies that derive much or all of their value from information contributed by users, that's a concession certain to be repeated. As the economic power of collaboration becomes clearer, most companies will likely find themselves in a similar position. The growing sophistication of Web-based services will ultimately reset the balance between producers and users, and undermine much of today's lopsided information laws.

As the SaaS model is fully deployed, the law of software may return to where it was before 1976. Unnecessary rights granted to information producers by copyright, patent, and the self-granted rights of licenses may be revoked. Even if they aren't, those rights may soon have little practical value. In the end, the regulation of information won't come from any body of law. It will come, for better and for worse, from the market.

Which is to say, it will come from the Law of Disruption.

CONCLUSION

Lessons Learned

The Law of Disruption, together with Moore's Law and Metcalfe's Law, is systematically rewriting the aging corpus of industrial-era laws. The result will be a new code, better suited to life in the digital age. In the midst of revolutionary change that is both fascinating and frightening, it's hard to look away. Confronted with the weird economics of information, the core principles of public law, private law, and information law are being turned upside down. Policymakers from the physical realm have increasingly less influence in digital life, while consumers, both individually and in virtual groups, have correspondingly more. The balance of power will rest with business leaders, who must learn to align themselves more with the latter group and less with the former. That, at first, will feel unnatural. But they'll get used to it.

Our new laws won't look much like the old ones. Treaties, statutes, regulations, and judicial opinions are giving way to more organic forms. The Declaration of Independence of digital life has already been written. Its Constitution, made up of wikis, terms of service agreements, privacy policies, and the software code itself, is now being drafted. Deliberations over changes to its rules and regulations will take place on blogs, social networks, and tweets. Dispute resolution will be outsourced within the cloud of computing resources and network users best suited to minimize transaction costs. This process, so far, has been driven by the users. Lawmakers and business leaders need to catch up quickly if they want to have a voice.

We have reviewed nine principles—the laws of disruption—that form the foundation for a new legal system. One way or the other, these principles will prevail. Open always wins. Whether the transition is relatively slow or fast, straight or zigzagged, peaceful or violent depends on all of us. Policymakers, business leaders, consumers, and citizens all have a critical part to play in the legal revolution. Throughout the book, I have given examples of both the productive and the not-so-productive contributions each group has made so far. Overall, governments should be taking a much less active role in the micromanagement of emerging technologies than they have the past ten years: they should stick to the macro and leave the micro alone. As government recedes, businesses and consumers have new obligations to work together to create equitable rules that will keep the information economy healthy.

The key lessons learned for each group, as well as few important "to do" items going forward, are summarized below.

POLICYMAKERS

In a prescient 1998 essay, legal scholar and federal judge Frank Easterbrook implored his colleagues to be wary of regulating disruptive technologies. "Beliefs lawyers hold about computers, and predictions they make about new technology, are highly likely to be false. This should make us hesitate to prescribe legal adaptations for cyberspace. The blind," he wrote, "are not good trailblazers." Easterbrook, who wrote the opinion in the Craigslist case that preserved immunity for the Web site's housing listings, practices what he preaches.

The best way to regulate innovation is to leave it alone. The most courageous decisions lawmakers have made about the Internet have been to protect it from outside interference, including their own. Section 230, as we saw, granted immunity to Web site operators for message boards, blogs, and other content written or posted by their users, ensuring a robust marketplace of ideas. Congress has repeatedly extended laws that prohibit federal or state regulators from charging taxes on Internet access. Regulators, including the FCC and the European Union, have generally resisted political pressure to tinker with the specifics of how e-commerce and more recent social networking applications find their way to new and profitable models of doing business. These and other antilaws ensure there is only one set of rules applied to online interactions. They also preempt local jurisdictions from shortsighted and dangerous experimentation, either to enforce local morals or to shore up sagging tax revenues.

Doing no harm is a good start. But the Law of Disruption demands more of governments. Encouraging innovation, through basic research grants and prodding emerging industries to self-regulate, is even better. Here the track record for government has been positive. Research sponsored by the former Defense Advanced Research Projects Agency led to the creation of the Internet itself, ensuring its standards remain both open and nonproprietary. Government-sponsored research paid for much of the development of the World Wide Web and other key building blocks of digital life. Semiprivate agencies, including the groups responsible for maintaining Internet addresses and domain names, act as a kind of digital traffic code, making sure everyone follows the same basic rules.

Tinkering with the machinery while it is spinning at top speed, on the other hand, is sure to cause injury to machine and mechanic alike. The nonrivalrous nature of information and the network effects they generate have lured antitrust regulators into the trap of equating stunning success with anticompetitive behavior. Information technology companies, granted monopolies through the operation of copyright and patent law, are demonized when the incentives work too well.

The case against Microsoft, in the United States and abroad, has cost a fortune and distracted an innovative company for years. But it has not helped one consumer one bit. Record fines, including $1.45 billion against chipmaker Intel in 2009, only encourage more punitive actions, which enrich the regulators but do nothing to fix market failures. The regulators are egged on by weaker competitors, who later find themselves on the receiving end. In the early days of the Obama administration, the Department of Justice has promised more, not less, aggressive interference with industry. Though high technology has not been specifically targeted, Google appears on everyone's short list. At a minimum, regulators must learn to restrain themselves from taking on market failures for which they have no remedy to propose.

In areas where governments should be providing regulatory leadership, lawmakers can't seem to resist doing the opposite. Instead of pampering the remarkable marketplace of ideas that digital life has generated, legislators have passed humiliating laws targeting specific content, including pornography and commercial speech in the United States and political speech abroad. Though these statutes are often symbolic and courts regularly overturn them, the damage is not negligible. For one thing, the residents of digital life are now convinced their elected officials are all cynics, hypocrites, or worse.

Lawmakers have also too often heeded the siren call to do *something*, anything, to prove that digital life is not a lawless frontier. The moment the media get hold of lurid but anecdotal tales of outrageous behavior, laws are debated and sometimes even enacted to cure harms that aren't fully defined or may find natural solutions. Cyberstalking, identity theft, spyware, cyberbullying—each of these may turn out to be a serious problem, or not. But legislating ahead of the technology helps no one and often leaves behind rules that trap those who were doing nothing wrong. When it's time for reelection, at least the lawmakers can say they tried.

Regulatory agencies, particularly the FCC, have behaved even worse. The agency's mission since its creation in 1934 has been to "make available, so far as possible, to all the people of the United States . . . rapid, efficient, Nation-wide and world-wide wire and radio communication service with adequate facilities at reasonable charges." Unexpectedly, the Internet has provided the opportunity of a lifetime to achieve that goal. But all the agency has done, with its baffling and dogged determination to see the world exactly as it looked when AT&T was ending its reign as a regulated monopoly, is slow the deployment and build-out of new infrastructure.

Both the legislative and the administrative levels of government are plagued by the serious problem of undue influence. Some of the worst examples of interference we have seen, including state government bans on the online sale of wine, caskets, dog medicine, and other goods, are nothing more than ham-fisted efforts by local industries to preserve profitable inefficiencies. While information-content industries have failed (so far) to force the adoption of the broadcast flag or to completely gut fair use, they have purchased plenty of victories, including the regular extension of copyright protection, even for authors long dead and presumably no longer in need of incentives to create.

What about the judiciary? In the wake of ill-conceived laws and desperate competitors, courts are invariably called upon to resolve some of the most serious border disputes between the law of the physical world and the Law of Disruption. Yet most judges have little understanding or experience with digital life, let alone the expertise to solve its most complicated problems.

Again, the best advice is to follow Judge Easterbrook's wise admonition not to innovate. His California colleagues in the Roommates.com case, however, declined to abstain, doing everyone a disservice. The Internet, they wrote, "is no longer a fragile new means of communication that could easily be smothered in the cradle by overzealous enforcement of laws and regulations applicable to brick-and-mortar businesses." The judges may be right or wrong about that. But they gave no facts to support their view. And it is not up to the court to decide in any event.

Two areas require immediate and positive attention: cyberterrorism and patent reform. The U.S. government, by its own admission, has failed since 9/11 to take even basic steps to secure the infrastructure of digital life from acts of terrorism. Instead, the apparatus of national security has been exploiting those weaknesses itself, offending core principles of the Bill of Rights in the process. Both trends must be reversed.

Meanwhile, after five years of proposed reforms to what everyone agrees is a broken patent system, nothing has changed beyond the better-late-than-never decision by the courts to undo the business-method patent, their own terrible invention. But here most of all, information technology is different. Experimentation is cheap and easy, and the life span of innovation is short. If information technology needs patent protection, it is not to the same degree or of the same kind as inventions, such as drugs, that require far more investment in both time and effort. We should either establish different rules for software or leave them entirely to the will of the market, which is to say, to the Law of Disruption.

BUSINESS LEADERS

Executives in high-tech and low-tech companies alike must demonstrate both leadership and restraint: leadership in shaping the rules of digital life where governments cannot or will not do so, and restraint in not exploiting old rules that may still be enforced but no longer make economic sense. To fulfill both roles, they must work to close the gaps created by the Law of Disruption between the world of the possible and the world of the customary, helping lawmakers and customers move up the curve more quickly. Educating the public about the benefits of new innovations and the real risks and opportunities they present is both an obvious and a doable reform. To achieve it, trade associations, lobbyists, and other external communicators must be reinvented to absorb and promote the new message.

Given the complexity of modern regulations, executives have historically delegated all legal matters to company and outside lawyers. In the transition from industrial law to digital law, however, CEOs and other executives must have a basic understanding of the current regulatory landscape. In my experience as both a lawyer and a management consultant, senior executives at even global technology leaders remain willfully ignorant of the most basic rules that govern how they do business. Only one business school I know of (Wharton) has a required course in business law. In high-technology and other information-intensive businesses, neither the CIO, the CFO, nor the CEO can tell the difference between copyright, trademark, and patent. Yet the success, if not the survival, of their business increasingly depends on it.

Worse, many executives labor under the delusion that they know more about these subjects than they actually do. Microsoft's Bill Gates was fortunate to have a lawyer for a father, but even Gates was caught badly off guard when regulators in the United States and abroad first began rattling the antitrust saber in his direction. Famously, Gates quickly immersed himself in the study of what even most lawyers considered arcane aspects of the law of competition. That, unfortunately, is neither a luxury nor an ability most executives share.

This is a lesson of life-and-death importance for entrepreneurs and start-up ventures in particular. Law, especially business law, is not intuitive or obvious. A little knowledge can be a very dangerous thing. In modern litigation, moreover, the merits have far less to do with outcomes than does funding. Having the winning argument in a lawsuit doesn't help if you can't afford to pursue it as far as your adversary can. RIM and its army of Blackberry users barely survived the meritless though well-funded legal attack of patent troll NTP. Linux users seem to have dodged the bullet fired by SCO, but there are other hunters in the forest, some with precision weapons.

As businesses shift the focus of their attention from wooing regulators to engaging customers, innovators will find they have a lot to learn about working with the latter as equal partners. Most CEOs have likely never read the warranties, terms of service, licensing, and other absurdly one-sided agreements that are foisted without much thought onto consumers. Company lawyers make modifications without consultation as a matter of course. Neither business leaders nor their customers could understand these documents even if they tried. The terms of use for the iTunes store is 9,000 words, all of them incomprehensible even to most lawyers. The Google privacy policy is better—it's only 2,000 words and actually makes sense. But the link to it is still the smallest thing on the Web site.

This is not an academic problem. As the Internet frontier develops and settles, these documents take on added significance in digital life. They are the foundations of its rules, its statement of fundamental rights, and its system for resolving conflicts. Going forward, these governing documents will have to be written in plain English, with meaningful involvement from the entire executive team as well as the users. As the revolt of Facebook members suggests, the choice is not whether but when to include customers in the conversation.

Given the uneven distribution of change between traditional law and the realities of online business, the tools and the temptation are always there to use the courts to gum up the works for competitors. It's a temptation that must be resisted. Litigation is expensive, distracting, and unpredictable. Many of the cases reviewed in this book have gone on for years without a definitive resolution. As we have seen, remands and reversals from an escalating succession of appeals are always possible. The granting or dissolution of injunctions, especially in patent cases, easily eclipses the actual legal merits of the case. Litigation to secure a better bargaining position as industries reform, as in the case of Cablevision's fight over DVRs with its suppliers, is destructive if not barbaric. And it often backfires when dubious precedents later reappear. Engage the real issues at the bargaining table. Don't deflect them in proceedings still conducted partly in Latin.

Perhaps the single most valuable change that can be made is to the role of company lawyers, both internal and external counsel. Business lawyers today operate, depending on your point of view, as lone rangers or necessary evils. Both roles are unsuitable for companies that want to establish competitive advantage in the business of digital life. If your general counsel isn't part of your strategic decision making, you're asking for trouble. And if your general counsel doesn't know what strategic decision making is—that is, if she doesn't understand business in general, let alone your business in particular—you're already in trouble. Like the developers of Facebook, you'll be hearing from your users sooner rather than later.

Ten years ago, when the Internet became strategic, so too did the role of the chief information officer. Today, as the Law of Disruption is remaking the legal system for life in the digital age, a similar upgrade is critical if business lawyers are to be effective. IBM, which fought government antitrust battles long before Microsoft was even born, was constantly at the mercy not so much of the Department of Justice but of its own lawyers. Former CEO John Opel is reported to have said that the legal department was the only one in IBM that didn't have a budget, and it exceeded it every year. It might be funnier if it wasn't true. The lawyers for Apple Records and Apple Computers thought they had worked out a clever solution to the companies' trademark dispute. But the settlement they drafted, largely ignorant of trends in computing visible at the time, caused even more problems down the line. The legal staff must be integrated into the business. Failure to do so will only lead to more dangerous collisions at the border of physical and digital life.

You need lawyers who are experts in business, especially in-house lawyers. As obvious as that might seem, it remains heresy in many businesses. Most corporate lawyers—inside and outside counsel—keep themselves far from the business details of the clients they serve. They see themselves as risk managers. If asked for their opinion about matters of corporate strategy, future products and services, or new technologies, they view their job only as pointing out the downsides, the dangers, and the reasons not to innovate. If you ask a lawyer, the answer is presumed to be no. Yet CIOs have learned to be full participants of the executive team. We need to begin training lawyers to do the same.

Business leaders and their newly enlightened legal counsel should focus their efforts on the development of an organic code of business created in collaboration with customers and developed outside the courts. The model for that effort would be the "law merchant," rules and tribunals that grew alongside expanded trade routes and markets during the Middle Ages. Rather than take their disputes to courts set up largely to handle feudal property disputes, merchants worked out their own rules and applied them in abbreviated proceedings overseen by senior merchants. The law merchant, the starting point for the modern Uniform Commercial Code, was efficient and specific. It evolved quickly to support rather than slow the development of new forms of commerce.

There are already signs of similar homegrown forms of dispute resolution in digital life. EBay tries to resolve disagreements between buyers and sellers of its global marketplace using largely automated online arbitration, for example. At the same time, the company has invested in technologies to help merchants police their brands and identify counterfeit goods, tools that Tiffany, Louis Vuitton, and others have decided to forgo in favor of litigation. Sometimes the gamble pays off. Ultimately, however, the Law of Disruption always wins.

INDIVIDUALS

The natives of digital life need little in the way of advice. The natural beneficiaries of the Law of Disruption, consumers are already driving most of the innovation and accompanying legal disruption described throughout this book. In that sense, the real challenge for policymakers and business leaders is to accelerate to a speed closer to that of their citizens and customers. Consumers, adopting whatever technologies the Law of Disruption puts in their path, are using their new tools not only to enjoy digital life but to construct it in ways that better match their aspirations for a more perfect union. A rich, robust world already awaits the new inhabitants of life online. As Moore's Law and Metcalfe's Law continue to work their magic, the inhabitants become more numerous and more interesting all the time.

A few suggestions, however, could remove a great deal of existing friction between users, and between users and their business and government counterparts. As information spreads more quickly and cheaply on Web sites, blogs, and collaborative tools such as Wikipedia, bad information often outpaces good. Be careful, in particular, of accepting common wisdom that often turns out to be legal myth. Throughout the book, I have tried to expose the most persistent urban legends I come across in my work as both an instructor and a consultant: the First Amendment does not protect freedom of speech from anyone but the government; there is no constitutional right to privacy, at least not in the United States, that protects you from employers, parents, or casual acquaintances; the "fair use" provision of copyright law knows no safe harbors, nor is there copyright protection for new words, or for brilliant ideas and insights that cannot be navigated through the treacherous waters of the patent system.

Social networking tools and other new media have given consumers increasing returns to scale in their ability to collaborate. These network effects translate to increased effectiveness in getting across their demands in both political and business negotiations. That new power comes with new responsibilities. For one, consumers must be more aware of the hidden agendas of those with whom they align. Some privacy advocates, as we saw, have religious, even apocalyptic, goals.

Or consider the Net Neutrality debate, which has perhaps most involved consumers in the process of deciding digital policy. Accelerated by the introduction of new high-speed technology and applications, the issue is little more than a new chapter in the ongoing struggle between content providers and access providers, who dragged mostly innocent Internet users into the fight on the false premise that the very soul of the Internet was at stake. The reality is something much less, and much more mercenary. Net Neutrality, to put it bluntly, is a shell game.

While the ability of user involvement to influence lawmakers and the FCC demonstrates the growing strength of the body politic of digital life, this is a bad example nevertheless. Consumers have been manipulated and misled by both sides. The result was the near enactment of more inappropriate and ultimately unenforceable legislation—more bad laws such as CAN-SPAM or the SPY ACT or the cyberstalking statute. It's a lesson in what not to do. Pitchforks down.

Users need to be more sophisticated in the ways they approach other complex problems facing their digital selves. Calls for legislation to combat identity theft and spam or to protect privacy increasingly fall on accommodating ears. But what is it users really want? Consumers can't agree on the kinds of e-mail they want banned, nor why they think traditional law enforcement is the institution best suited to implement it. The vast majority of users, according to most surveys, worry about online privacy, but they also want protection from terrorists and other violent criminals. Regulators dutifully enact rules requiring search engines, cell phone companies, and ISPs to retain less and then more data at the same time, a hopeless mess that leaves everyone feeling cheated and let down. Don't approach legislators with problems. Approach them with plausible solutions ready for implementation. And don't approach them at all when technology can provide a lower transaction-cost remedy.

In flexing new consumer muscle in the marketplace, the track record for consumers has been more promising. Consumers have successfully fought off numerous attempts to subvert the non-rivalrous properties of information. As media companies more fully embrace digital distribution, DRM and other forms of copy overprotection are proving difficult to enforce. So are limits on DVR usage, and closed networks for cell phones. Creative reuse of information in mash-ups of all kinds of content is flourishing, despite the overprotections of copyright. Most of that reuse is supportive, not destructive, of the underlying content. Open-source software, particularly Linux and Firefox, is slowly gaining in popularity over closed-market leaders. Cloud computing promises to disconnect even more false linkages between technologies, letting users create whatever technical environment best suits their needs. Users like open, and open, as we saw, always wins in the end.

The technology of digital life has also helped its residents win political battles. Digital natives aspire to a society that is free, democratic, and egalitarian—the principles on which the Internet protocols are themselves created and enhanced. Through the EFF, ACLU, CDT, and other nonprofits organized to defend their rights, they have fought off a variety of content regulations, civil liberties invasions, and abusive patents, setting important legal precedents in the process. The survival of the self-governed Second Life environment and the failure of its more heavy-handed competitor, SIMS Online, suggest perhaps that users really can vote with their wallets.

LESSONS LEARNED

Over the next few years, many of the laws reviewed in this book may become the subject of significant reform. Privacy law may be updated in the United States and Europe to reflect the realities of persistent digital life. Local ordinances on free speech, electronic surveillance, and other human rights may find new meaning and new unity. A truly neutral infrastructure—one free of government regulation and not subject to the whims of powerful lobbyists and other vested interests—may smooth the spread of information technology to the large segments of the world's population that don't have it. Legal institutions responsible for regulating competition, enforcing criminal laws, and deterring the risk of terrorism may wake up to the unique characteristics and evolving needs of a new generation. Perhaps we'll even find a new metaphor for regulating the flow of information, one that fits better with the realities of a frictionless digital environment and a culture of collaboration and creative reuse.

Or perhaps not. The end result won't make much difference. The law, to paraphrase Brooks Adams, will either change to meet the new reality or collapse. In its present form much of it is law in name only, largely unenforceable and taken seriously by a shrinking segment of the population. Another decade and it may simply be forgotten.

A similar fate befell a body of law known as sumptuary, which carefully regulated the kinds of clothing that could be worn in public. Sumptuary law was a way of keeping the classes separate, as much a set of restrictions on the rich as on the poor. In Elizabethan England, for example, only the first-born son of a knight could wear silk on his nightcap or on his spurs; the punishment for defiance was three months in jail. But as the middle class continued to expand, the value of sumptuary diminished. Over time, rich and poor alike came to pay less and less attention to it, and enforcement ultimately ceased. In many jurisdictions, sumptuary laws stayed on the books, where they remain today in a kind of legal limbo, dead but not buried.

The same fate may await much of the law of the industrial age. The Law of Disruption works in strange ways. But it always works.

ACKNOWLEDGMENTS

For careful and extremely helpful readings of all or part of the manuscript, I am indebted to Hank Barry, Peter Christy, John Doggett, John Donohue, Eric Goldman, David Hornik, Simon Olson, Richard Posner, Christopher Sprigman, and Dennis Summers. Their comments and suggestions have improved the book far more than I had any right to expect.

I owe particular thanks to Joshua de Larios-Heiman, who served as research assistant, bartender, and coach.

At William Morris Agency, I am grateful for the advice and counsel of Suzanne Gluck and Eric Lupfer. Eric snagged my wayward proposal in midair and painstakingly brought it back down to earth, one idea at a time. He continues to provide advice, insight, and moral support.

At Basic Books, my thanks to everyone involved in the production and marketing of the manuscript, most of all my editor, Tim Sullivan, who demonstrated both patience and discipline when each was required. My thanks as well to John Sherer, Michele Jacob, Trent Knoss, Alix Sleight, and Sandra Beris.

Many of the concepts and examples in this book were developed in courses I taught at both Northwestern University School of Law and the University of California–Berkeley. As always, I'm grateful to my students for their challenging questions, impossible hypotheticals, and openness to new ideas.

I would also like to acknowledge the Stanford Law School Center for Internet & Society and its director, Lawrence Lessig, for having me as one of its nonresident fellows since 2005.

For encouragement, advice, and other support, special thanks to Eric Apel, Nancy Bacal, Ed Baker, Laura Boxer, Leigh Buchanan, Shirlee Citron,

L. Gordon Crovitz, Mike Davies, Lisa de Larios-Heiman, Tara Desautels, Paul Elie, Bronwyn Fryer, David Greenwald, Hollis Heimbouch, Aaron Holby, Steven Levitt, Dan'l Lewin, Andy Lippman, Larry Loo, Sarah Loo, John Mahaney, Kevin Maney, Joe Marino, Heidi Mason, Paul Nunes, Breid O'Brien, Kirsten Sandberg, Margaret Spring, and David Van Zandt. Thanks as well to Judd Antin and Kevin Ashton.

BIBLIOGRAPHY

Albrecht, Katherine, and Liz McIntyre. *The Spychips Threat.* Nashville: Nelson Current, 2006.

Benkler, Yochai. *The Wealth of Networks.* New Haven, CT: Yale University Press, 2006.

Coase, R. H. *The Firm, the Market, and the Law.* Chicago: University of Chicago Press, 1988.

Davis, Erik. *TechGnosis.* New York: Three Rivers Press, 1998.

Downes, Larry. *The Strategy Machine.* New York: HarperBusiness, 2002.

Downes, Larry, and Chunka Mui. *Unleashing the Killer App.* Cambridge, MA: Harvard Business School Press, 1998.

Friedlander, Amy. *Natural Monopoly and Universal Service.* Washington, DC: Corporation for National Research Initiatives, 1995.

Friedman, Lawrence. *Guiding Life's Dark Secrets.* Stanford, CA: Stanford University Press, 2007.

Friedman, Thomas L. *The World Is Flat.* New York: Farrar, Straus, and Giroux, 2006.

Goldsmith, Jack, and Tim Wu. *Who Controls the Internet?* New York: Oxford University Press, 2006.

Heller, Michael. *The Gridlock Economy.* New York: Basic Books, 2008.

Kuhn, Thomas. *The Structure of Scientific Revolutions.* 3d ed. Chicago: University of Chicago Press, 1996.

Landes, William L., and Richard A. Posner. *The Economic Structure of Intellectual Property Law.* Cambridge, MA: Belknap Press, 2003.

Lessig, Lawrence. *Code Version 2.0.* New York: Basic Books, 2006.

_____. *Free Culture.* New York: Penguin Books, 2004.

_____. *The Future of Ideas.* New York: Vintage Books, 2001.

Levi, Edward H. *An Introduction to Legal Reasoning.* Chicago: University of Chicago Press, 1949.

Levitt, Steven D., and Stephen J. Dubner. *Freakonomics.* New York: William Morrow, 2006.

Llewellyn, Karl N. *Bramble Bush.* New York: Oceana Publications, 1999.

Markoff, John. *What the Dormouse Said.* New York: Penguin Books, 2005.

Negroponte, Nicholas. *Being Digital.* New York: Alfred A. Knopf, 1995.

Posner, Richard A. *How Judges Think.* Cambridge, MA: Harvard University Press, 2008.

_____. *Not a Suicide Pact: The Constitution in a Time of National Emergency.* New York: Oxford University Press, 2006.

Rosen, Jeff. *The Unwanted Gaze.* New York: Random House, 2000.

Solove, Daniel J. *Understanding Privacy.* Cambridge, MA: Harvard University Press, 2008.

Tapscott, Don, and Anthony D. Williams. *Wikinomics.* New York: Portfolio, 2006.

Turner, Frederick Jackson. *The Frontier in American History.* New York: Dover, 1996.

United States National Commission on New Technological Uses of Copyrighted Works. *Final Report.* Washington, DC: Library of Congress, 1979.

White, Lynn, Jr. *Medieval Technology and Social Change.* London: Oxford University Press, 1964.

Williamson, Oliver E. *Markets and Hierarchies.* New York: Free Press, 1993.

Zittrain, Jonathan. *The Future of the Internet—and How to Stop It.* New Haven, CT: Yale University Press, 2008.

INDEX